D1145240

COUNTER
REVOLUTION

COUNTER
REVOLUTION

The Tesco Story

DAVID POWELL

GraftonBooks
A Division of HarperCollins*Publishers*

GraftonBooks
A Division of HarperCollins*Publishers*
77–85 Fulham Palace Road,
Hammersmith, London W6 8JB

Published by GraftonBooks 1991

Copyright © David Powell 1991

British Library Cataloguing in Publication Data
Powell, David
Counter revolution : the Tesco story.
1. Great Britain. Supermarkets. Tesco, history
I. Title
381.14806541

ISBN 0–246–13564–6

Phototypeset by Computape (Pickering) Ltd, North Yorkshire
Printed in Great Britain by
HarperCollinsManufacturing Glasgow

All rights reserved. No part of this publication may be
reproduced, stored in a retrieval system, or transmitted,
in any form or by any means, electronic, mechanical,
photocopying, recording or otherwise, without the prior
permission of the publisher.

CONTENTS

PREFACE AND
ACKNOWLEDGEMENTS

In March 1979, Sir Jack Cohen visited Tesco's latest flagship store, a frail old man confined to a wheelchair, dwarfed by his own creation. For half an hour he sat alone in the gallery above the main concourse, watching the crowds below, and briefly it must have seemed that whilst everything had changed, everything remained essentially the same, that he was back amongst the noise and the clamour of the East End market where the whole rumbustious affair had begun half a century before.

Six days later Cohen died, for an obituary writer in the *Daily Mirror* to reflect on 'the man who became a legend in his own lifetime'. Herein lies the problem of writing the history of Tesco: it is less a matter of dissociating Cohen from the company that he founded than of separating out the legend from the facts. Ultimately, of course, all biography is subjective, a conceit that it is possible to tidy up the past to satisfy a biographer's designs, to impose some order where, so often, none existed. And what is true in general is true in particular of the story of Tesco and Cohen. Brilliant, mercurial, charismatic he may have been, but methodical, never. That was not his way, and for the first tearaway years of the company's life, it bore the imprimatur of the man itself – of deals done and bargains struck with a fine contempt for convention.

At times, in fact, it appeared that he was carried away with the sheer zest of living – careless for tomorrow, voracious for today – a man born out of his time. Possibly this was the making of the legend, that having cast himself in the role of the privateer who enjoyed nothing more than a skirmish with the triple deckers of retailing, he found himself trapped in the past; that even as he ran up his colours, Slasher Jack was already part way to becoming an anachronism. No question, the media loved his swash and buckle, but time was not on his side; the progress of those systems and structures ('Computers, comschmuters! Marketing, schmarketing!') that represented for him all that he most despised, the equipage of organisation men, was inexorable.

Yet it was this new generation of management which, during Tesco's times of troubles, was to save the company not so much from itself as from Jack Cohen. For half a century he had imposed his will on his creation, dictating its policy, determining its character, and to outsiders he could do no wrong. The headlines still blazoned the exploits of 'Sir Save-A-Lot', the public still regarded him as the housewife's friend. That image and actuality were in conflict made little difference; that the image remained credible was all, a reaffir-mation of the man himself.

Seven years before Cohen was born, Oscar Wilde had written: 'Every great man nowadays has his disciples', and in his lifetime Cohen had more than enough disciples to be able to ignore Wilde's rider that 'it is always Judas who writes the biography'. A man who lived for the moment, it is doubtful whether he would have given a damn for what he would have regarded as a posthumous betrayal, confident that when placed in their true perspective his achievements would outweigh his faults. And with reason. If the last years of Cohen's reign at Tesco had all the qualities of tragedy, of a man who had outlived his time, yet could not accept that his time was past, then for the rest he had built success upon success, creating a retail empire from a £30 investment in war surplus stock – and the *chutzpah* of his ancestry.

Indeed, without a grasp of the background from which he came, the history of the early development of Tesco is incomprehensible, for the two are inseparable. A Whitechapel ghetto before the First World War shaped the man and thus helped form the culture of Tesco in the first years of its life.

Now, of course, all that has changed. The days of piling it high and selling it cheap have long gone, and Tesco bears little relation-ship to the company that Cohen once knew. Here, possibly, is the essence of the tragedy: that he could sit, a lonely man, above the concourse of the Pitsea store, realising that he was yesterday's man.

Of course, so much is speculation, but then so is much biography, a cat's-cradle of half-digested facts and musty recollections, of dog-eared records and time-distorted reminiscences each open to individual interpretation. As such, it would be invidious to list all those who have helped to make this book possible, for there are altogether too many of them – the memories of those men and women who in the past sixty years have played a part in the making of Tesco.

This said, however, a handful deserve special mention, not least Hyman Kreitman, Sir Leslie Porter, Daisy Hyams, Jim Pennell and Laurie Don for sharing their recollections so readily; Sir Ian MacLaurin for his wholehearted support during the two years it has taken to bring this work to completion; the present board of Tesco (especially David Malpas and Mike Darnell) for their patience with what must have seemed my inexhaustible curiosity; and finally, Mike Boxall, until recently the company secretary, and his secretary, Pat Roberts. To them all, my thanks.

And my thanks also to John Harper, Liz Mandeville and Ted McFadyen for the time they have devoted to reading the manuscript, and their constructive comments on its contents. Which only leaves me to thank Maggie Symons. The job of a researcher is an unenviable one, to do so much of the devilling yet to get so little of the credit. In this case, however, much of the credit for seeing this book to completion is due to her. Indeed, without the logic she has applied to sifting and interpreting a mass of frequently contradictory information, and to her penetrating insights into the myriad characters who have made up this biography, *Counter Revolution* would never have appeared.

But enough, the work is complete. All that I can hope is that it does credit to all those, past and present, who have contributed to the Tesco story.

David Powell
Lewes

1. THE CITY OF DREADFUL NIGHT

1898–1919

'From him I should like a true
tale of the City of Dreadful
Night.'

William Morris (1888)

Number Six, Sander Street no longer exists, a casualty first of the Blitz, then of developers bent on razing the stews of London's East End. If a start was to be made on building a brave new world, then what better place to begin than in this underbelly of the capital, a violent and noisome place which for three centuries and more had served as a reminder that London was, indeed, two cities: the one, an illustration of that benign, if partial, providence for which generations of the more fortunate had thanked their gods; the other, behind God and mammon's back.

Sprawling eastwards from the Tower, an embarrassment as much to tender consciences as to bourgeois sensibilities, the East End had changed little since Henry Mayhew's portrait of the life and labour of London's poor in the decade of the Great Exhibition, since Charles Booth's pioneering study of the character of poverty at the high-noon of Empire. A dark and secret place, it haunted the Victorian psyche, and while the fiction of Arthur Morrison and Sax Rohmer titivated genteel fears, there could be no denying the facts of the Houndsditch murders, or Jack the Ripper or …

And polite society would lower its voice – 'Not in front of the children, dear' – for this was a London which it preferred to forget. As Jack London wrote at the opening of his minor classic, *People of the Abyss*, the place was a no-man's land, as he learned when enquiring at Thomas Cook's about tours of the area. They could package him to Darkest Africa or Innermost Tibet, but as to the East End: 'You can't do it, you know,' said the human emporium of routes and fares. 'It is – ahem – unusual. We receive no calls to take travellers there, and we know nothing whatsoever about the place at all.'

The frontier of respectability was drawn in the tone of voice: that out there, only a couple of miles east of Ludgate Circus, there was another world, far removed from the prissy decencies of Victorian London; a giant and motionless Kraken whose poverty, as J. H. Mackay wrote in *The Anarchists*, 'encircles with its mighty tentacles the life and wealth of the City and the West End'. In the late eighteenth century, the German visitor von Archeholtz had been appalled by the contrast between the mean houses and crooked streets of 'this other City' and the elegance of Westminster and Mayfair, and conditions had deteriorated throughout the decades that followed.

As the Port of London grew to become the largest harbourage in recorded history, as the wealth of London burgeoned to become the capital market of the world, so the East End spawned. Dependent on the Thames and relying on the network of communications (roads, railways, canals) that tentacled out from the docks, the area was as much a clearing-house of humanity as of trade. When the government proposed a tax on matches in 1886, Westminster had been invaded by a deputation of 'filthy and haggard harridans' – the East End match girls – whom the London which saw them for the first time regarded as sub-human; whilst a handful of years later, during his campaign to win a living wage for dockers, the radical union leader John Burns continually had to remind his members to behave like human beings, and not to drink themselves into insensibility whenever they had a few coppers to spare.

The condition was indigenous, a momentary escape from 'that hell of poverty' where life was crowded, hugger-mugger, into inadequate housing (in 1889 more than 490,000 people were living three to a room), that lacked all but the most basic sanitation (the infant mortality rate in London's East End in the same year totalled 43.3 per thousand); and where successive generations of immigrants (Irish, Indians, Chinese) hunted for work where there was little to be found, the Unemployed Registration Committee reporting in

December 1887: 'We have the particulars of over 100,000 men, women and children plunged into the direst destitution resulting from want of work.'

This was the heartland of that Darkest England (as William Booth, founder of the Salvation Army, entitled his best-seller), where the young Jewish refugee Avroam Cohen finally settled in the mid-1880s. He was not alone. In 1882 a quarter of a million Jewish families fled westwards across Europe to escape the growing savagery of their Tsarist overlords. They came from Russia and Poland, Latvia and Lithuania, carrying all they possessed with them – a pilgrimage in search of a promised land. For half a century, Tsarist Jewry had faced growing persecution – the closure of synagogues and schools; the selective conscription for all youths between twelve and twenty-five years of age; the banishment of entire communities and the creation of ghettoes.

On Palm Sunday, 1871, an Odessa mob turned on the Jewish quarter, and the authorities did nothing to intervene. The Tsarist regime, growing increasingly unpopular, had found its scapegoat – the Jews – and in the following decade the pogrom became an instrument of government in principle as in practice – an Imperial ukase of 1881 exhorted all Christians to punish Jews at Eastertide. As the persecution mounted, so the Jews fled, and if the United States was their *goldene medina*, then many got no further than London – and so the *stetl* came to the East End.

At first it must have seemed to Avroam Cohen that he had exchanged one nightmare for another, that the brutalism that he had left behind him was matched by a new brutalism, of which Professor Julian Huxley had written recently: 'I have seen the Polynesian savaging ... before the missionary or the blackbirder or the beach-comber got to him. With all his savaging, he was not half so savage, so unclean, so irreclaimable, as the tenant of a tenement in an East London slum.' At least, in the ghettoes, there was a common enemy, whereas here the danger was everywhere, and faceless. The Commissioner of Police might boast that 'London is the safest capital in the world', yet violent crime was indigenous to the East End, and in 1888 the anti-semitism of large sections of the community was heightened by the rumour that the Ripper himself was a Jew.

The story was completely unfounded, but nonetheless it momentarily fused all the fears and suspicions of the Jewish newcomers.

Isolated by their language, and concentrated in ghettoes of their own making, they appeared an alien community in an alien world, the more so when it seemed as if they could well threaten the jobs of the existing population. By the last decade of the nineteenth century, the Jewish worker had become a byword for the new economic man celebrated by Samuel Smiles – thrifty, diligent and willing to forgo the shorter hours and improved working conditions that had been imposed by the nascent unions on unwilling employers.

As Beatrice Potter, one of Charles Booth's investigators, who later became the wife of Sidney Webb, wrote: 'Polish Jews and Englishwomen will do any work, at any price, under any conditions … the Jew is unique in possessing neither a minimum nor a maximum; he will accept the lowest terms rather than remain out of employment; as he rises in the world new wants stimulate him to increased activity of effort, and no amount of effort causes him to slacken his indefatigable activity.'

In their struggle to obtain recognition, these qualities did not endear the burgeoning Jewish community either to the unions or to their members, and as hostility grew, so it heightened the Jews' innate sense of difference, driving them further in on themselves. By the 1890s there were sixteen synagogues within a five-minute walk of Whitechapel High Street serving the still expanding Jewish population, most of whom worked at the so-called 'immigrant trades', especially tailoring.

Since the mid-1850s there had been a small colony of Jewish bespoke tailors in the West End, but in the following years the development of ready-to-wear lines, allied to a consistent increase in disposable incomes, led to an explosive growth in the tailoring business, and by 1887 almost a third of the new immigrants were directly or indirectly involved in the trade. The sweat shop had become a feature of Whitechapel life. Booth's survey records more than a thousand small workshops in the district, the majority employed at general tailoring, the rest specialising in vests, trousers and children's clothes.

In general, working conditions in the sweat shops were appalling, the hours punitive and the pay pitiful, as little as eleven shillings for an eighty-four-hour week. In 1888, a House of Lords Select Committee, established to investigate the sweating system, took evidence from one Myer Wilchinski, lately of Carlish in Tsarist

Poland. It could well have been Avroam Cohen's story. Like Cohen, Wilchinski had fled westwards; like Cohen, he was willing to work at 'anything that would bring the scantiest means of existence', and like Cohen, he had taken to tailoring.

'I ... closed with a tailor who offered to teach me a trade and give me lodgings and coffee for three weeks, and six shillings a week afterwards, until I learned one branch of the trade ... The room we worked in was used for cooking also, and there I had to sleep on the floor. The wife helped as much as she could at the trade, besides doing all the work of the house and the (three) children. A young woman worked the machine from eight every morning till nine at night, for three shillings a day; not often making a full week's work. My work was at first to keep up a good fire with coke, and soap the seams and edges; and the elbow grease I used was considerable. I had to get up in the morning about half past five, and we finished at night between ten and eleven, and turned out every week about thirty coats, which came to about £4.'

This was not so much the life, more the existence that Avroam Cohen must have come to know well in his early years as a tailor in Whitechapel – a toil-worn and punishing existence in a punishing and brutish world. Small wonder that he became something of an autocrat in later life. To survive the experiences first of a Polish ghetto and then of London's East End demanded both shrewdness and resilience and when, on 29 October 1898, he stood in the small bedroom of 6 Sander Street, Whitechapel, and held his second son, Jacob, in his arms, he must have wondered what the future would bring.

The years since Avroam arrived in London had been hard but fruitful ones. He had established himself as a journeyman tailor, had married Sime (always a somewhat shadowy figure in the Cohen household), and moved into a home of his own. A patriarchal figure, and intensely religious, he determined to bring up his family in the faith which had provided a staple for Jewry for more than two millennia, and which continued to provide an identity for the immigrants of Whitechapel.

Privately, they despised the lackadaisical ways and violent behaviour of their East End neighbours. Although there was excessive overcrowding within the Whitechapel area, it was not accompanied by the same level of poverty that marked out Lime-house and Hoxton and the Irish quarter south of the Whitechapel road. Judaism saw to that. Learned and memorised from generation to generation, it had proved a powerful shield against persecution, a nomadic culture which had survived continual harassment, as it was later to survive the ghettoes and concentration camps of Nazi Germany.

The synagogue was the nucleus of this world, as Joe Jacobs was later to describe in his autobiography *Out of the Ghetto*: 'In those days ... it was common practice for the fathers to be accompanied by their sons, to proceed on foot in best clothes to the synagogues on Friday evening at sundown, and early again on Saturday morning, and yet again before sundown on the same day.' Jacobs himself lived within three hundred yards of seven synagogues, and their influence was all-pervading, stressing the value of home and family and the benefits of education.

So often condemned to a life of wandering, Jewry has long invested the home with a near-mystic significance, that quiet place in which to raise the children on which the future of the family and Jewry itself depend. In such circumstances, the role of the mother is paramount. She is responsible for child-bearing and child-rearing, and it is instructive that Booth found that infant mortality in Whitechapel was well below the norm for the East End, and that child prostitution amongst the Jewish community was virtually unknown, in contrast to other ethnic groups.

If the synagogue and the home were parts of the whole, education made up this trinity of childhood. Compared with prevailing East End attitudes, largely compounded of a hostility to, and a suspicion of, all forms of schooling, the Jews of the Whitechapel ghetto placed great store on the value of education. One Inspector's report of the early 1890s noted: 'They [Jewish children] are keen and intelligent, they have an interest in all that concerns the welfare of our country. They are bright, are superior intellectually, are excellent workers in school and anxious to learn. They are superior in faculty, in industry and in perseverance.'

There is a note of justifiable pride in Joe Jacobs' catalogue of the later achievements of this small, expatriate community: 'The Jews were great ones for having their children educated. We produced doctors, teachers, scientists and musicians, etc. There are professional men of the highest calibre practising all over the world who began right here ... It was the heritage that produced Arnold Wesker, Bernard Cops, Harold Pinter, Wolf Mankovitz, as well as Lionel Bart and Alfie Bass ... '

Jacobs' list is seemingly inexhaustible, the product of the dynamic culture of the Whitechapel ghetto at the turn of the century which was to be Jacob Cohen's inheritance – not that he was aware of it in the early years of his life. Avroam, a strict disciplinarian, little given to pleasure, ruled the household as he managed his business – autocratically. He had climbed the hierarchy of tailoring since his apprentice days, and was now a small employer on his own account, working from home as a sub-contractor to a number of manufacturers, making up their garments for sale to shops.

The work was seasonal, and the life of the Cohen household was closely geared to the fluctuation in demand for Avroam's output. During the high season, in the spring and autumn, all else was subordinate to the iron discipline of the workshop, and for ten hours a day the house in Sander Street was silent, save for the insistent rattle of foot-pedalled sewing machines and Avroam's occasional, quietly spoken instructions. For the rest, for Sime and her children, life was conducted *sotto voce*. They had learned, well enough, what it was to cross Avroam. As Proverbs xii has it: 'He that spareth the rod hateth his son' – and at times Jack Cohen must have wondered at how painful love could be.

But life was not all work, and during his slack periods Avroam would march his small family down to the Commercial Road to kit them out in Eton suits and straw boaters, or take them for an afternoon's outing in the nearby Victoria Park. Overall, the impression is of a home starved of laughter, cowed by the commanding figure of Avroam, who imposed his will as much on his wife as on his four children and from whom his second son was already restless to escape.

In the early 1900s, the Cohens moved from Sander Street to a four-bedroom house in nearby Rutland Street. Although considerably more spacious, there was still no avoiding the fact that what Sime called 'home' was, in reality, little more than an appendage to a workshop. Jack would spend long hours watching his father at work, a miniature figure in an elemental world. The experience had a profound influence on young Cohen's later career, but meanwhile he may well have wondered at the drudgery of it all, while counting down the days until the time came when, like his elder brother, Morris, he could enrol at the Rutland Street School.

The school records noting that six-year-old Jacob Cohen was enrolled in the infants' class in the autumn term of 1904 have long gone, and nothing remains of the once forbidding place, imprisoned by its high brick walls. If this was freedom for the young Cohen, it was of a paradoxical kind. The syllabus was limited and the classroom discipline severe, and it was only at break that Jack was able to find himself, a small but by no means puny figure, who soon learned to hold his own in that often violent playground. He was no more than an average pupil, showing no signs of the prodigious skill with figures which later enabled him to do five- and six-figure calculations in his head.

Ambitious for their children, Avroam and Sime may well have been disappointed by their son's studied indifference to scholasticism. No question, he was bright, very bright, but he wouldn't apply himself. For eight years his reports told much the same story ('Lacks application ... Must try harder'), and for eight years he progressed more by default than design through the educational hierarchy, remaining a pupil at Rutland Street after the family moved out of Whitechapel to 26 Darnley Road, Hackney.

Although less than a couple of miles north of Rutland Street, the solid, five-bedroomed house was a world away from the one the Cohens had left behind. True, the place was more spacious, thus allowing Avroam to expand his workroom, but that was secondary to its social significance. Within two decades of arriving in London, the more successful émigrés were already dispersing, abandoning their tight-knit ghetto in pursuit of status as much as space. In those early days Hackney was the limit of the Cohens' ambition.

When he was fourteen, Jacob left school, and after a short spell working in the markets with his brother-in-law, Morris Israel, he joined his father in the tailoring business. Albeit unconsciously, his worst fears were realised, fears of a life spent in the stifling environs of a sweat shop, far removed from the freedom he had found in the markets. As a greener he worked throughout the day and long into the night buttonholing. The going rate for the job was a halfpenny a buttonhole, and Jacob was soon skilled enough to be producing sixteen an hour – though Avroam only paid him pocket money.

Jacob's sister Rachel was to be married, and Avroam was saving for her wedding.

Where there had been resentment before, now there was growing hostility between father and son, the more so when Sime died in 1915 and Avroam remarried shortly afterwards. Jacob's world was closing in around him. Trapped in a job that he hated, in a home where he found little love, beholden to a father who he suspected would always treat him as a second son, never as an equal, he searched for a way of escape – and in March 1917, at the age of eighteen, Jacob Cohen enlisted with the Royal Flying Corps. The war had been raging for three years, and many of his old school-friends had already marched away to the shambles of Ypres and the Somme. Now he was to join them – 64535, Air Mechanic Cohen, J.

Eighteen years in the closed world of the East End had done little to prepare him for barrack-room life in Aldershot; for being numbered off, a cypher; for days lived at double time and subject, always, to some anonymous authority; for nights filled with bluster and browbeating and, just occasionally, the whispered taunt: kike. Until then he had had little first-hand experience of anti-Semitism, though it was a bogey that had haunted his childhood; a story of persecution told and retold by Avroam and Sime and the elders of Whitechapel but always remote. Until now, when they called him Jew. Suddenly it was as if his whole inheritance was encompassed in that one word, that all the hurt of the past was crystallised in himself.

Again, he had escaped into a trap, and much later he was to recall the unhappiness of those early days in the forces when he sought to reconcile himself to his birthright and adjust to the identity of Jack rather than Jacob Cohen. Once he would never have believed that he could have missed Darnley Road, but now ... With his basic training complete, Jack was posted to Roehampton to work as a rigger on the barrage balloons which defended the skies of south London. Slowly, diffidently, he began to build friendships and with them came a growing acceptance by the unit itself which, late in the year, was posted first to Marseilles and then to the Middle East.

The Mediterranean crossing passed without incident until the troopship *Osmanieh* entered the harbour at Alexandria, where it was holed by a torpedo from an enemy submarine. Within minutes the order came to abandon ship, but the lifeboat to which Jack had been assigned overturned on hitting the water. Unable to swim, he struggled desperately to keep afloat, but without the assistance of a nurse he may well have drowned. For four hours she kept him afloat and then, when rescued, disappeared. Although he made numerous attempts to trace her, they never met again.

He spent a brief spell in hospital before his unit was ordered into the desert in support of Allenby's army thrusting north into Palestine. On 9 December 1917, Jerusalem fell and for Cohen the irony must have been inescapable – that he, a Jew, should have helped to liberate the Promised Land from the Turks for the British! A joke in the best Yiddish tradition, it was something he was never to forget. The Foreign Secretary, Arthur Balfour, might issue his declaration ('His Majesty's Government view with favour the establishment in Palestine of a national home for the Jewish people'), but he was far removed from the frontline of prejudice with which the young aircraftsman lived every day.

Even after his discharge from the RFC following a bout of malaria, the memory remained, emotional scar tissue, and when he returned home to Darnley Street in 1919 Jack Cohen had come of age.

Almost three-quarters of a million Britons had died for the peace of 1918, but when it came it offered little to the survivors. The Prime Minister, Lloyd George, had promised much but he had little chance of redeeming his pledge: four years of war had seen to that. Crippled by debt (it was only in 1922 that the government finally negotiated the repayment of a £2 billion loan from the United States), and with an economy geared to wartime production, Britain was in poor shape to wage the peace. The situation worsened when demobilisation began. Although the programme itself was damned by confusion and delay, more than 2.1 million men had been discharged by November 1919. Half of them discovered that their old jobs had either disappeared or were held by someone else, often a woman or a man who had escaped conscription.

For many it seemed that they had waged a war only to lose the peace, and in the spring of 1919 there were momentary fears of revolution. At Shoreham, Dover and Folkestone servicemen awaiting discharge came close to mutiny; in Luton ex-servicemen burned down the town hall and assaulted the police station, and similar disturbances occurred in Wolverhampton, Salisbury, Coventry and

Swindon; in Cardiff, Liverpool and Glasgow there were race riots directed primarily against West Indian seamen who had been recruited into the merchant navy. August was marked by a series of savage clashes between the police and demonstrators in Greenwich, Edmonton, Barking and Brixton, culminating in the so-called Battle of Wood Green (in north London) when several hundred young people attacked the police.

If this was peace, then Jack Cohen must have wondered what he had fought for. Briefly, London had shared a common cause, but once again it was becoming two cities. 'Up West' at a Victory Night ball at the Berkeley Hotel, a captain in the Tenth Hussars had led the diners in a riotous toast to 'The Fox Hunt', as socialites danced the Armistice Hop and toasted the peace in champagne. Meanwhile the *Daily Herald* reported on the growing impoverishment of the East End.

At the core of London's economy, the area had thrived during the war, but the armistice put an end to that. Within weeks, the giant Woolwich Arsenal had closed, and while the rag trade suffered from the collapse in demand for military uniforms, a slump in world trade led to massive lay-offs in the docklands. The bitterness of the experience, the rejection of the survivors of the bloodiest war that history had known, was to scar a whole generation. The *Herald* wondered whether the revellers who had rung their bells on Victory Night would soon be wringing their hands. Cohen already had the answer. Like so many others, his General Service and Victory medals were mocked by the reality of the peace. Once they had meant something, but now he locked them away and, borrowing a suit from his brother, enlisted in the ranks of the unemployed. The poet Edmund Blunden was right: 'The war had won, and would go on winning.'

Years later in his official biography, *Pile It High, Sell It Cheap*, Cohen recalled: 'I wanted work, something to rely on. Unemployment is a useless, wasteful and almost immoral thing. Imagine healthy young men hanging about the streets. It was a hateful sight. I did not want the dole, just work. This was our due anyway after the war. My pension and unemployment payment could not by any stretch of the imagination be regarded as compensation for the chance to earn myself a living.'

The will was there, if the way was not immediately apparent. Indeed, there was only one thing of which he was sure: that he would not rejoin Avroam at his work benches in Darnley Road. He had quit the business to escape his father as much as the tedium of tailoring, and his two years of service had strengthened his determination to be his own man. His homecoming had been warm enough, but the welcome was short-lived, soon replaced by the brooding silences ruled over by his father and by the begrudging acceptance of his step-mother. For a while he had forgotten how stifling the life at number 26 had been. His return provided him with a salutary reminder. The place was a trap, its solid and hard-won respectability crushing out his individuality and leaving him feeling like the *golem* of Jewish folk-lore, a wraith-like figure always struggling to be free.

Eight years before he had momentarily found a measure of freedom working in the markets with his brother-in-law, and for all its tight discipline, he had found it again in the Flying Corps. Now his freedom would have to be of his own making. The question was how to achieve it. As the pace of demobilisation accelerated, so the queues for 'Jobs Vacant' lengthened and the sense of demoralisation became almost palpable. As winter turned to spring Jack began to doubt whether this was what he really wanted, to hawk himself in a market when there was no demand.

The idea of going it alone was tempting. The problem was where to begin. He had little capital and limited skills, yet the alternative – joining Avroam – meant resigning himself to living permanently in his father's shadow, in a house where he felt himself to be a stranger. The offer of a place in the business had been made not once, but many times, persuasively at first, but with mounting insistence until it had become a clash of wills – the now-ageing autocrat and his headstrong son, locked into a struggle as to whether Jack Cohen should be free or not.

It must have seemed that all his life had been a preparation for this – the school, where he had early learned to be streetwise; the RFC, where the poison of anti-Semitism had taught him the penance of Jewry; the job queues, where he had learned that promises easily made are as easily broken, the promises, not least, of politicians. Once, possibly, he would have bent to his father's will. No longer. A Jew with faith only in himself, he would settle for nothing less than independence. In the late spring of 1919 Jack Cohen hired a barrow with his £30 service gratuity, stocked it with ex-NAAFI goods and pushed it into the markets of the East End.

2. THE SECOND OLDEST PROFESSION

1919–30

'I cannot sit still, James, and
hear you abuse the shopocracy.'

Christopher North (1835)

Street markets are a place of legend, the distillation of 8,000 years of commercial history. As long ago as 6500 BC the Natufian settlers of the Jordan Valley had begun trading their surplus products with the nomadic tribes that passed through their territory on the way to new hunting grounds – corn for furs, wine for meat. However primitive the arrangement, it marked the birth of the market economy, though Jack Cohen can have had little idea of what he was heir to that spring day of 1919. Careless of history, his only concern was to find a pitch for his barrow, then talk up his wares. As for the past, there was altogether too much of it.

Always the practical man, he was profoundly suspicious of theory, a profitless occupation. Now if there had been a margin in peddling history, it would have been different; as it was, all he knew was that a barrow was a barrow was a barrow, and he had to unload it by the end of the day. Two thousand years before, a trader in the market at Pompeii had thought much the same thing, scrawling *Salve Lucrum* (Hail Profit) on the wall behind his stall. Aristotle may have despised the credo ('Citizens should not lead the life of mechanics or tradesmen, for such a life is ignoble and inimical to virtue'); nonetheless, it was the lever that had moved the world, though the onset of the Industrial Revolution in the late eighteenth century was to mark a clean break with what had formerly been a largely agricultural-mercantile economy.

Within half a century, the emergence of such great industrial centres as Glasgow, Birmingham and Newcastle had transformed the socio-economy of Britain, but it was Manchester that captured the public's imagination – 'as great a human exploit as Athens', according to Disraeli. Between 1783, with the opening of the town's first cotton mill, and 1851, the year of the Great Exhibition in London, Manchester's population rose from 17,000 to 303,300, causing Thomas Carlyle to exclaim: 'Hast tho' heard, with sound ears, the awakening of a Manchester Monday morning, at half past five by the clock, the rushing off of its thousand mills, like the boom of an Atlantic tide? 10,000 times 10,000 spools and spindles all set humming there. It is perhaps, if tho' knew it well, sublime as Niagara, or more so.'

The world was astounded, first by the sheer magnitude of the miracle, more belatedly by the contrast between wealth and poverty that the miracle entailed. As a Manchester clergyman, Canon Parkinson, was to write in 1845: 'There is not a town in the world where the distance between rich and poor is so great, or the barrier between them so difficult to cross' – a condition graphically illustrated in the retail hierarchy of the city.

In 1772, only two shopkeepers were listed in Manchester; seventy years later there were almost 1,500, a high proportion concentrated in the central shopping area, which was largely the preserve of the middle class. But if the bourgeoisie shopped in the Exchange and St Anne's Square (or their counterparts in the other industrial cities and towns throughout Britain), what of the great mass of the population who, in Lancashire and Cheshire in the 1840s, were living on an average wage of nine shillings and sixpence a week?

For them, the street market remained the staple of retailing, and in *The Condition of the Working Class in England* (1845), Frederick Engels was to provide a vivid insight into prevailing conditions, of traders selling moulting potatoes, wilted vegetables, rancid butter and 'meat lean, tough, taken from old, often diseased cattle, or such as have died a natural death, and not even fresh then, often half decayed. The sellers are usually small hucksters, who buy up inferior goods, and can sell them cheaply by reason of their badness ...

'On the 6th of January, 1844 (if I am not greatly mistaken), a court leet was held in Manchester, when eleven butchers were fined for having tainted meat … In one case, sixty-four stuffed Christmas geese were seized, which had proved unsaleable in Liverpool, and had been forwarded to Manchester, where they were brought to the market foul and rotten. All the particulars, with names and fines, were published at the time in the *Manchester Guardian*.'

The condition was general, rather than particular, though Henry Mayhew was to cast the markets in a considerably more romantic light. In 1860, he estimated there were some 30,000 costermongers (defined as 'street sellers attending the London green and "fish" markets') working in the capital, varying from 4,000 daily at Covent Garden in the summer, to 1,000 per market morning during the winter.

'The street sellers are to be seen in the greatest numbers at the London street markets on a Saturday night. Here, and in the shops immediately adjoining, the working classes generally purchase their Sunday dinner. Indeed, the scene in these parts has more of a character of a fair than a market. There are hundreds of stalls, and every stall has its one or two lights … these, with the sparkling ground-glass globes of the tea dealers' shops, and the butchers' gaslights streaming and fluttering in the wind, like flags of flame, pour forth such a flood of light, that at a distance the whole atmosphere immediately above the spot is as lurid as if the street was on fire.'

The conjunction of shops and stalls trading side by side is significant, for in the second half of the nineteenth century the traditional market was to come under increasing pressure from fixed-place retailing. If the Industrial Revolution had posed the problem of providing adequate foodstuffs for an exploding population (in the hundred years to 1900 Britain's population more than doubled), then it was also to provide the answers.

The long-term storage of perishable food-stuffs had defeated the ingenuity of man until 1806, when the Frenchman Nicholas Appert devised a method for preserving meat, fruit and vegetables in glass bottles by subjecting them to heat to destroy bacteria. Six years later, having substituted tin for glass, Bryan Donkin established the world's first canning plant in the East End, and in little more than half a century the growth of the canning industry was to open up the demand of world markets to previously inaccessible regions (notably, South and North America, and Australia) with their huge production potential.

As with canning, so with refrigeration. In the 1830s an American, Jacob Perkins, had developed and patented a primitive ice-making machine, and in 1876 the world's first refrigerated ship, the SS *Frigorifique*, sailed from Buenos Aires for Rouen with a cargo of frozen meat. Six years later, the clipper *Dunedin* berthed at London's East India Dock with a refrigerated shipment of meat and dairy produce, an event which *The Times* was to describe as 'a feat which must have a place in commercial, indeed, in political annals'.

Allied to the rapid extension of the rail network, and the substitution of steam for sail at sea, it appeared that the world had finally solved the perennial problem of matching supply to demand, especially for industrialised nations. In Britain the imports of wheat, sugar, tea and cheese doubled and of butter and lard quadrupled in the forty years to 1905, whilst the annual import of meat rose from 0.2 lb per head in 1875 to 23 lb per head only thirty years later. Such figures not only reveal the extent of the technological revolution which transformed British eating habits in the second half of the nineteenth century, but also the improvement in wage levels which had funded a consistent rise in the standard of living.

Individually, each of the above factors, whether technological, economic or social, would have had a significant bearing on the retail structure; collectively they were to transform the nature of retailing, destabilising the long-standing if delicate balance that had existed between shopkeepers and stallholders. With the emergence of new and increasingly advanced techniques and of an increasingly affluent public becoming more sophisticated in its demands, fixed-place shopping began to make significant inroads into the traditional preserves of the market.

Initially the pace may have been slow, the number of registered costermongers even showing an increase to 1900, but it was inexorable nonetheless. In 1871, Thomas Lipton opened his first shop in Glasgow; by the turn of the century, the Maypole and Home and Colonial groups were each operating more than 150 shops; whilst in 1909, F. W. Woolworth opened its first UK branch in Liverpool. They were among the forerunners of a retailing revolution of which James Jeffreys wrote in his book *Retail Trading in Britain, 1850–1950*:

'The large-scale retailing organisations that emerged to meet this [working class demand] were ... those which practised to the greatest extent economies in buying and selling techniques, those that used standardised methods and sold standardised goods, those that took the shop to the customer rather than expecting the customer to come to the shop, and those that directly and indirectly emphasised price appeal. The multiple shop and the co-operative forms of large-scale retailing fulfilled these requirements.'

By the outbreak of the First World War there were 39,700 outlets operated by multiples with ten or more branches, and the numbers were still increasing, in large part at the expense of market traders. Indeed, it is arguable that 8,000 years of history were coming to an end when Jack Cohen first pushed his barrow into the Well Street market. In Britain's case, what had once been the core of retailing was already becoming a marginalised, if colourful, anachronism.

The street market was to Jack Cohen what Jack Cohen was to the street market. Tough and uncompromising, each was ideally suited to the other, though that first day in Well Street he may have wondered whether he would survive the rigours of costermongering. It was a matter not so much of finding a pitch (eventually an established trader allowed him to use a part of her stand for a nominal rent), more of mastering the cut-and-thrust of the business, of touting himself as much as his wares in competition with the old hands of the market. He had no need to worry. By the close of business he had sold £4 worth of surplus NAAFI goods (Maconochie's Paste, Lyle's Golden Syrup), and made a profit of £1.

Avroam might disapprove (to the orthodox Jew street trading was a *déclassé* occupation) but Cohen had found his métier. The sheer exuberance of the market captivated him, and within days he had mastered its techniques. Witty, irreverent and with growing self-confidence, he would patter his customers into a sale – tinned milk ('Not threepence, not twopence, it's yours for a penny'), and broken biscuits ('Looking for a bargain? Me, I'm giving things away'), and golden syrup ('You names your price and you takes your choice'). One of them recalled: 'I can hear the old customers in Well Street now, when they used to come up to his stall and say, "Can I have a tin of jam until Friday, Jack?" and him saying, "Yes, girl, I'll trust you till Friday", always with a chuckle.'

In the pinched world of the East End, where price was the measure of all things, Jack Cohen was as much an entertainer as a tradesman, and as his patter improved, so his sales rose. 'I felt it was good to make £1 in one day. It was money, something I needed if I was going to make something of myself. Besides, I found an excitement and a thrill about market trading that only those who have ever stood and tried to sell by the most basic techniques of all can ever understand.'

The lessons he learned in those early days were to have far-reaching consequences; meanwhile his only concern was to develop his embryonic business. The opportunities were there; all that was required was the nerve to take them, and within six months of moving into Well Street he was working in at least two other markets, buying goods at cut prices and selling at cut-price margins.

As unemployment continued to rise, reaching over two million by the summer of 1921, the number of East End families living below the poverty line increased — not that Cohen or the street traders of Hoxton or Hackney or the Caledonian Road needed any lessons in the meaning of hardship. It was a condition they lived with every day, and while they made no pretence at philanthropy their cut-price trading was to play an important part in eking out the subsistence budget of London's working class during those hungry years — to the anger of manufacturers and suppliers who operated what was, in effect, a price-fixing ring.

As far back as the 1880s an embryo form of resale price mainte-nance had made its appearance in the grocery business. By the 1920s the practice was well established, with trade associations fixing the price of more than thirty per cent of all consumer goods. For the more affluent, the increased cost was little more than a minor inconvenience; for the poor, the handful of coppers which price maintenance added to their weekly budget was a punishing impo-sition — and one which costermongers treated with the contempt it deserved. Whilst members of the various 'rings' refused to wholesale their goods to steet markets, a complex underground of dealers existed who traded in bulk lots, frequently of salvaged or damaged goods ('seconds').

It was from them that Cohen bought the stock which enabled him to trim his margins to the bone — though always at a profit. If he was to succeed, it would be at the rate of a penny here and a halfpenny there, but he was confident that his latent skills with figures could keep track of his accounts. 'If I had any talent, it was mental arithmetic and a good memory. The combination paid me on the right side, never letting me down.' The remark captures something of the bravura of the man himself, the archetypal entrepreneur, quick to seize an opportunity but slow to appreciate the minutiae of its management.

After a day in the markets, he would return to his father's home with his pockets stuffed with receipts and folding money, to fall asleep, exhausted, whilst trying to balance his accounts. The only thing of which he was certain was that he was trading at a profit. What more did he need to know? It was an attitude that was to colour Cohen's entire approach to business. Abstractions were all very well as far as they went, but they did not go far enough. Ultimately, a feel for the market and a good head for figures was what business was all about; as for the rest ... As late as the 1950s he would compute the Tesco profit and loss account in his head!

For all his self-assurance, however, even the twenty-one-year-old Cohen recognised that he could not continue to hoard his takings indefinitely, and in November 1920 he opened a bank account with the Old Town Hall branch of the Midland Bank in Hackney. The rapid growth of his business in the severely depressed yet intensely competitive environment of London's street markets was beginning to impress his family (one Friday in the Caledonian market he had even astonished himself by turning over more than £100 in a day), though they were not so keen when it came to sharing Darnley Road with his growing volume of stock.

What had once been a trickle of goods had now turned into a flood. Handcarts and trucks trundled up to the front door of number 26 to deliver crates and cartons and containers which soon spilled over from Jack's bedroom into the hallway and then into that *sanctus sanctorum* of the household, the workroom.

The irony of the situation escaped Avroam; while his own business remained depressed due to the sluggishness of post-war demand, his son's business prospered to the point where Avroam's home was no longer his own. It was not a situation that could continue indefinitely, and eventually Jack found first a small lock-up stable in Clarence Road, Clapton, and later a makeshift warehouse under the arches in Upper Clapton Road, adjoining the tramyard of the Servitor Brush Company.

While his family were delighted to have their home to themselves again, Cohen exploited the move to expand his business further. After a couple of years in the markets, he had not only become adept at buying, but also recognised that such skills might well be turned to his own benefit. No question, street traders were born salesmen, but the same could not be said of their capacity as buyers. It was a gap in the market waiting to be filled, and with the rapid growth of stocks in his new warehouse, Cohen was quick to fill it.

The parable of the talents might not be part of the Jewish tradition, but who was he to ignore good advice? Since he had first invested his gratuity in a barrow-load of goods, his business had developed to the point where he was now operating out of half a dozen markets; he had purchased a horse and cart to supply his stalls and he was fast winning a reputation as a supplier on his own account. Investment was clearly the name of the game – though in 1923 he had equally pressing matters to occupy him.

At a wedding reception for one of his seemingly innumerable relatives, Cohen had met Sarah 'Cissie' Fox, the only daughter of a Russian émigré who now worked as a master tailor making suits for Aquascutum. Jack became a regular visitor to the Foxes' home in Westbourne Park, where Cissie was soon enlisted to balance his books at the end of each day's trading. In the autumn of 1923, their engagement was announced and on 29 January 1924, Cissie and Jack were married. Cissie contributed a £500 'dowry' which, together with wedding gifts totalling £130, they paid into a Post Office savings account.

The young couple's first home, rented for twenty-seven shillings and sixpence a week, was in Gore Road, Hackney, and it was here that their first child, Irene, was born in 1926. A second child, Shirley, was born four years later. Both daughters were to marry men destined to become, in their turn, chairmen of Tesco. Not that Jack could have read the future that January day of 1924. Indeed, all that he could be sure of was that the wedding gifts would provide him with the ready money to finance his next venture – buying household soap at £15 a ton, and retailing it at a profit of £20.

All that remained to be done was to find outlets for the stock. In response to a series of advertisements in the local press, Cohen recruited agents to go out and peddle his new and sure-fire line. The outcome was disastrous. The orders came in, but the agents, and their takings, disappeared. Apparently the parable of the talents had taken too little account of human nature. Jack Cohen had been comprehensively conned.

The setback may have refined Cohen's cynicism (from this time on he became increasingly cautious about trading on credit), but it did nothing to discourage his enthusiasm. Although modest by late twentieth-century standards, the success of the Upper Clapton Road operation was unquestionable. In the late summer of 1924 Cohen added a new and significant dimension to his market operations. A consummate buyer, always on the alert for new trading opportunities, his meeting with T. E. Stockwell, a partner in the tea-importing and blending business of Torring and Stockwell, led to a deal under which Cohen would buy bulk tea at ninepence a pound and sell it in half-pound packets at sixpence a time.

Only one problem remained: 'We had then and there to think of a name for the market brand I would sell. Well, we scratched our heads and finally came up with the name TESCO, incorporating his initials and the first two letters of my surname.'

It was a propitious occasion. The deal was an instant success: within weeks housewives were clamouring for the brand, and on one day alone Cohen sold almost 450 lb of Tesco tea from his barrows. Once more he had taken an initiative that his competitors were quick to appreciate, and as the queue outside the Upper Clapton Road warehouse lengthened, so his order from Torring and Stockwell rose. All the while, his market operations continued to expand: Monday, Hoxton or Hammersmith; Tuesday, Well Street; Wednesday, Chatsworth Road, Hackney; Thursday, Bermondsey; Friday, the Caledonian Cattle Market; and Saturday, whichever site promised the best return.

Six days a week, for upwards of fifteen hours a day, Cohen peddled his stock or managed his warehouse with a small team of helpers recruited from the family – his nephews Jack and Mossie Vanger and Cissie's brother Harry. The conditions in which they often had to operate were as tough as their schedule (the rule for Hoxton was 'Always hold your hand over your money and, if necessary, be prepared to run'), and in Cohen's first venture south of the river the police threatened to run him in for causing an obstruction in Frith Road, Croydon.

Whether from manufacturers or wholesalers, shopkeepers or the police, street traders were under continuous pressure, the more so when the London County Council laid a Bill before Parliament in the spring of 1927 in a further attempt to curb their operations. If enacted, it would have meant the end for many traders. With Olympian condescension, *The Times* reflected that 'though they do not serve everybody, they serve thousands more cheaply than the shops serve them', but that was poor consolation. Doubtless, the costers provided a service, but often at some cost to themselves. At New Year 1926, Cohen's private account stood at £128 and his assets totalled £453, small return for six years of back-breaking effort. Yet now the retail lobby was agitating for a new clamp-down on market traders.

It was the old, old story, the two faces of what the nineteenth century was pleased to call 'the shopocracy'. Unquestionably, street traders affected the profits of fixed-place retailers, but there was more to it than this. From behind the new-found respectability of their counters and plate-glass windows, shopkeepers regarded the costers with contempt, a reminder of their own not-so-distant past. And so they waged a quiet war on their own origins. As late as 1947 the economist Herman Levy wrote in *The Shops of Britain*, for the International Library of Sociology and Reconstruction: 'Proposals from the National Federation of Grocers and the Provision Dealers' Association that the future expansion of street stalls and barrows … should be limited, possibly by legislation, should be strongly resisted. It is only where the retail trade associations are taken as the opinion of "the trade" that no word of praise or support is found for these non-shop outlets.'

The attitude remains symptomatic of much of the retail sector which has always been concerned more with defending the status quo than with adapting to changing circumstances – a criticism that could never be levelled at Cohen. On the contrary, it was not because he did not enjoy the hustle of market trading, more because he recognised that it offered limited opportunities for expansion, that he first began to consider the possibility of opening a shop of his own.

Despite all the auguries, 1927 proved to be a good year for Cohen. In little more than twelve months, he tripled his personal account and doubled his assets whilst in 1928 his turnover may well have exceeded £23,000 – though this figure is speculative, for he was still loath to keep formal accounts. The market outlets were still trading satisfactorily, but for the moment it appeared as if wholesaling might become the major growth sector. The business was expanding fast, and began to accelerate at breakneck pace following a deal struck with Cyril Carter of Amalgamated Dairies at the Grocers' International Exhibition in 1930.

Amalgamated had over-stocked on a line of New Zealand canned milk, Snowflake. The product, as Carter explained, was so thick as to be cloying, but that did not deter Cohen. Twenty-four hours after their first meeting, he bought 500 cases, each containing 48 tins, for £250 to hustle in the market: 'Extra thick, creamy Snowflake. Extra thick, extra value.' At a profit of three shillings a case, he could not obtain enough of the line to stock not only his own barrows but also those of other market traders and wholesalers. Upper Clapton Road was close to breaking point; within eighteen months Cohen had unloaded 87,000 cases of Snowflake, and it was only the cool of Albert Carpenter that brought some semblance of sanity to the growing chaos.

A one-time clerk with W. D. Harvest, a City food merchant, Carpenter was all that Cohen was not. Where the one was cautious, the other was impulsive; where the one was fastidious, the other was flamboyant. As Cohen himself was to say of their partnership: 'When I took Mr Carpenter on, I was seriously worried whether I could afford to employ a man rather than boys. I made my own invoices out personally, and kept cash about my person. It took Mr Carpenter some eight or nine months to straighten matters out, and it was during this time that the foundation of my business was laid by a lucky venture into bigger transactions.'

Arguably, Cohen would have been quite incapable of managing this expansion without Carpenter. Ten years in the markets had taught him much, but at heart he remained a costermonger, a slight but cavalier figure more concerned with dealing than with the fine details of a balance sheet. A trait that was to become the hallmark of his whole career, the impetuosity that brooked no arguments made Cohen none the easier to work with, the more so as his confidence burgeoned. All right, so he had made mistakes, and the memory of the household soap fiasco still niggled, but as for the rest, his instinct had always proved correct.

Once Avroam and the family had deprecated his decision to go into the markets. No longer. Once friends had urged caution about his expansion into the wholesale sector. No longer. Once well-wishers had advised him against over-extending his business. No longer. At the age of thirty-two, confident in the belief that life helped those who helped themselves, Jack Cohen determined that he was going to help himself to more than six days of trading in London's street markets and a wholesale business in the Upper Clapton Road. In November 1930, he opened his first indoor stall in the Tooting Arcade, south London.

3. THE LONG WEEKEND

1930–9

'It is quite likely that fish-and-chips,
art-silk stockings, tinned salmon ... the movies,
the radio, strong tea, and the football
pools have between them averted revolution.'

George Orwell
The Road to Wigan Pier (1937)

The inter-war years marked a significant shift in Britain's economy and, once again, Cohen's instinct served him well. The wiseacres of that dismal science, economics, might peddle their jeremiads, but he traded in a more tangible commodity, and the Tooting stall did roaring business in tinned and packaged foods that first Christmas of 1930. Only a year had passed since the Great Crash, but already there were signs of revival in London and the south-east – in contrast to much of the rest of Britain.

The north–south divide (a convenient, if misleading, description for the spatial polarisation of the economy) is not new. Disraeli first coined the term 'The Two Nations' as the sub-title for his novel *Sibyl*, published in 1845, and almost a century later, George Orwell commented on the phenomenon in *The Road to Wigan Pier*: 'There is a real difference between north and south, and there is at least a tinge of truth in that picture of southern England as one enormous Brighton inhabited by lounge lizards.' As for the north, it was 'a strange country', its great conurbations having first been ravaged, and then left destitute by industry.

The slow but inexorable decline of Britain's industrial base had begun long since. In 1800, British industrial output accounted for almost forty per cent of the world's total. By 1930 it was a quarter of that figure. However, the conviction remained that Britain was still the workshop of the world, careless of the warning expressed by the Liberal Industrial Enquiry's publication *Britain's Industrial Future* (1928): 'Certain staple industries are proving unable to provide the established standards of life for their workers, with the results reflected either in low wages, in unemployment, or in both. Yet these industries occupy a position of exceptional importance in our national life ... It would be impossible to view their decline with the same comparative equanimity with which we have been able in the past to view the decline of other industries against which the tide of fashion and economic opportunity has turned.'

The sense of *déjà vu* is inescapable. Seemingly only the terminology of crisis changes, and during the 1930s the evidence of crisis was there for all to see, not least in the punishing levels of unemployment in the major industrialised regions of Wales, Scotland and the north of England, though, as *Good Housekeeping* remarked, those on the dole were 'the only people who have money today'. To its essentially middle-class readership, this notion perpetuated the illusion that the unemployed were no better than scroungers. To those drawing the full benefit of thirty-two shillings a week for a couple with two children, it mocked the reality of their everyday lives, one cereal company printing on the back of their packs recommendations on how they could balance their weekly budgets, Orwell itemising their typical shopping list: meat – two shillings and sixpence; flour – three and fourpence; yeast – fourpence; potatoes – a shilling; dripping – tenpence; margarine – tenpence; bacon – one and twopence; sugar – one and ninepence; tea – a shilling; jam – sevenpence; peas and cabbage – sixpence; Quaker oats – fourpence.

And even this, it seemed, was extravagant: one correspondent to the *News of the World* submitted her weekly budget, which allowed three shillings and elevenpence for food! In such conditions, it was hardly to be wondered at that shops in Britain's depressed areas were themselves severely depressed, giving credit to their customers in order to stay in business. Indeed, as Richard Hoggart wrote in *The Uses of Literacy* (1957): 'The grocer, whose corner shop is the housewives' club as it is in most kinds of district, will hardly prosper unless he respects the forms of the neighbourhood. Newcomers may pin to the shelf at the back of the counter one of those notices which the local jobbing printers produce, "Please Do Not Ask For Credit As a Refusal Might Offend", but whether the notice stays up or not most of them have to start giving "tick" before long. Many housewives remember how obliging their grocer was during the depression; he knew that they had not enough money to pay off the bill each week, that he might have to wait months, but if he did not serve them there would have been no customers, so he kept on and weathered it, or shut up shop after a time.'

Credit trading was neither a new practice, nor one confined solely to depressed regions of the 1930s. In *The Wheels of Commerce*, Fernand Braudel argues that it was the principal reason for the development of fixed-place retailing in medieval times, though it was long the preserve of the gentry, there being more than a smidgen of truth in the caution that the last man they paid was their tailor. With the onset of industrialisation the practice became much more widespread to the point where, by the turn of the twentieth century, 'tick' had become a feature of working class culture, just as the first phase of industrialisation itself was ending.

For more than a century, Britain's primary industries – coal and steel – had powered the economy, but by the 1920s there were signs of the emergence of a new generation of industries (electrical engineering, motor manufacturing, chemicals), many of which were located in the West Midlands and the Home Counties. In short, a quiet revolution was occurring in Britain's socio-economy, powered in large part by changing consumer demands.

Indeed, once the infra-structure of industrialisation was in place and the basic necessities of the majority of the population had been satisfied, it was inevitable that new demands would emerge. As early as 1890, the economist J. A. Hobson remarked, somewhat caustically, that 'the stimulation of new ideas provided by city life has constantly and rapidly enlarged the scope of desires of the poorer classes', and ten years later Charles Booth was noting that where formerly correspondents to his surveys had asked, 'What shall we eat, what drink, and wherewithal shall we be clothed?', they were now asking, 'How shall we be amused?'

The condition was by no means universal, and for the working class this new-found affluence (in itself a relative term) might prove a fragile thing, as it was to discover in the years immediately after the

First World War. Nonetheless the markets were quick to capitalise on changing consumer tastes. The exact relationship between supply and demand is always hard to determine, though evidence suggests that as disposable income rises the money devoted to purchasing food-stuffs peaks out, the marginal increments being spent first on durable and then on more luxurious items; hence, in part, the sharp decline in the percentage of household income (from 80% to 35%) spent on food in Britain between 1900 and 1939.

Although this overall figure disguised wide regional variations, it could not disguise the fact that the early 1930s marked a rapid upturn in the growth of the southern economy, largely to supply the growing demand for new consumer durables. Much of the north might remain chronically depressed, but then it was indeed a 'strange country', and the habitués of the Ritz were as startled by the appearance of a hundred hunger marchers asking for tea as their predecessors had been shocked by the East End match girls half a century before. The mood in the Midlands and the south of England was to become progressively more bullish as the 1930s advanced. The 'sunrise' industries were booming, and with them the southern economy. In the inter-war years, employment in the chemical industry doubled, in part to meet demand for such new products as synthetic fibres (more especially rayon) and dyes. There was an equally rapid take-off demand for a new range of electrical goods – vacuum cleaners, electric irons and what was fancifully termed 'the miracle of the age', the wireless, more than two million radio licences being issued in 1939.

The car, however, was to provide the single most visible and dramatic symbol of change. In 1913, Britain was producing 34,000 motor vehicles annually, and motoring was still regarded as the pastime of the wealthy; but in 1922, the first mass-produced Austin Seven sold for £225 and by 1939 the motor industry, concentrated largely around Birmingham, Coventry and Luton, was producing 507,000 cars and trucks. Shortly before the outbreak of the Second World War more than two million families owned a car of their own and the *Daily Herald* remarked: 'Rather than churchgoing, it has now become the fashion for families to polish up their God on Sunday morning.' At the same time, the extension of the suburban rail network was having a remarkable effect on the lifestyle of the south-east.

For all of its 2,000-year history, London had remained remarkably compact until the early nineteenth century, and although its population doubled in the next fifty years its radius increased only marginally. By 1914, however, the capital was fast outgrowing its original boundaries, and while the Great Eastern Railway was ordered by Parliament to run cheap trains for workmen to Tottenham and Leytonstone, the upper and middle classes were already developing their own enclaves, many in south and west London. The commuter age had dawned.

The process accelerated in the inter-war years, in part to cope with population pressures (between 1921 and 1938, the south-east and the Midlands accounted for 80% of the population growth in England and Wales); in part, due to the electrification of the rail network (there was a five-fold extension of London's effective commuter radius between 1920 and 1930); in part, as a result of social changes produced by economic developments, not least the shift from manual to white-collar employment in the service industries burgeoning in London and the Home Counties.

As London doubled and then re-doubled in size, so the demand for housing escalated. In 1902, the architect Raymond Unwin had written: 'How to provide for the Housing of the People is a problem to which our larger municipalities are now being compelled to find a solution' – and in the inter-war years four million new homes were built, almost two-thirds by private developers, and a high proportion concentrated in the new suburbs that sprawled around London.

A combination of depressed land prices and low building costs, allied on the one hand to improved communications and on the other to the emergence of a new white-collar labour force on regular salaries, powered the expansion. Between 1920 and 1938, the average salary of the urban commuter rose by 23%, and his improved rating as a mortgage risk provided the trigger for the development of the £500 house ('Deposit £25, Repayments per twenty-five shillings a week'). Comfortably distanced from the humdrum of life, aesthetes such as Osbert Lancaster were appalled by the development of what they termed 'Bypass Variegated'. In *Pillar to Post, the Pocket Lamp of Architecture* (1935), Lancaster wrote: 'As one passes by, one can amuse one's self by classifying the various contributions which past styles have made to this infernal amalgam: here are some quaint gables culled from Art Nouveau surmounting a façade that is plainly Modernistic in inspiration; there the twisted beams and lead panes of Stockbroker's Tudor are happily contrasted with bright green tiles of obviously Pseudish origin; next door some terra cotta plaques, Pont Street Dutch in character, enliven a white wood Wimbledon Transitional porch ... Notice the skill with which the houses are disposed, which ensures that the largest possible area of the countryside is ruined; see how carefully each householder is provided with a clear view into the most private offices of his next-door neighbour.'

The critics might scoff, but for millions the suburban semi was a domestic miracle. The overcrowding that they had known for so long was a thing of the past. For the first time they had 'room in which to breathe' (this from a developer's brochure), most houses having three bedrooms and a bathroom on the first floor, two living rooms and a kitchen downstairs, and a small garden of their own.

If the plan of houses was changing, so were their furnishings. With the growth in white-collar employment an increasing number of women were entering the work force so that time-saving devices were becoming an increasingly important feature in the home. The old fixtures and fittings, cumbersome and difficult to clean, no longer served, and the demand was for more functional designs, while a range of new labour-saving fittings were to become *de rigueur* in the kitchen with its organised cupboard space, tiling and white enamel fittings. For most, much of the drudgery of house-keeping remained, only a minuscule proportion of homes being able to afford such new-fangled luxuries as refrigerators and washing machines. Nonetheless, the pattern of domestic life was slowly being transformed, and with it, the pattern of retailing.

Late romantics such as E. M. Forster might deplore the change. Careless of reality, for them the past was an idyll, whilst as for the future, Forster wrote in *The Abinger Pageant* (1934): 'Houses. Houses. Houses! You came from them and must go back to them. Houses and bungalows, hotels, restaurants and flats, arterial roads, bypasses, petrol pumps and pylons – are these going to be England? Are these man's final triumphs?'

Jealous of their privileges, they had no wish to share them with a future that was already in the making.

Jack Cohen was to be a beneficiary of the metamorphosis of the

Home Counties during the 1930s. Ten years of successful street trading had bolstered his confidence and refined his ambition. Already something of a legend amongst the fraternity of coster-mongers, he could still patter with the best of them, but while they were willing to settle for twopence halfpenny margins he had other, more expansive ideas. The Bargain Centre in Tooting was a beginning, not an end in itself.

For an investment of £500, and supplied with goods from his warehouse, the unit had proved what fixed-trading could achieve within six months of its opening. Although little more than an enclosed stand, with its goods being auctioned off to passing customers, it provided Cohen with a regular salary of between £10 and £12 a week, after all overheads had been paid. It was a small enough return for the effort required, but if only he could develop a chain of thirty, fifty, or even a hundred such units … Or better still, conventional shops!

The ideas were unformulated, a rag-bag vision without definition and powered solely by Cohen's ambition. The future was out there, waiting to be taken, but he preferred to trade from day-to-day, suspicious of any talk of long-term planning. It was all very well for Albert Carpenter to go on about the need for some kind of management strategy from his fastness in the Upper Clapton Road, but that's not where the profits were made. It was in the markets, on the streets, that the real business was done, and that was Cohen's natural environment.

For all his ambitions, he remained a barrow-boy at heart, quick as a Cockney sparrow to scent the crumbs of a deal. The soap fiasco still rankled, but that could be put down to experience, and at the age of thirty-three, Cohen's instinct was to think big. The risks involved were proportional to the investment incurred, but so were the profits. If nothing more, that was the lesson not only of the Tooting venture but also of the Tesco tea and Snowflake deals. In the spring of 1931 the experience was to be reinforced with the purchase of 3,750 crates of tinned salmon to be sold under the name Red Glow. Housewives loved it, traders clamoured for it, and Cohen turned a profit of £3,000.

Almost by chance, Cohen had evolved a formula which, by permutating his options, was to help minimise his risk in the years immediately ahead. His overriding objective was to expand his retail operation, but if all else failed he still had a fall-back position in the warehouse business on the Upper Clapton Road. Meanwhile, he opened his second covered-market venture in Chatham in May 1931, before going into partnership with Mick Kaye, a distant relative of his wife.

Returning from a day trip to Margate in 1931 the two men spotted a vacant, central-area site in Dartford, raised £1,000 to develop it, and opened for business in the late summer. Small and unpretentious, with an open front where goods were auctioned 'at prices never seen before in Dartford', it led first to the formation of Bargain Centres (Dartford), and then, in 1938, to the establishment of the Pricerite chain.

A quarter of a century later, in the spring of 1963, Pricerite was to go public, though the offer document made no mention of Kaye's association with Cohen. The omission is all the more surprising as Cohen had retained a half stake in the company until 1956, when he sold his share to Kaye for £10,000. Superficially, the explanation is straightforward: Kaye suspected that Cohen had betrayed him by helping his nephew, Sidney Ingram, to extend his Anthony Jackson Foodfare operation into north-east Kent, which Kaye regarded as Pricerite's trading preserve. The underlying reason may be more complicated, however.

Retailing has always been a cut-throat business. To succeed in the market or on the High Street in everyday competition with the opposition – competition on stock, on price, on quality, on service – demands that skill be matched by nerve, flair by ruthlessness. Indeed, retailing is a world of two faces: the one, engaging, turned outward to the customer; the other, implacable, turned inward on the competition. Both are the prerequisites of survival – and the Jewish traders who came out of the East End *stetl* survived better than most.

In half a century the Kayes and the Ingrams and the Cohens each built empires for themselves, and this at a time of intensifying competition amongst existing retailers. During the inter-war years, the number of multiples with ten or more branches rose by 44%, the number with twenty-five branches by 68%, whilst by 1939 the Co-op was trading through 24,000 shops, a 150% increase in two decades. This was the nature of the competition, well-established and jealous of its market share, with which the new generation of

Jewish retailers had to compete – besides competing amongst themselves.

To the world at large, they gave the appearance of an extended family, presenting a united face against criticism. In private, it was very different. Until Albert Carpenter arrived Cohen had recruited almost exclusively from among his relatives, however distant the relationship, an arrangement that worked admirably – for as long as it was remembered who was the Governor.

Inspired by Cohen's success, however, certain of his protégés sought to become his imitators, which was where the trouble began. Case-hardened by his time in the markets, Cohen was unwilling to play second best to any man, and while both families were quick to weave a conspiracy of silence around the post-war rift with Kaye, the disagreement was symptomatic of much that was to follow.

By the summer of 1931, Cohen's business was doing almost too well, yet still he hankered as much for the status as for the profits to be achieved by opening a conventional shop. Tooting and Chatham and Dartford were all very well as far as they went, but they did not go far enough either in catering for the Governor's ambition or in meeting the demands of a new generation of consumers.

The Home Counties' economy was becoming more buoyant by the day, and customers were 'trading up'. Once, possibly, they had been happy with the street and indoor markets. No longer. Price was still important, but their new-found respectability demanded a new-found respectability in the places in which they shopped, and it was this that Cohen determined to provide.

The archetypal coster was turning conventional and, in the process, transforming the hotch-potch of enterprises that he had patched together over the previous decade. However, there is no evidence to suggest that Cohen was pursuing a planned policy. Quite the reverse; it is more than likely that he would have scorned such a notion, preferring to rely on his day-to-day 'feel for the market'. This said, there was an underlying consistency in the embryo company's development. Since his early days in Well Street, Cohen had been trading progressively up-market, and in the autumn of 1931 he opened his first conventional shops at Green Lane, Becontree, and Burnt Oak, Edmonton.

Each unit was under 500 square feet but nonetheless they

provided Cohen with a bridgehead into the new middle-class markets of the suburbs whilst giving him an entrée to established manufacturers and wholesalers who refused to do business with market traders dealing in cut-price lines. True, they operated a price ring; and true, he had been amongst their foremost competitors, but now he, Jack Cohen, could deal with the best of them – although Albert Carpenter must have wondered exactly what that would mean.

Conditions in the minute offices at Upper Clapton Road were chaotic, and deteriorating fast. More than sixty years after she joined the embryo company in 1931 as the office girl-cum-general factotum, Daisy Hyams can still recall her first days at work: of running the gauntlet of the constant procession of market traders arriving to collect their goods as she tried to label new stocks in the warehouse; of checking the cash, then paying the penny fare to the Midland Bank, Mare Street, to pay in the takings, while Cohen and his cronies retired for a drink in the King's Head next door. The scene she conjures up has an almost Dickensian quality – the ill-lit office, the piles of copper and silver on the second-hand desk beneath the bleary window, the stacks of dusty bills and receipts, the grimy oil stove in the corner brewing up the ubiquitous 'cuppa' – yet this was the nerve centre of Cohen's operation, where Carpenter struggled to impose some semblance of management discipline, with little idea of what might happen from one day to the next.

Caught up in a fury of activity – of wheeling here and dealing there – Cohen remained stubbornly unaware either of the need to communicate his intentions or of the necessity to regulate his books. In the early days it may have been all very well for him to balance the accounts in his head, but those days had long gone. With a six-figure turnover, the heterogeneous mix that passed for the group demanded more than Cohen's head for figures, but while paying lip-service to the need for rationalisation he continued to ignore his own best intentions.

Ultimately the situation was untenable. Cohen's dynamism was outstripping his management capacity, and without the intervention of the accountant Frank Cooper in 1931 it is likely that the young company would have blown itself apart. Bernard Lazarus, Cohen's lawyer, effected the introductions. Shocked at the chaotic state of his client's records, he suggested that Cohen set about regularising his affairs and warned him to get himself a good accountant – or face the consequences with the Inland Revenue. In the late summer of 1931 Lazarus began to explore the possibility of establishing a registered company to consolidate Cohen's holdings, whilst Cooper began a four-month probe into the Cohen enterprise.

Like Lazarus, he was horrified by the confusion he found – scraps of paper passing for invoices, bills on the back of envelopes, receipts for long-closed deals. The whole thing verged on the anarchic, and but for Carpenter it would have been even worse. For almost a year he had been doing his best to rationalise the irrational, but without being fully in Cohen's confidence it had been an almost impossible task.

The miracle was not so much that the whole haphazard enterprise had survived, as that it had prospered. Cooper's draft balance sheet of December 1931 revealed – annual sales: £119,000; cash in hand: £929; balance at the bank: £2,000. On 1 January 1932, Cohen received his first audited and properly maintained set of books – though the tax returns remained a problem. As late as October 1934, Cohen was protesting to the Inland Revenue that during his early years in business 'the keeping of books and accounts was a useless procedure', and three years later Cooper was still trying to reach an agreement with the Inspector of Taxes arising from the long-entangled state of Cohen's private and business affairs: 'We have pleasure in enclosing Capital Statement depicting Assets and Liabilities of the business conducted by Mr J. E. Cohen as at the 31st December, 1924, to the 31st December, 1931 inclusive ... We would point out that up to September, 1931, the accounting records maintained by Mr J. E. Cohen were inaccurate and inadequate ... The papers and books of the above were disjointed up to 1930, during which period Mr Cohen controlled everything, including the making of invoices as no office staff was employed.'

Addressed to the Chief Inspector of Taxes, Inquiry Branch, the letter indicates the gravity of Cohen's situation in the early 1930s. It was in an attempt to resolve the problem that Lazarus proposed the wholesale restructuring of Cohen's affairs in December 1931.

In order to provide Cooper with the time essential to clarify and then to regulate Cohen's finances, he argued that the overriding need was to establish a clear division between Cohen's personal finances and those of his enterprises. There is no record of Cohen's reaction, but the immediate result was the formation of two private companies (one under the name of J. E. Cohen and Company Ltd, the other Tesco Stores Ltd), each with paid-up capital of £100, and each with two directors – Jack and Cissie Cohen.

Whether or not Cohen himself was wholehearted in support of the arrangement is unknown. Always something of a loner, he may well have begrudged the loss of the old freedoms that he had struggled so long and so hard to find. Twelve years had passed since he had gone it alone, twelve profitable years, yet now he was being ensnared with paper chains. Whatever his private opinion, however, he had little option but to agree to what was to prove his biggest deal – and on 28 January 1932, the Registrar at Companies House filed revised details of the private limited company, Tesco Stores.

The name sounded well, Tesco Stores Limited, but the reality was somewhat different. Under the revised details, the issued capital in the Cohens' name had been increased to £1,425 in one-pound shares, yet the company's actual trading assets still remained small – a warehouse, a couple of market stands, half a dozen pitches, two small shops and a handful of devoted employees. They were small enough resources to pit against the extent and the expertise of the competition – of the Co-ops, and Internationals, and Sainsburys – but this was to discount Cohen's zest as much for business as for life. He had a formal company, so now he would make it work.

Undisciplined and ruthless he may have been, but he never lacked the nerve for a challenge, and the challenge to Tesco was clear. If the established multiples were invading the new suburbs that spawned around London, then that is where Tesco should be. Becontree and Burnt Oak had established the point, though they were already in need of reorganisation. The practice of auctioning goods from the shop fronts no longer served their new clientele and in October 1932 Cohen's latest recruit, Thomas Freake, suggested that he drop the technique.

In his early thirties, and with ten years' experience of managing a shop in Islington, Freake was to play a key role in the expansion of Tesco in the pre-war years, providing a counterweight to Cohen's natural extravagance. As with Carpenter, Freake was prudent, whilst Cohen was impulsive; though when he suggested the conversion first of Burnt Oak, then of Becontree, Cohen readily agreed. The idea was to retain the market atmosphere, but without customers having to wait to see what goods happened to be on offer. As Freake said later, 'We conceived the plan of putting in a small counter but fronting the store with two pyramids of goods on open display. The façade was to be given the name Tesco.'

The Burnt Oak alterations cost £50, and weekly sales doubled to £300. The company had discovered the format of piling it high and selling it cheap which, with modifications, was to survive for the next fifteen years. But if the conversions had proved themselves, the need now was to find new sites. For all the company's limited resources, and for all the competition, the task was not as difficult as Cohen may first have imagined. Driven by the decentralisation of the population, and underwritten by developers, the demand for new housing appeared to be virtually insatiable, and with the new homes came shopping parades.

Twenty years after the end of the Second World War, Edward Lotery, one of a new generation of property developers who opened up London's suburbs during the 1930s, recalled the land rush of those days. Obtaining an option on a piece of open land in an area scheduled for housing, he would first commission architects' drawings for a parade of new shops, then invite a major multiple such as Woolworth's to take the anchor site. After that, there was little to do but wait as other retailers clamoured for neighbouring properties.

In *The Property Boom* (1967), Oliver Marriot wrote, 'Thus Lotery and his competitors took shops to the new middle class ... as serried rows of semis ate into the countryside in patterns dictated by the railways and the underground lines ... Jack Cohen, chairman and founder of the now £90 million Tesco grocery chain, told me: "Edward Lotery was responsible for Tesco's becoming a multiple. We would go out in his car in the morning around his developments and come back with six more shops. He would pay for the shop fronts and fittings, then on opening day we would give all the customers a 2 lb bag of sugar free and bang, there was your new shopping centre."'

Elm Park and Wimbledon, Enfield and Staines, Ealing and Hornchurch – within three years of the formation of the company, the Tesco logo was becoming a familiar feature of London suburbia. The shops were there for the picking, and most at peppercorn rents – Croydon for £250 a year, Watford for £175. It was an exhilarating, wildcat time. Planning constraints were minimal and it seemed that the whole world, or that part of it bounded by the Home Counties, was caught up in some giant bonanza which offered a new way of life for millions of people.

Ultimately it was people that Cohen and Freake were about, and not only the new generation of customers with their stuccoed semis and their Austin Sevens. As the company continued its headlong expansion through the 1930s, signing a deal for a new store one day, opening a new store the next, staffing posed a growing problem. It was not difficult to recruit managers at the going rate of between £3 and £4 a week, and assistants for twenty-five shillings, but retaining them was a different matter. The work was hard, and the hours long.

Legislation was underway to restrict the length of the working week (forty-four hours for those under sixteen, forty-eight hours for women and sixteen- to eighteen-year-olds), though it had little effect until after the Second World War. William Careswell, manager of a North London store, remembers, 'The manager arrived to open up between seven and eight in the morning, to put out the benches and pile them up with all sorts of tins, like pineapple chunks – one for threepence halfpenny, two for sixpence halfpenny. We were all cut price. All this was stacked on the pavement, and that's where the frontsman would have to stand, trying to sell what he'd got. It isn't like it is now. You weren't allowed to leave. When it got dark the lights outside went on, and you went on selling. There were lots of people shopping late. Housewives used to wait until their husbands came home on Friday or Saturday with the wages, and then they used to come and shop. Often it was well after nine before we saw off our last customers, and it was only then that we closed.'

If the hours were gruelling, so were the working conditions. Muriel Needs, who ran the Union Street, Reading, branch before the war, recalls: 'When we had a delivery, and like as not it would come around lunchtime, it would have to be dropped at the end of the road, and be stuck there all afternoon. Eventually, when things quietened down, we'd have to pick it up with a trolley, move it down the road, then carry the lot upstairs – eighty pounds of cheese at a time, and the sugar in twenty-eight-pound sacks.'

After this came the preparation. Although packaged goods were taking a growing market share, a high proportion of stock in the 1930s still came in bulk that first had to be broken down, then weighed up for the sugar and dried fruit to be packed into bags with galvanised wooden spoons, the cheese and butter and bacon prepared, then laid out. Alicia Reeves ran the Tesco store in Wantage, Berkshire, for twenty-seven years: 'Sometimes I sold four eighty-pound cheeses a week. These came in big wooden crates, each holding two cheeses and all wired up. I still have the jemmy and pliers I used for opening them. After getting them out the job was to skin them. Sometimes the wrappers were so hard to pull off that I blistered all the tops of my fingers, so that in the end I had to get a galvanised bath, fill it with water, then put the cheeses in to soak the skins.'

Initially, much of the stock was the result of Cohen's own buying expeditions. The old habits died hard, and he still could not resist a deal, more especially if it meant beating Resale Price Maintenance imposed by the more respectable manufacturers. For all their new-found airs and graces, there was nothing that housewives liked better than a bargain, whether stock from fire-damaged properties or tinned products from salvaged vessels. And as Cohen bought, so he sold. Alfred Howe, who joined Tesco in 1933, recalls, 'I remember he bought a consignment of Skipper sardines from a boat which I think was half sunk, though it got into port. He sent around sheets of emery paper with a covering note: "Take off the labels, clean off the rust and sell them for twopence a tin." We did, they were lovely, the customers couldn't get enough of them.'

But while much of the old freebooter in Cohen remained, the times were moving against him. There was little point in trying to move up-market if all the while he continued to play the rapparee. Inevitably, it created a conflict of image, and whilst shoppers still enjoyed the Tesco special offers (one week a can of pineapple, with a pint of Hartley's jelly free; the next a tin of Libby's salmon given away with every ten shillings spent), they not only ran counter to the practice of established groups such as Lipton's and Sainsbury's, but also posed a growing threat to the company's sources of supply.

Manufacturers such as Cadbury and Ovaltine knew Cohen's reputation for dealing with cut-price wholesalers well enough, but with a growing number of outlets, Tesco needed to guarantee the supply of manufacturers' stocks and exploit the national promotion of their standardised lines: Kelloggs 'The Sunshine Breakfast', Beechams, 'Worth a Guinea a Box.' Except at the top end of the market, the days of individualised production and marketing were numbered. Rationalisation was becoming the rule, leading to the growing power of a diminishing number of manufacturers which, in its turn, led to increasing homogeneity in the pattern of consumer demand.

Freake was quick to recognise the danger. The price-busting methods that Cohen had employed so successfully for so long were now threatening his entire operation. Unless Tesco conformed to the manufacturers' rules as fixed by their various trade associations, there was a very real danger that the company would be blacklisted. A memorandum to all warehouse customers dated 19 January 1935 indicated the gravity of the situation: 'Please note that it is imperative that you do not lend or sell Ovaltine or any other proprietary line to any other traders whatsoever. Failure to comply with this request must definitely mean that we shall have to stop your supplies as well as having our own supplies stopped.'

There was no escaping the implication: either put up or shut up. Three years had passed since Cohen had formally registered his company, and Freake was unwilling to see either the time or the effort go to waste. Appointed to oversee all the Tesco's stores, now numbering more than forty, he was loath to jeopardise the future for the sake of a few bargain deals, though it proved easier to eliminate the problem than to tackle the more deep-rooted practice of buncing, the retailers' argot for fiddling. The extent of buncing was neatly encapsulated in Cohen's advice to his pre-war managers: 'I don't mind if you're making a bob for yourself, as long as you're making two for me.'

How they did so was neither his nor Tesco's concern. In effect, each manager was his own profit centre, selling at whatever price he thought reasonable. Whether he obtained his supplies direct from the warehouse or via company reps made no difference as long as he showed a profit on stock. An open invitation to private enterprise, the variations on a theme of buncing were as various as they were ingenious.

David Jarman, who joined Tesco as a manager in Sudbury Hill in the mid-1930s, says, 'If a manager had stocks that were marked up by the warehouse as being twopence cheaper than anywhere else, but he could unload them for only a penny cheaper, there was his profit, and that was buncing.'

Alfred Howe: 'Some of the reps would come in and try to push an article: "Take fifty cases of so-and-so," they'd say, and my reply would be "I'll take fifty, and ten cases free" – and that'd be the profit on the deal.'

The extent of buncing depended entirely on individual managers, but it was always the customer who bore the cost. As Mr Jarman now says, it was robbing the public whether for personal or corporate gain, and both Cohen and Freake openly encouraged the practice. Entrepreneurs themselves, they recognised the need for entrepreneurship in others. Indeed, if they were to hold down wages, what better incentive could a manager have than to know that a percentage of the takings, albeit below the line, were his? By 1935, Tesco was employing some forty embryo entrepreneurs in shops throughout the Greater London area!

Since the hiatus of 1931, Cohen was almost half way to achieving his ambition of establishing a chain of a hundred stores and, with no let-up in the development programme, demand was already out-stripping the capacity of the Upper Clapton Road warehouse. Ten years before, when he had paid his first rent of £100 a year on the premises, it may have seemed that his hopes had been realised, but now the old building and its darkling office were altogether too small, outgrown by the expansion of Tesco.

Late in 1934, Cohen had earmarked a site for development on Angel Road, Edmonton. The owner was willing to dispose of the land, and in August 1935 the first Tesco House was opened, at a total cost of £50,000, £20,000 of which was raised from the Halifax Building Society. For Daisy Hyams, the move was little less than a culture shock: 'I can't describe the feelings when we moved into the new building with a proper office layout, furnished by Heals, and with all the facilities we lacked at Upper Clapton Road, which even when extra offices were obtained in the tramyards was a grim place to work.'

Many old practices were still retained, however: the cardboard shoeboxes for storing the records, the red exercise books for price lists (Tesco tea at one and sixpence a pound, butter at eight and threepence a case). The ultimate test of their utility appears to have been whether they worked, which they did, in managing both the accounts of the burgeoning chain and the increasingly complex stock of the warehouse. With a floor area of 41,000 square feet, and capable of servicing up to 200 stores, it was among the most advanced units of its kind in the country.

The place was a whirlwind of activity. Although the move had led to the company's withdrawal from selling to street traders, in part because the traders themselves found the new site inaccessible, in part to reduce further the risk of manufacturers' sanctions, the volume of stock handled was increasing and the distribution network expanding by the day. Where once a second-hand ambulance, later replaced by a charabanc with boarded-up windows, had sufficed for deliveries, there were now ten Tesco vans and trucks.

Jim Harrow, who first joined Cohen as a boy in the Croydon market, recalls, 'I would load up between seven and half past eleven in the evening, then drive through the night to be at Bedminster, in Bristol, before moving on to Bridgwater. I would then take seven hours' sleep at a suitable bed and breakfast stop for three and sixpence before haring back to Edmonton.'

There the process would begin all over again. Working a fifty-four-hour week, the twenty-four-man warehouse team under Avron 'Darkie' Rose shifted thousands of tons of bulk stock a year, with only a couple of trolleys and no automation to help them. Years later, Cohen was still to measure an employee's quality by whether he could hump one box, or two, while he set an example by driving himself harder than anyone else. His energy was inexhaustible, even when it came to practising his own eccentric methods of quality control.

According to Jimmy Hogarth, a northerner taken on in the warehouse in 1936, 'He had his main office and a toilet and a little kitchen where he used to sample all the products coming in, seated at a small table. Whether or not he knew their quality, he would still buy them, taste them, then dump them down the lavatory, peas and all. He blocked it up so often with products that it became a sort of standing joke.'

The remark tells much about the atmosphere of Tesco House in the days before the outbreak of the Second World War. As with the stores, the work schedule was tough, even punishing, but the head office staff still remained comparatively small – and the feeling of a family concern remained. Cohen was the Governor, Freake ran the stores, Carpenter kept the books, and each of them was a hard taskmaster, but formality had yet to come. There was no time for ceremony, there was too much to do.

In 1935, the company was turning over some £40,000 a week, and in the next four years store openings averaged one a month. The mood was ebullient, dynamic – in less than a decade Tesco had become a force to be reckoned with in London retailing – and as the company continued to extend its coverage, Cohen's search for sites took him farther and farther afield. He had learned something of development and planning from Lotery, but much of the old impulsiveness remained, and more than once he stopped his car on seeing a vacant store in a promising site, to clinch a deal within the day.

And behind Cohen came Freake, setting up shop and recruiting staff. As the company expanded, so its reputation among retailers increased, not least for the autonomy which it offered its managers. Other chains were tightly regulated, but at Tesco each manager was his own man, responsible for directing his own affairs. Stan Maunder joined Tesco as a manager in 1942:

'I enjoyed my work, even though I sometimes started at half past five or six in the morning. If you worked for Tesco and you had an idea which was practical and showed a profit, you could put it into operation. You couldn't do that with other companies. You had to do exactly what they told you. At David Greig they even measured the position of the butter slab, and if you moved it half an inch you were told off. Tesco was another world, where you could use flair and initiative, which is what I liked.'

The rewards were considerable (for a period the company even operated a rudimentary profit-sharing scheme, offering managers a 1¼% commission on sales), but the pressures were intense. Operating as always on fine margins, Tesco had no room for failures, and the quarterly stock check was the ultimate yardstick of a manager's abilities. Two poor results, and he was out – Freake, or one of the team of three inspectors he now employed, would see to that. At times, it must have seemed to managers that they were not just competing with their High Street rivals, or even against the management of Tesco House, but against themselves as well.

The stimulus worked. Cohen's dynamism was infectious. The alchemy of motivation is difficult enough to define, and how to communicate it is now a study in itself, carefully quantified by the whey-faced boffins who lurk around the corners of power. Cohen would have remained an enigma to them, a complex personality conforming to none of their rules. Yet this was the man, shrewd and capricious, ruthless and charismatic, who in the long weekend of the inter-war years had laid the foundations of a retail empire with his £30 investment in a barrow in London's East End. By 1939, Tesco had more than a hundred small stores trading in London and the Home Counties, and as he listened to Neville Chamberlain announcing that Sunday morning of 3 September that Britain was once again at war, Cohen must have wondered at the difference those years had made and pondered, for an instant, whether his ambitions were now at an end.

4. THE STORM OF WAR

1939–45

'In war, food is a most fundamental
and decisive factor. If food goes,
everything goes.'

Robert Boothby, MP
House of Commons (July 1940)

Britain's food policy was in a shambles at the outbreak of the Second World War. As early as 1933 the government had decided that rationing should be introduced if another major war occurred, and in 1936 a Food (Defence Plans) Department had been established. As is so often the case, however, good intentions disguised the reality, for in September 1939 the country was quite incapable of feeding itself from its own resources in the event of a prolonged war.

For a century, British agriculture had been in a state of near-continuous decline. Where once the country had been largely self-sufficient as far as staple foodstuffs were concerned, the growth of cheap imports had undercut the home market to the point where, in 1913, Lloyd George was deploring the fact that '£300 million worth of the products of the soil were being imported from abroad which could have been grown here'.

The remark was echoed in a Commons debate of January 1940. Leading an attack on the government's neglect of the agricultural sector, the now ageing Welsh Wizard concluded: 'The last war was decided on food shortage ... Germany collapsed for lack of food. We survived, largely through the food programme which converted 3,250,000 acres of grassland into arable land.'

As with Louis XVIII, however, it seemed that the government

had forgotten nothing and learnt nothing. During the agricultural depression of the inter-war years, some 3.5 million acres had been taken out of production, and more than 250,000 skilled workers had left the industry, so that by 1939 as much as two-thirds of all UK food supplies were once again coming from abroad, including 87% of cereals, 73% of sugar, 69% of cheese, 51% of meat, 39% of eggs, and 25% of vegetables. If the war was short, the situation was just about tenable. Given prolonged hostilities allied to a concerted attack on Britain's shipping lanes, and there was a very real risk that the country would starve.

The phoney war temporarily disguised the magnitude of the danger, but with the fall of France in June 1940 the full extent of Britain's vulnerability was exposed. The Germans controlled a coastline reaching from northern Norway to the Spanish frontier, whilst with Italy's opportunist entry into the war the Mediterranean sea routes were effectively closed. Simplistically, Lord Beaverbrook suggested that Britain should grow more and eat less, but in Whitehall a more realistic attitude prevailed. The Ministry of Agriculture knew well enough that the damage inflicted on agriculture could not be corrected overnight – it was three years before Britain became 70% self-sufficient – while at the Ministry of Food Lord Woolton launched a campaign which in the coming years was to transform Britain's eating habits.

As Woolton wrote later: 'The organisation of the ministry had been carefully planned before the war by civil servants. They had based their plans on the experience of Lords Davenport and Rhondda, the Ministers of Food in the First World War who ... were the creators of a system of rationing which operated then. But there was a difference. Rationing and restrictions were introduced in the First World War to meet emergencies which had arisen. The planners – wisely with the Black Book of the history of the first ministry ever before them – had built up conditions for the new ministry to operate at once should war break out.'

He was too kind. The bureaucrats may have handled the machinery of registration for ration books and the subsequent introduction of rationing in January 1940 well enough, but their minister, William Morrison, was unwilling to mount total war on the kitchen front, and the ministry failed to communicate the urgency of the problem to the general public. Britain was facing a crisis, yet the ministry appeared to be more concerned with the minutiae of administration than with mobilising shopkeepers and housewives to help win the war on the home front. Twice during the winter of 1940 there were heated debates in the Commons over 'the muddle in food distribution', much of it directed at the inadequacy of food controls themselves.

While rationing had been introduced on essential foodstuffs, luxuries were left to find their own price levels, and public opinion quickly hardened against the minster for attempting to maintain pre-war trading practices when the need was for more rationing and stricter price controls to ensure that the entire population obtained food at prices they could afford. On 2 April 1940, Morrison resigned, to be replaced the following day by Lord Woolton.

The change in style was immediate, perceptible and fortuitous. On 4 June, the last of the 338,000 Allied troops were lifted off the beaches of Dunkirk, and Britain was left facing Germany alone. The phoney war was over, but Woolton had already set about energising his department and activating a publicity campaign to enlist support for his programme. Initially, rationing had only covered bacon, ham, butter, sugar and meat, but in July 1940 it was extended to include tea, margarine and cooking fats, and eight months later jams, preserves and syrup were added to the list.

There were minor variations in individual allowances – pregnant women and young children, for example, received additional milk quotas – but by mid-1941 the average ration had stabilised at two ounces of butter per head per week, two ounces of fat, four ounces of margarine, twelve ounces of sugar, two ounces of tea, two ounces of cheese, four ounces of jam or syrup, one shilling and twopence worth of meat – and one egg per fortnight.

It was a tough regime, and needed to be, for the Battle of the Atlantic was intensifying by the day. In February 1941, 400,000 tons of Allied shipping was lost due to enemy action, in March 500,000 tons, whilst in the following two months U-boats sank 142 merchant vessels and air attacks accounted for a further 179. Britain's lifeline with the world was close to breaking point, and as supplies diminished, so wholesale prices for food and clothing rose, and the opportunities for racketeering increased. Determined to maintain an equitable distribution of supplies and to peg price inflation, Woolton extended rationing in December 1941, by introducing a points system on certain canned goods and luxury commodities.

Under the new scheme, all customers were allocated sixteen points for any four-week period, which they could then exchange for different sorts of foods, each commodity being given a points value: for instance, a tin of red salmon took the whole of one's monthly allocation of points, whereas a tin of sardines was only three points. Unlike the previous system, under which customers had to register at specific shops, they could now buy their goods wherever they liked, retailers exchanging their points coupons at Food Offices and receiving vouchers in return which they would then send with their reorders to wholesalers.

Inevitably there was grumbling (always a useful safety valve in times of crisis), but considering the magnitude of an operation that embraced the entire food chain from farmers through manufacturers, wholesalers and retailers to Britain's fourteen million families, the system was fair and met one of Woolton's cardinal requirements: to ensure that 'everyone received the minimum amount of protein and vitamins necessary to ensure good health'. Shortly before the outbreak of war, one of the world's leading nutritionists, Sir John (later Lord) Boyd Orr, had published a blistering report on Britain's dietary shortcomings which, amongst other things, revealed that a quarter of the population was in some way malnourished. Within months of the outbreak of war, the revelation spurred the government to adopt a scientifically formulated diet, based on the identification of the protein, fats, vitamins and carbohydrates needed for good health.

The breakthrough was timely, enabling Woolton and his ministry to devise a balanced wartime diet, which was then assiduously promoted through newspapers, in cinemas (Food Flashes in soap-opera style), and on the memorable Kitchen Front, a five-minute spot that followed the eight o'clock news on the radio every day. The conditioning was inescapable ('Remember, nearly half of our food comes from across the sea. Here is your part in the fight for victory'), though certain of the ministry's more exotic dishes were to provide a rich source of material for humorists – Woolton pie, whale meat steaks, and the ill-fated *snoek piquante* ('take one tin of snoek, four spring onions, and two tablespoons of sugar ...'). All that *Food Facts* failed to mention was that snoek itself was virtually inedible.

But while *bons viveurs* may have regarded such dishes as gastronomic disasters, the so-called 'welfare diet' of the war and immediate post-war years led to a consistent improvement in health standards for the majority of the population.

Housewives queuing for their weekly rations did not necessarily appreciate this at the time, however. By the third year of the war, the queue had become a feature of the British way of life, a hardship to be borne with a combination of good humour, resignation and intense irritation. As one London housewife, quoted in Calder and Sheridan's book *Speak for Yourself* (1985), recalled: 'People arrive before the shops open at nine. Other people discovering this arrive earlier the next day. Still more arrive earlier on subsequent days. The position is so ugly that at nine police are regulating the queues ... There are many shops blitzed, and those functioning have too small staffs to give reasonable service to these terrible queues.'

Those functioning had too small staffs! The remark tells as much about the history of retail employment as it does about the future development of the industry. Until the mid-nineteenth century, it had been virtually unthinkable that upper- or middle-class women should work except, as a last resort, as a governess, whilst jobs for working-class women were confined largely to agriculture, the textile industries of Lancashire and Yorkshire, and domestic service (the 1851 census registered 905,000 women in domestic employment).

Important as they were, women effectively remained an underclass, marriage confirming both their social status and their subordinate role in society. However, whilst this had always been the case, there were tentative signs of change. Although the benefits of an economic upturn in the third quarter of the nineteenth century were by no means universally shared, there was a general improvement in the standard of living, and in the first age of mass consumption advertisers were quick to recognise not only the potential of the housewife's increasing spending power but also the fact that a growing number of women were generating incomes on their own account.

The relationship was a symbiotic one, the image of the new and, by implication, liberated woman of the copywriters simply reflecting a fundamental change that was taking place in the socio-economy with the emergence of a new range of employment opportunities for women. Albeit hesitant at first, the development was to do as much to revolutionise women's perception of themselves as it was to revolutionise the future job market.

Driven by the expansion of service industries, allied to the introduction of the typewriter (advertised by one company as 'the ideal tool for young ladies to operate'), there was an explosive growth in the number of clerical jobs open to women, their number increasing by 400 per cent in the half century to 1911. And as with office staff, so with teaching and nursing and retailing; overall employment in the so-called 'white blouse' sector rose by 161 per cent between 1881 and 1911.

Although preferable to manual employment, working conditions in the service sector were still punishing, more especially for shop assistants. The hours were long, a minimum of sixty a week, the pay was poor, averaging around £30 a year for those with 'living-in' accommodation, and against the opposition of the retail lobby an assortment of reform proposals foundered on the timidity of successive administrations.

The First World War brought a temporary improvement in the situation, mass mobilisation leading equally to a demand for, and a belated appreciation of, women's role in the workforce. With the peace, however, Lloyd George and the Liberals set about persuading women to return to 'home and hearth', and it was not until 1928, after half a century of campaigning, that a Shops Act was passed limiting opening, and thus working, hours; it was also the year in which women finally won equality of suffrage.

The events may have been coincidental, but the conjunction was appropriate. The issue of retail employment may have been subordinate to the 'Votes for Women' campaign, but the former certainly lifted the level of women's consciousness which, in its turn, found powerful expression in the suffragette movement; whilst, conversely, the latter must have nerved a growing number of women to demand not only the vote but also improved working conditions for themselves and their colleagues.

Even then, patronage still prevailed. The liberated woman was all very well in theory, whereas in practice Virginia Woolf was to note in 1938: 'Our class is the weakest of all classes in the state.' It took the Second World War to re-establish women's work credentials. From the first call-ups of 1939, manufacturing and service industries began to lose manpower and, for a second time in a quarter of a century, women were recruited to take their places. By 1940, it was estimated that Britain was 100,000 workers short of its needs, and little more than three years later 90,000 women were working on the land, and a further 467,000 serving with the armed forces.

Women's war effort was to compel universal admiration. In 1942, the US War Department issued a leaflet to all GIs arriving in Britain for the first time. Hyperbole aside, it revealed the new mood that was abroad: 'British women have proved themselves in this war. They have stuck to their posts near burning ammunition dumps; they have delivered messages afoot after their motorcycles have been blasted from beneath them; they have pulled aviators from burning planes. There isn't a single record of a British woman in the uniformed services quitting her post, or failing in her duty under fire. When you see a girl in uniform with a bit of ribbon on her tunic, remember she didn't get it for knitting more socks than anyone else in Ipswich.'

Clearly, it is impossible to assess the exact impact on women of their wartime experiences, though it is equally clear that they were to have a significant bearing on the subsequent emergence of feminism. Again they had escaped the stereotype of 'the little woman', but this time there would be no meek return to domesticity, no submissive acceptance of second class citizenship. Two world wars had taught women growing militancy.

So much, however, meant little to customers queuing for their weekly ration in the ill-stocked and understaffed shops of the wartime years. All the old courtesy, it seemed, had gone, one more victim of the war effort, and if the author and dilettante W. McQueen Pope could rue the passing of 'the servile shopkeeper', then Harold Wicker of the London Co-operative Society was to sound the death knell for personal service. In 1942, and harassed by shortage of staff, he opened Britain's first self-service store at Romford, in Essex. Operated by the Co-op, and measuring little more than two hundred square feet, it was the shape of things to come.

Within minutes of Neville Chamberlain's announcement that war had been declared that September day of 1939, the banshee wail of sirens sounded over London. It was a practice alert, but for Jack

Cohen it must have triggered memories of a not-so-distant past; of that day twenty-two years before when he had enlisted with the RFC; of that night in an Aldershot barrack-room when he had first heard the whispered taunt: kike. Now there were dark rumours of a new and more terrible pogrom, with Hitler raging, 'Perish Judah.' Momentarily it must have seemed to Cohen as if past and present had fused, that the brutishness of the barrack-room had seeded and multiplied until now the German legions marched to the battle song: 'When Jewish blood spurts under the knife', to make a hazard of everything for which he had hoped and worked – his family, his home, but most of all his business.

Ironically, the war was to prove a godsend for Tesco. A privateer by inclination, and implacable by force of circumstance, Cohen had little time and less sympathy for the niceties of bureaucracy, for the regulations and directives and the endless form-filling that implied that he was no longer the master of his own concern. Surely he had proved his astuteness in building a business from nothing in less than two decades, yet now it seemed that there were others who knew his business better then he did himself.

The reaction was understandable, but it disguised the fact that by the very nature of its success Tesco needed a period of calm to consolidate its position in the market. In the five pre-war years the company had expanded at breakneck pace, and for all Freake's management expertise, for all Carpenter's financial acumen, the need remained to rationalise the future of the company, to establish where it was going, and how.

Cohen might not have accepted this; the quintessential coster, he still preferred to wheel and deal, but he was quick to recognise that as a multiple, albeit a small one, Tesco was in an advantageous position at the outbreak of war. Indeed, his longstanding practice of buying in excess of known demand in the hope of making a quick turn was now to stand the company in good stead, not only in attracting new customers but also in its dealings with the Ministry of Food.

To fix the allocation of unrationed goods, all retailers had to supply the ministry with records of their food purchases between 1936 and 1939. Although far from sophisticated, Carpenter's efforts to make sense of the chaos which he had inherited now paid a handsome dividend, as Daisy Hyams recalls: 'Fortunately we had all the records the ministry required. I wouldn't say they were highly organised, most of them were kept in cartons and shoeboxes and that sort of thing. Nevertheless, they were there, and I went through every invoice and put in a return to the Ministry of Food. From these invoices we were given an allocation of goods in short supply, such as canned goods from abroad, fruit, meat and vegetables.'

Based on Cohen's buying forays, Tesco's allocations were generous, and significantly reinforced the company's attraction when rationing was introduced. Two months after the outbreak of war, all customers had to register with a grocer of their choice if, from January 1940, they were to obtain their rationed goods – tea, sugar, butter, bacon. For all the importance of such staples, it was Tesco's stock of goods, as yet unrationed, that gave it added customer appeal.

The trick was neatly played: new custom was generated by Tesco's extended stock which, in its turn, generated increased supplies based, as they were, upon the custom registered at individual stores. Cohen may have had his doubts about bureaucracy, but even he was compelled to admit the elegant simplicity of this closed circle of supply and demand. But if Tesco was the main financial beneficiary of the scheme, Cohen himself inaugurated an in-store programme that ensured fair shares for all.

In 1939, the company introduced a points system for all its registered customers to ensure the equitable distribution of unrationed goods. It was a pioneering venture that not only did much to establish Tesco's reputation as a fair dealer but was also to find an imitator in the points system introduced by the Ministry of Food in 1941. Possibly the bureaucrats tucked in the wartime fastness of North Wales knew nothing of Cohen's initiative, and clearly the extension of the original rationing system was motivated by national interests rather than me-tooism. Nonetheless, the two schemes bore a remarkable similarity, and it may have been that as a member of the Ministry of Food's Food Trade Emergency Committee Cohen mentioned his scheme to a Whitehall mandarin for it to be processed through the corridors of power to re-emerge as the directive which led to points rationing.

Whatever the truth, one thing is certain: that in December 1941, the Ministry introduced its own points system, after almost two years in which Tesco and its rivals had enjoyed the benefits of trading in what amounted to a captive market – at the expense of the smaller independents and corner shops. Operating on extended credit, which wholesalers became increasingly unwilling to advance, and trading on limited stocks, many found it increasingly difficult to compete with the multiple's cash and buying power. The Ministry reported in 1941: 'On the whole, wartime conditions favour the multiples, who are more highly capitalised and organised than the independent trader.'

Certainly Tesco's gross profits show a consistent growth in the early years of war, from £105,000 in the year ending 31 December 1938, to £131,000 at the close of 1941, for all the constraints and hazards involved in retailing. With the fall of France in June 1940 the Channel became the front line, and brought London within easy striking distance of the Luftwaffe operating from aerodromes on the French coast. By early July, the Battle of Britain was gaining momentum, and the capital was under siege. Day in and day out, German aircraft pounded the city, razing whole streets and driving the population underground, as Alfred Howes recalls: 'I used to leave home in Battersea at six o'clock in the morning, and sometimes the bombs would be dropping all the way to the shop. Quite often when I got to the [underground] station to come home I would find no trains. Just under the Thames there were floodgates across the lines, in case the bombs went straight through. When they shut the gates, that was it. You couldn't get through and like everyone else I had to sleep in the station. When the "all clear" went and they opened the gates I'd go home and have a quick wash and shave, then go back to work. I never went out with anyone, my mates, not anyone, because I never saw them.'

The story was commonplace during the Blitz. Daisy Hyams had to change buses as many as five times, taking up to two and a half hours to reach the office, where she would take up her position in the strong room each time the alert sounded: 'It was the place where all our records were kept, and built under the stairs. Because it was reinforced, I used to go and sit in there for hours during air raids.'

Next door, in the warehouse, the crew built a shelter of packing cases, though not entirely as a safety precaution. Jimmy Hogarth: 'As most of the crates held pineapples and peaches, the shelter began to disappear as soon as it was completed!'

The remark is made lightly, forgetful of the everyday fear that the next one might have your name on it or, worse still, that of one of your family; of the growing fatigue of working a nine or ten hour day, then having to fire-watch in a store by night; of the frustration of having to make do with whatever was available, which was never enough to satisfy the customer. Daisy Hyams: 'No wonder people got frustrated and took it out on us, when they had to queue for almost everything whatever the weather was like – rain, wind, cold. And as often as not, and for all their queuing, the sign would go up "Sold Out" before they reached the head of the line. I remember if I was late getting to the store I wouldn't get anything. Even though I was in the business, I still had to queue.'

And always, and inescapably, there were the forms, forms to rationalise the irrational and to regulate the irregular; a bureaucratic nightmare, managed by bureaucrats. Shadowy figures, but armed with extensive powers, food inspectors kept a close watch on stores, examining papers, questioning staff and enforcing the growing volume of directives – directives on shop opening hours and energy saving, directives on food prices and staffing levels, and – notably for Margery Ketchell, in the absence of her husband the wartime manageress of Tesco's Teddington store – directives on salvageable material:

'I was the first person to be fined for burning paper rubbish. There was a man called the salvage man, and he collected all the rubbish cartons and things for the war effort. I was very naughty; some cartons had got tatty and damp out the back, and I didn't like having rubbish about, so I burned it. I got split on by someone and had to go to court where I was fined £2. It was awful. The following day it was in the papers saying I'd gone on the wrong path.'

The war brought other changes. Where once keen pricing had been Tesco's major selling point, prices were now fixed by the ministry; where once 'buncing' had been prevalent, it was now to be replaced by a growing traffic in under-the-counter deals. By the third year of the war, and with forms proliferating in inverse proportion to the availability of supplies, opportunities to beat the system burgeoned, and Mrs Ketchell still remembers being approached by a police officer with the offer to drop her case in return for half a pound of unrationed butter.

Blackmail? Certainly, but then it was only part of an extensive network of dealing that the ministry was unable to stamp out. Which is hardly surprising. At one level, the black market, there were considerable financial incentives to trade in commodities in short supply; at another, and altogether more informally, retail staff were always under continuous pressure from family and fair-weather friends to provide them with 'a little extra on the side'. David Jarman was managing a Tesco store in 1942 when the inspector called.

'He came straight to the point and said I was in trouble. When I asked why, he said I'd sent in last week's coupons instead of the current ones. I told him I'd find out what had happened as the case could come to court, and found that a local butcher was operating a ring which involved my own girls.

'It was a simple enough scheme. In those days, there were different-coloured coupons for each week, and what he was doing was cutting out all the old coupons in his own customers' books, then giving them to my girls. All they had to do then was wait until I counted out my own *bona fide* coupons, as many as a hundred thousand a week, which I'd put in an envelope and leave on my desk.

'Maybe it was careless of me, because that's when they'd make the switch. One of them would call me into the warehouse to get something off the most inaccessible top shelf, and one of the others would swop the dud coupons for the genuine ones, which they'd then hand over to the butcher who'd give them free meat. I suppose it wasn't a big racket, though it almost landed me in court.'

As shortages of trained staff and stock increased, so the pressure on managers grew, to compound all their other difficulties. By 1943, the tide of war was turning, but conditions on the home front remained austere. Now boredom threatened the shops. Having once tidied the store and distributed the rations there was little left for staff to do, as Muriel Needs, of the Tesco store in Union Street, Reading, recalls: 'Mr Greenslade, one of our inspectors, came looking for me in the shop one day. I wasn't there, and the girls told him I'd gone to the Vaudeville Cinema, where Boots now is. He came in through the side door to find me, and I remember thinking "Crikey, this is it." Luckily, I think he knew how it was. There wasn't much to do in the shop in those days and we used to close at four o'clock.'

The condition was endemic. Little by little the dynamism that had been a feature of Tesco's growth was dwindling. A mood of resignation set in: the humdrum and the hardship, the restrictions and the regulations were essential for the war effort, it was true, and yet, and yet …

To Cohen it must have seemed that he was watching his business waste away piecemeal. Morale is the measure of any company's vitality, the more so in multiple retailing, diversified as it is. Given a sense of purpose, stores develop their own trading momentum, but by the middle years of the war the thrust and enthusiasm that had given Tesco its particular identity were gone. There was a job to do, and it would be done. As for the rest, there was only tedium.

To Cohen the condition was anathema, the antithesis of all that he represented. Restless to the point of hyperactivity, he became increasingly frustrated that whilst this was a war to which he, too, was deeply committed, there was so little in practice to occupy him. True, he still took his turn at fire-watching at Tesco House. True, he still toured his stores in an effort to bolster flagging morale. True, he still sat on interminable committees to administer this and regulate that, but there was no real stimulus in a business becalmed by bureaucracy, in which there was no place for his entrepreneurial skills.

It was a situation that Cohen was incapable of tolerating for long. Now in his early forties, he was not a man to be sidelined, and in 1940 he made his first private investment in landholding. Ostensibly the venture – the purchase of a half-acre nursery at Enfield, north London – was to help secure Tesco's lines of supply for fresh fruit and vegetables, though it was to prove of considerably greater significance for Cohen himself.

Within two years, and having spent £10,000 buying and improving a second, much larger nursery at nearby Cheshunt, Cohen was devoting an increasing amount of his time and energy to his horticultural business. For two decades, Tesco had dominated his thinking, but now the Cockney trader turned farmer with all the enthusiasm he had once applied to piling it high and selling it cheap. Freake was quite capable of looking after 'the shop' for the duration, whilst Cohen discovered a new purpose in life, the more so after buying a 340-acre holding near Maldon in Essex.

In 1944, Goldhanger Fruit Farms was registered with a nominal capital of £100. A private company controlled by the Cohen family, it was not only to become a pioneer of the frozen food business but was also to develop an extensive canning facility supplying own-label goods and bottled fruit and jams in the post-war years. For Cohen, however, farming proved to be only an interlude in the business of managing Tesco.

For all his temporary disenchantment, the company had shown near-consistent growth in turnover and profit during the six years of war, though it had singularly failed to identify a development which, in the years ahead, was to transform the entire pattern of retailing. As early as 1935, on a visit to the United States, Cohen had noted that first, embryonic development of self-service shopping, and on a second visit shortly before the outbreak of war, he had been impressed by the rapid evolution of the technique. Rumour had it that supermarketing was revolutionising the retail industry, that this was where the future lay.

For all its advantages, not least in helping to resolve the staff shortages that emerged during the war, Cohen failed to adopt the system in Tesco, even though it is probable that he heard of Harold Wicker's experiment at Romford. Possibly he felt that it was too big an initiative to take in wartime, or possibly he was too concerned with his farming enterprises to think through the benefits to be gained from introducing self-service into the company. Whatever the reason, it was thirteen years after his first visit to the States before the company explored the possibility of supermarketing, and by that time Britain had been at peace for more than three years.

Meanwhile, the war had been financially profitable for Tesco. Indeed, as the ministry had forecast, multiples had gained in market share from independents, due both to their organisation and to their buying power. Against this, however, had to be set the damage done to morale within the company itself. As the war progressed, so it sapped vitality, depriving Tesco of what had been its unique selling point – the drive and purpose that had been a feature of the company during the 1930s. Supplies were never enough, queues were never ending, customers were never satisfied, and the bureaucracy appeared to have developed a life force of its own.

In short, and for all the profit and loss account, Tesco's morale was at a low ebb at the end of the war, the crucial need being to revive the company's spirits, a role that Cohen was admirably suited to play. Physically unprepossessing he may have been, once going so far as to liken himself to a Brooke Bond chimpanzee, but he had a zest for business that was infectious. If he could sell 'seconds' to housewives in Well Street at the close of the First World War, then he could just as well sell enthusiasm to his staff at the close of the Second. The difference, and it continued to escape him throughout his career, was that he was no longer trading stock from a market stall; rather he was running a company which, even before the declaration of war, had been turning over some £40,000 a week.

But while the war had provided the company with an opportunity to consolidate its pre-war growth, they had been wasted years when it came to devising a strategy for post-war development. Old habits die hard, and hostile as he was to all forms of forward planning Cohen continued to trade on instinct, confident in his 'feel' for the market and in his own judgement. In the immediate post-war years, his intuition was to pay handsome dividends. In the longer term, it was to have other and more damaging consequences.

5. THE END OF
THE BEGINNING

1945–50

'When I get my civvy clothes on,
Oh, how happy I shall be.'

Second World War song

The war in Europe ended on 7 May 1945, and three months later, on 14 August, the Japanese sued for peace, nine days after the first atomic bomb had exploded in the sunlit skies above Hiroshima. The mood in Britain was euphoric, and the crowd that burned Hitler's effigy on a pyre of ration books in Trafalgar Square were celebrating the future they had been promised as much as the victory they had won. This time there would be no mistakes, the war would not be allowed to win for a second time.

Indeed, memories of the flawed peace of 1919 had so radicalised Britain that the 'khaki' election of July 1945 led to the outright rejection of Winston Churchill and the landslide victory of Labour. In his clipped voice the new Prime Minister, Clement Attlee, might warn of 'the difficult days ahead', but the country was in no mood for caveats. As early as 1940, *The Times* had modified its politics to such an extent that it could reflect: 'If we speak of equality, we do not mean political equality nullified by social and economic privilege', whilst in 1942 the Beveridge Report not only indicated the 'Five Great Evils' of 'Want, Disease, Ignorance, Squalor and Idleness', it also advanced a comprehensive programme for their elimination.

The vision was a compelling one, to build 'not for the glory of rulers and races but for the happiness of the common man'; the problem was how to finance it. Once again, Britain was virtually bankrupt: its foreign investments further dissipated to pay for the war; its new foreign debts totalling £3,000,000,000; almost half of its shipping at the bottom of the sea; and its exports running at less than a third of the pre-war total. Even this was not all. Although demobilisation was progressing smoothly by the close of 1945, it was estimated that 8.5 million men and women were still doing war work, whilst manufacturing industry was short of five million workers needed to power Britain's exports and, hence, economic recovery.

Small wonder that Attlee advised caution or that Britain celebrated an austere Christmas that first year of peace. Where, six months before, there had been high expectations, there was now growing an appreciation that to achieve Beveridge's goals with a broken-backed economy would take as much time as sacrifice, and while it was all very well for Labour to press ahead with its plans for the creation of a welfare state, that was cold comfort for housewives who still queued for their bob's worth of meat and screw of tea. Above all else, the ration book had come to symbolise everything they had come to hate. With it, there was little enough. Without it, there was virtually nothing – little food, no clothes and few of the small luxuries that made life bearable.

Even before the war's end a Housewives' League had been formed by the wife of a suburban vicar to campaign against queuing. Within months, the league had a national membership of thousands, an essentially middle-class, highly articulate lobby that served as a focus for the disenchantment of women as much with the government's rationing policies as with shopkeepers whom many had come to regard as sub-agents of the state. As Paul Addison wrote in *Now the War is Over* (1985): 'There was a tremendous amount of government interference. It ran down to all kinds of domestic detail. It was very irksome. Endless forms, endless filling in of forms for almost everything. You had bread tickets, food tickets, clothes tickets, petrol tickets, coal tickets, coal was rationed.'

The litany is significant as much for what it reveals as for what it conceals: a deep-rooted suspicion of the interventionist state. At high cost, Britain had just won a war against totalitarianism, yet for many in the Housewives' League it seemed that Labour was adopting bureaucratic means to achieve much the same totalitarian ends. Thirty years after the movement adopted a demand for reduction of government intervention in family life, the writer

Anthony Burgess interpreted George Orwell's classic novel *1984* as a commentary on the state of post-war Britain: a bureaucratic nightmare.

By mid-1946, the Cabinet was actively studying ways of re-enlisting women into industry, and by the end of the year had launched a promotional campaign directed at recruiting women in the thirty-five-to-fifty age bracket, among them 300,000 married women who had been employed (many for the first time) during the war. As a result of the higher wage levels in manufacturing, staff shortages emerged in the retail sector which, in their turn, powered the shift to self-service.

Staffing problems were not the sole reason for the development of a system which, within a quarter of a century, was to transform the whole character of shopping. Of comparable importance, the old and leisurely notion of counter service was passing. The war had brought a change of tempo to life, introducing a sense of urgency, a feeling that time was at a premium. Where formerly shopping trips had often been regarded as leisurely social affairs, a growing number of working wives and mothers was now concerned with time-saving rather than with personal service. The class divide remained; Lord Sainsbury once recalled being accosted by a judge's wife in Purley complaining that 'I had no right to expect the customer to do the work the assistants had done in the past', but the development was not to be gainsaid, for all the initial antipathy of the more well-to-do and, in many cases, of local planners.

As a critic, Margaret Thomas, was later to note in her book *Built Environment Quality*: 'Planners were not at all happy about the ways of some innovators, but increasingly the shopping public came to love the self-service store and the High Street supermarket, and voted with their feet. Most of these shops were in town and district centres, accessible on foot from neighbouring streets and by public transport from further afield. Small traders, both nearby and in neighbourhood shop groups, experienced powerful competition. The overall effect was to draw into High Streets some of the food spending which otherwise might be carried on in local shops.'

But if this was to be the shape of tomorrow's world, of consumerism powered by rising affluence allied to the availability of an ever-extending range of goods, then it still seemed to be a world away when Attlee drafted the goodwill message that decorated the

Christmas hoardings of 1947: 'I want to thank all those women who are staying on at work and all those who are now joining in the drive for greater production. Our united efforts in the coming twelve months will determine the future prosperity of our people.'

Attlee's cryptic message, and what it implied for the future role of women, not only crystallised the fears of the Housewives' League but also highlighted the innate conflict between needs and expectations that was a central feature of the immediate post-war years. For all of the government's exhortations during what the *Sunday Despatch* called 'the phoney peace', the reality was that the essentials of life were in desperately short supply and, rather than improving, conditions appeared to be deteriorating by the day.

That much of Europe was close to starvation made little difference, and when bread first went on the ration following a cut in American grain supplies there was a general outcry, the Master Bakers mobbing the Minister of Food at Central Hall and the *Daily Sketch* fulminating: 'If this is the peace, then surely we are entitled to ask: Who won the war?' Inexorably, the hopes of 1945 were being whittled away. No question that unemployment was virtually non-existent. No question that by 1947 manufacturing output was almost back to its pre-war level. But such statistics counted for little when everyday conditions remained so austere.

Britain, it seemed, was slowly becoming inured to a spartan regime, and the launch of Christian Dior's New Look did little to compensate for the announcement of further cuts in the ration following the sterling crisis of 1947, triggered by the precipitate foreclosure of an American loan agreement. All the talk was of an 'economic Dunkirk', and whilst the *Daily Express* blazoned 'Less ... Less ... Less' across its front page, and Attlee asked for 10% more effort to turn the economic tide, tobacconists hung 'Sold Out' notices in their windows, and butchers only opened on a couple of days a week.

For a second time in less than thirty years, it seemed that the dream was turning sour, yet the appearance was deceptive. Whilst instant gratification had to be deferred, Britain was well on the road to recovery by 1950. In the previous five years, more than a million permanent new homes had been built, major legislation relating to health and education and planning had been enacted, a new code of industrial practices had been thrashed out (including the establishment of Wages Councils which, among other things, brought 1,250,000 shop workers under statutory wage regulations), and the economy was booming. Britain, it was claimed, could make it, and there was growing evidence to support the claim – with industrial production 50% and exports 67% higher than in 1946.

With economic recovery came increasing freedom. In 1949, the President of the Board of Trade, Harold Wilson, had announced that he was going to make a 'bonfire of controls', and in June 1950 *The Economist* observed: 'The leaders of the Labour Party have always said that the restrictive controls, especially those which are unpopular, would be removed as soon as it was possible to do so without running any risk of the rationing of necessities "by the purse" or of creating unemployment. That time, in many lines, has come. It may very well be that the Labour Party, so long as it had a secure majority, had a bias towards making these relaxations later rather than sooner ... but the government are, in substance, only doing what they said they always would do.'

Wilson's bonfire, however, had been lit too late. The age of austerity had gone on for too long. That the sacrifices of the immediate post-war years had been necessary for Britain's economic survival now carried little weight with the electorate. The dis-enchantment had gone too deep, and when the Conservatives entered the election of October 1951 on the pledge of making 'a dash for freedom', Churchill was returned to reap the rewards of the blood, sweat and tears as much of the peace as of the war.

Jack Cohen's hopes for the peace were soon disappointed. Tesco had done well out of the war, its gross turnover rising by 18%, but they had been wasted years as far as his entrepreneurial skills were concerned. Always restless to be up and doing (in later years, he was to hand out brass tie-pins engraved with the legend YCDBSOYA – You Can't Do Business Sitting On Your *Armchair*), for him the frustrations of trading by diktat had grown increasingly unbearable. But surely with peace declared, conditions would return to normal, and he would be able to indulge once again in the old cut-and-thrust at which he excelled? He was soon to learn otherwise.

As the high summer of 1945 gave way to the siege economy that followed, it must have seemed to Cohen that the best years of his life were wasting away. The elders of his childhood synagogue had been fond of quoting Job – 'We are but of yesterday, because our days upon earth are a shadow' – but they were wrong. There was more to it than that, much more. In his mid-forties, with a quarter of a century of successful retailing behind him, he was not a man to live in the shadow of yesterday when so much remained to be done.

There is no record of exactly when, or even why, Cohen began to consider the benefits to be realised from floating Tesco as a public company. Possibly it was because the practice became fashionable in the post-war years, possibly because a neighbour who worked on the Stock Exchange interested him in the prospect of raising capital for his company, or possibly because it offered an outlet for all his repressed energies.

More than a year after the end of the war, retailing was still trading within the straitjacket of restrictions, and it may well have seemed that going public would do as much to relieve his boredom as it would provide Tesco with the finance necessary to venture into self-servicing. Since his first Romford experiment, Harold Wicker, of the London Co-operative Society, had been promoting the system, and Cohen was to confirm the benefits to be achieved on his first post-war visit to the United States. He was astounded by what he found:

'The improvements since my last visit were beyond belief. There were the great names of American food retailing – Safeway, Atlantic and Pacific, Food Fare – all up to their necks in supermarket trading … There were gleaming palaces, well lit, roomy and clean. One of the most impressive developments concerned the packaging of goods. New materials, radical new designs, bright labels, clear price markings, and the women not only carried baskets, they pushed trolleys. It was Utopia for a retailer … The noise from the cash registers was music to any trader's ears.'

This was the stuff to excite Cohen ('I could not wait to get home, I was bursting to have a go'), whose own embryonic chain still operated very largely out of small, open-fronted premises, with roller shutters in place of windows. Seven years before, on a previous visit to the States, he had seen the future, and ignored its potential. It would not happen a second time. There was too much at stake. Within half a decade, 45% of US grocery outlets had been converted to self-service, to command almost 80% of all grocery sales. The lesson was a simple one – that the new system minimised operational costs whilst maximising returns – and by 1947 Cohen was determined to apply it to Tesco.

There was little to distinguish 67A St Peter's Street, St Albans, from many other Tesco stores. Small and unprepossessing, it provided few hints of the role that it was to play in revolutionising Tesco. Thirty-seven-year-old Redford Fisher was the manager, and his takings averaged around £350 a week, though the word was that, with the introduction of self-service, his turnover would rise and his overheads fall.

Although constrained by government cash limits on conversion costs, and with the re-designed interior consisting of little more than wall shelving, a central island and a National Cash Register till by the door, the first week's takings at the re-opened store topped £450, the second week's £600. Seemingly, local shoppers enjoyed the experience of serving themselves, not least of impulse-buying from the open shelves, and weekly takings were soon averaging £500 a week. As a test market, it appeared that self-service had proved itself, and what was good for St Peter's Street would be good for Tesco as a whole – as long as the capital was available to undertake the conversions.

Whatever Cohen's personal motives for going public, they must have been fuelled by his growing conviction of the need to raise funds if he was to go into the wholesale transformation of his company. Privately, he may have suspected that such a move would dissipate his own control of the business, but publicly there was no escaping the fact that without additional finance there would be little hope of modernising or expanding the company and thus remaining on competitive terms with rivals such as the Co-op and Sainsbury. The skill would be in balancing out both interests.

Almost thirty years had passed since he had staked his First War gratuity on a market stall, thirty years in which he had grafted first to build a business, then to establish a dynasty. The ambition may have been inchoate, a personal daemon, but it was there, nonetheless. Driven by long ages of persecution, and haunted always by a sense of insecurity, of the age-old tale of the Wandering Jew, the search for some notional permanence, an intangible yet irrevocable thing, has powered more men to success than Jack Cohen. And now Cohen was caught in its snare. Once, maybe, he had hoped for no more than to make a steady living, whereas now the priority was as much to safeguard his interests in Tesco as to generate new capital for the company.

Through the summer and into the autumn of 1947, Cohen laid his plans for going public with the help of his long-time friend Bernard Lazarus and the corporate lawyers Slaughter and May. For all of the war years, and despite the virtual freeze on post-war expansion, Tesco was in good shape. As the director in charge of retail operations, Thomas Freake (now backed by four inspectors) kept tight control of the company's 110 stores, whilst Carpenter and Daisy Hyams managed the administration of a group whose fixed assets now totalled more than £120,000.

By November, Cohen's plans were close to finalisation, and on the 27th a new private company, Tesco Stores (Holdings) Ltd, was incorporated under the Companies Act of 1929 (Appendix 1A). The move, involving the consolidation of all Cohen's subsidiary operations, was a formality in advance of the public share offer, and the new company was given an authorised and fully paid up capital of £300,000 in 1,200,000 shares of five shillings each, of which Cohen took 1,172,910 and 200 were scheduled to be issued for cash. Three weeks later, on Friday 19 December, 250,000 of Cohen's shares were offered on the market at fifteen shillings each. While these amounted to less than a quarter of the total shareholding, the company was no longer Cohen's private bailiwick – though he was well on his way to making his first million.

As for Tesco, if Cohen had any fears about its long-term control, he had no immediate cause for concern. As Chairman of the new company, he remained its majority shareholder with 922,910 shares, whilst two of his fellow directors, Carpenter and Freake, held only 16,715 shares between them. For all that Tesco was now a public company, it appeared that the private succession was assured, the more so since Hyman Kreitman, who had married Cohen's eldest daughter, Irene, was the fourth member of the board. Whether on a vote at the annual meeting, or a head count of directors, it remained a family concern – a situation whose long-term consequences were presaged by growing differences with Freake.

Appointed Assistant Managing Director of the new company, Freake was as unhappy with his small (11,133) shareholding as he was with his role in the new management. During his seventeen

years with Tesco, Cohen had emphasised his importance to the
business as much as he had relied on his retailing skills, but now
Freake had been given what he regarded as a derisory stake in its
future, whilst appearing to have a diminishing influence on its policy
decisions. As to the former, Cohen categorically denied that he had
ever promised Freake a 5% shareholding, in place of the 1% he
received; as to the latter, it was too soon to burgeon into one of
those damaging feuds that were to wrack Tesco's upper management over the next two decades.

By his fiftieth birthday in 1948, Cohen was a self-made autocrat,
increasingly intolerant of contradictions. Whether Tesco was in
private or public hands, he was the boss, for all Freake's talk of
accountability. In theory the notion was all very fine. In practice it
was no better than those other abstractions – long-term planning
and financial controls and suchlike – peddled by sophists who had
little or no experience of retailing on the ground. What he wanted
about him was 'two-box men' (one of Cohen's favourite axioms,
referring to the load-bearing capacity of his staff), not pedants, and
they would play the game by his rules, or not at all.

Cohen's bruising management style was to generate growing
tensions in the years ahead, but in the meantime Freake watched and
bided his time. In its first year of operation as a public company,
Tesco showed a substantial post-tax profit, due in part to the gradual
relaxation of wartime restrictions, though there were troubles at St
Albans. After twelve months of self-service trading, the St Peter's
Street store was reconverted to counter service, though the reasons
given for the decision vary widely. The received opinion, as noted in
the board minutes, was that it was demanding 'too much executive
time' (a phrase which may disguise the suspicion that a great deal of
pilfering had been taking place), though Daisy Hyams believed that
the limited range of goods due to rationing was not sufficient to
attract customers, whilst Kreitman suspected that St Albans was too
middle-class an area to conduct such a trial successfully.

Certainly, subsequent experience was to bear out his view. In the
decades ahead, it was the lower income groups which were the first
to take advantage of the savings to be achieved from the application
of economies of scale to retailing, in contrast to the innate conserva-
tism of middle-class shoppers who, in many instances, proved
actively hostile to such innovations. Whatever the reason, however,

St Peter's reverted to counter service, to be re-converted successfully to self-service for a second time in 1949.

Somewhat enigmatically, the annual report for the year ending December 1949 noted that 'one of our shops was converted into a self-service unit with the object of indicating to the board the possibilities of this type of trading' – without making any mention of the previous aborted experiment. Twelve months later, the Chairman's address was to be equally enigmatic, though on a more personal issue:

'You will have seen in the directors' report a reference to an alteration in the business of Edmonton Packers Ltd, and to an action pending between Mr T. E. Freake and two of the subsidiary companies. It would not be proper for me to make any comment on these matters except to say that they have a good defence to Mr Freake's action. Arising out of Mr Freake's resignation, your board propose at a suitable opportunity to fill the vacancy on the board.'

The omissions were more significant than the admission. Privately, Freake had always resented Hyman Kreitman's appointment to the board. Whatever the reasons for the move, he suspected that it reflected as much on his own ability as on Cohen's determination to retain absolute control of the company, and in the two years since the company had gone public he had felt increasingly boxed in by the family. The board minutes for the period are vague to the point of opacity, though they suggest that critical decisions were subject to little discussion and agreed 'on the nod', the take-over of Knowles Bros (Merchants) Ltd in December 1949 being reported to the board only after Cohen had closed the deal.

It was another six months before matters finally came to a head. The directors' report for 1950 stated baldly that Freake had tendered his resignation 'on grounds, as he alleged, that decisions with which he was in disagreement had been made without reference to him'. What these disagreements were is not specified, though it is possible that they were connected with a deal under which Goldhanger Fruit Farms, a private company controlled by Cohen, took over a part of the small Tesco subsidiary, Edmonton Packers.

As early as July 1949, with Edmonton experiencing 'considerable difficulty in the manufacture of preserves and similar products', Goldhanger had bought out its raw materials and equipment. In December of the same year, however, Goldhanger were still shown to be owing Edmonton Packers £33,505, and while this was soon paid off, the issue of the relationship between the two companies and Tesco continued to exercise the board. It may be no coincidence that Freake's resignation in June 1950 occurred at much the same time as the Goldhanger–Edmonton hiatus. Once again, however, the record of events in the minutes is obscure, disguising more than it reveals.

In fact, only one thing is certain: Freake must have been deeply disillusioned even to consider taking legal action against a company which he had done so much to create. If Tesco had been the product of Cohen's flair, then it was Freake's retailing skills which, in large part, had been responsible for the everyday direction of the business for two decades. Yet now it seemed that Cohen regarded him at best as some kind of management supernumerary, at worst as expendable. Individually, the slights were bad enough – the derisive share offer, his isolation on the board, and finally his concern about certain aspects of the Goldhanger–Edmonton affair – cumulatively, they led to Freake's resignation on 16 June 1950.

Almost exactly two years later, Freake's action for breach of contract came before the courts, for him to withdraw the case after the first day's hearing, the judge ordering that damages be found in favour of Tesco. Cohen and Freake met only once more, and neither of them ever revealed what occurred during those troubled days of the late 1940s, Freake insisting that he had no wish to rake up old quarrels.

Whilst the full story remains untold, however, Freake's doubts about Tesco's future under what was effectively a new management team were forcibly borne out by the company's performance in the years immediately after going public. In 1948, the company had returned a post-tax profit of £41,800; in 1949 it had fallen to almost half, due, it was stated, to rising costs that Tesco was unable to pass on to the customer. The following year, profits fell by a further 30%, and although they recovered slightly in 1951 they did not regain their 1948 levels until 1954 – five years after Wilson had made his 'bonfire' of controls, and three years after the newly elected Conservative government had launched Britain on its 'dash for freedom'.

Why? What went wrong? How was it that Tesco, at one time the retail pace-setter, failed to capitalise on the final abolition of wartime regulations and the subsequent boom in consumer expenditure? In view of the secrecy surrounding this period, it is only possible to hypothesise, though the secrecy itself suggests that something was seriously amiss. Indeed, it is the obscurities that cloak the period that fuel the suspicion that there was considerably more to Freake's departure than a simple falling-out between Cohen and himself. Precisely what went on in the Tesco boardroom in the days after the company went public, and, coincidentally, did this have anything to do with the company's deteriorating performance in a resurgent economy?

Ultimately, the answer may well lie in Cohen's silence. If the suspicions surrounding the affair, and its consequences, had no foundation, he would have been among the first to refute the rumours. As it is, his silence suggests that he recognised the gravity of his own mistake first in alienating, then in losing Freake. Without doubt Kreitman was to make a significant contribution to the company in the years ahead, but in his early days he had virtually no practical experience of grocery retailing, in contrast to Freake's acknowledged talents. Yet it appears that Cohen favoured Kreitman over Freake, and all for what? To establish a dynasty? If so, then he placed the future of the newly fledged public company at risk for an ambition he was never to achieve.

6. A NOISE OF
CASH REGISTERS

1951–9

'It *was* nice, wasn't it, last year,
Festival Year? It was the nicest thing
that happened in England in the
whole of my life.'

Marghanita Laski
The *Observer*, 1952

For Cohen, it may well have seemed that the war only ended with the Conservative election victory of October 1951. Careless as much of the problems that faced Britain in the immediate post-war years as of the Labour government's achievement in reviving a back-broken economy, Cohen was all for the Tory election slogan of making 'a dash for freedom'. Now, at last, he was to be freed of the pettyfogging rules and regulations that had cramped his entrepreneurial style for so long.

And Tesco? For more than half its trading life the company had been prevented from pursuing its own trading policies, an agent of bureaucrats better suited to shuffling forms than turning profits. Now Jack Cohen would show them what business was really about, for there could be no question, the demand was there. Seemingly, the whole mood of the country was changing, and if the 1951 Festival of Britain symbolised the new, adventurous spirit that was abroad, then the accession of the young Queen Elizabeth II the following year gave rise to talk of 'the dawn of a second Elizabethan age'.

Heady stuff, certainly, but there was mounting evidence that Britain could afford to indulge her new-found taste for freedom.

Since the war's end, unemployment had been running at less than 2% of the total workforce, and although the average weekly earnings of men over twenty-one stood at only £8.6s. a week in 1951 there were clear indications of an incipient wage push. The Conservatives talked up freedom, and the unions took them at their word, especially when encouraged by the rhetoric of the Chancellor of the Exchequer, R. A. Butler, who pondered in 1954: 'Why should we not aim to double our standard of living in the next twenty-five years?'

Butler was already being overtaken by events. In the decade to 1961 wage increases kept well ahead of the Retail Price Index, rising by almost a hundred per cent to £15.7s., whilst between 1955 and 1969 average weekly earnings rose by 130%, against a 78% rise in retail prices. And this was not all. Two world wars had taught women to value their independence, and in the twenty years to 1971 the number of women in employment rose by almost twenty-five per cent.

If the trend was further to reinforce household spending power, it was also to exert a powerful shaping effect on the British lifestyle. Where, before the war, there had been a steady if limited demand for the new consumer durables entering the market (refrigerators, washing machines, electric irons and the like), these now became the essential equipment of a new generation of working women, freeing them to enter the labour market which, in its turn, was to help generate the income that was to power the consumer boom of the 1950s and 1960s.

The growth of car ownership provided the single, most visible symbol of the radical change that was taking place in the British socio-economy. Still largely a middle-class preserve in the pre-war years, private car ownership doubled from just over two million to more than four million in the ten years to 1957, the major part of this expansion being concentrated amongst skilled workers and lower-paid white-collar workers. This was freedom of a new sort, representing social as much as personal mobility.

Apparently, the whole world was turned upside down. Where once there had been hardship, there was now relative affluence. Where once there had been privilege, there was now a caring society. Where once there had been division, Harold Macmillan captured the mood of the times when he asserted that 'every man and woman and child in this country deserve their fair share of the future that we are building today'.

As always, Britain's retailers provided the shop window for such change. Free to sell what they liked, where they liked, to customers who could shop how they liked, where they liked, the 1950s marked the take-off of the quiet revolution which, in subsequent decades, was to transform the entire structure of British retailing.

With the lifting of all controls came a surge in food expenditure. Virtually every item in the standard shopping basket, save such wartime staples as bread and potatoes, showed a consistent increase in sales throughout the 1950s, when food accounted for a third of all household expenditure.

Estimates of household food consumption, 1950–1960
(Ounces per person per week)

	1950	1960
Liquid milk (pints)	4.78	4.84
Cheese	2.54	3.04
Butter	4.56	5.68
Lard/cooking fats	3.11	2.63
Eggs (number)	3.46	4.46
Sugar	10.13	17.76
Total meat	30.49	35.89
Fresh green vegetables	13.81	15.34
Other fresh vegetables	11.38	9.13

This table, taken from John Burnett's history of diet in England, *Plenty and Want* (1979), is not inclusive, for due to lack of detailed information it gives no hint of the growing demand for convenience foods. However, as Burnett records, Bird's Eye had established a quick frozen-food operation in East Anglia as early as 1945, though by 1947 its UK output totalled only £250,000. Fifteen years later, frozen-food expenditure in the UK had risen 260-fold to £80 million, the take-off of a dietary revolution powered in part by the demands of working housewives, in part by the re-equipment of kitchens, and in part by the growing techological investment in the food business.

As tastes and techniques changed, so did Britain's shops. For half a century the corner shop and small independent had been under mounting pressure from multiple traders, and the post-war years compounded their problems. Operating on limited capital and often trading on fine margins (in 1961 some 177,000 independents were working on a turnover of £5,000 or less a year), small shopkeepers found it increasingly difficult not only to compete with the financial muscle of major retail groups but also to adapt to changing social trends.

According to a 1966 government study, *The Distributive Trades in Great Britain*: 'Nearly 70,000 shops owned by multiples (including multiple department stores) were recorded in the 1961 census of distribution ... Multiple retailers are the type of retail organisation which have shown the fastest growth in the last few years. They raised their total share of the trade from 22% in 1950 to 29% in 1961, when the value of their sales was in the region of £2,850 million. In the food trades their turnover increased by 42% between 1957 and 1961 alone, compared with 11% for independent retailers and only 3% for co-operative societies. Both increased numbers of shops and increased sales per shop contributed to this expansion. The increase in sales per shop (24%) was above that for retail establishments generally (18%).'

Powered by rising incomes and increasing public mobility (by the late 1950s one family in three owned a car), allied to the fundamental changes taking place in the home and the workplace (by the early 1960s almost eight million women were in either full- or part-time employment), British consumers delighted in their bid for freedom during the 1950s. If, in 1959, Harold Macmillan was to contemplate that Britain had never had it so good, who were British retailers to disagree?

Jack Cohen had it right in 1951: freedom was to work wonders for British retailing, though as far as Tesco was concerned he got the formula wrong. Despite the growth market, for three years to 1954 the company's trading profits fell below those achieved in the austerity days of 1948 when even bread and potatoes were placed on the ration. The setback was only temporary, yet it provided the first clear evidence of the innate weaknesses of Cohen's management style.

But in 1950 who was to gainsay him, or to question his

authority? Thomas Freake had gone, and only Cohen's son-in-law, Hyman Kreitman, and his long-standing placeman, Arthur Carpenter, remained on the Tesco board. Both were good men, though the former still lacked the in-depth knowledge of the food business essential to managing a multiple retailer, whilst the latter certainly posed no threat to Cohen's hegemony. As if jealous of power, and fearful of any challenge to his ascendancy, Cohen had created a management team which, whilst it might serve to perpetuate his own authority, was to pose immediate problems for Tesco.

Undoubtedly, Cohen had been proved more often right than wrong in the previous two decades. Since he and T. E. Stockwell had invented the name Tesco, it had become a talisman of success, but the practices that applied in the 1920s and 1930s had less and less place in the new look world of the 1950s. The old, well-tried formula of piling it high and selling it cheap out of small stores had diminishing relevance as an increasingly affluent public became more discriminating, whilst this was no longer a world in which it was possible to play games in the head with a profit and loss account.

As Laurie Don, who became Company Secretary of Tesco in 1961 and later Managing Director of Bejam, says, 'I think that you can build a business up with figures on the back of an envelope, and one saw other companies reaching that sort of stage. Ultimately, however, they all faced the same sort of problem, that too much control was vested in the proprietor who wouldn't allow anyone from outside in. But the time has to come when that must change, when a company grows too big to be one man's preserve.'

In this way, Cohen was caught up in a paradox of his own making, for in attempting to retain absolute control of the company he was undermining the very thing that he wished to achieve – the future expansion of Tesco. It was all very well to be called 'the Governor', and to recall his days in the market, but in a company which, by 1951, employed more than a thousand people in over a hundred stores, some delegation of power was becoming essential, the more so when there was a need for a fundamental shift in trading methods if Tesco was to remain competitive.

A quiet-spoken and diffident man, whose father had run one of the country's largest footwear manufacturers before the war, Hyman Kreitman was quick to recognise this. If the times were changing, then Tesco must change with them – or go to the wall. As always, however, there was trouble with Cohen. Tony Di Angeli, the doyen of retailer journalists and longtime editor of *The Grocer*, says: 'Mr Kreitman was a cautious man, though he was always innovative and open to new ideas which made him clash with Jack, who couldn't see the need to spend money.' The comment requires a coda, for while Cohen was keen enough to deal in lines where he felt he could turn a quick profit (on an early visit to South Africa, he bought 100,000 tins of baked beans, which it took Tesco five years to unload), he was considerably more wary about being committed to longer-term investments.

The conflict turned as much upon age differences as upon attitudes. A month after the General Election of 1951, Cohen celebrated his fifty-third birthday, and while he took the past as his touchstone, Kreitman, in his mid-thirties, was more concerned with the future. And this was not all. There was possibly an altogether deeper and more subtle factor in play. As with his own father, Avroam, there was already more than a touch of the autocrat in Cohen, and as he had had to fight against the stigma of always being the second son, so Kreitman had to fight against the inheritance of being the son-in-law. At best, it was an uneasy relationship; at worst, a damaging one which, in latter years, was to lead to savage and hurtful disputes, Cohen continually testing Kreitman's patience, and frustrating Kreitman's plans to the point where, more than once, they almost came to blows.

Laurie Don recalls: 'Jack was a wicked old man in many ways, he could spot a weakness and take advantage of it, and he would needle Hyman all the time. It didn't help that they were all in a tight family. Hyman could never get away, even having to spend his Friday nights round at the Cohen household. Later on in the sixties, he often wouldn't turn up for work on the Monday morning, because they had had a row on Friday night.'

Challenged about his behaviour, Cohen was quick to show remorse. Robin Behar, whose father became a director of Tesco in 1962, remembered the aftermath of one family row, which had closed with a five-minute harangue from Cohen: 'I told him afterwards that he was a dreadful old man, behaving like that in front of me, someone who wasn't even in the family. Eventually his face crumpled and he looked very contrite, and asked me if I really thought he was awful.'

Mercurial as he was, and as quick to remorse as to anger, the old Adam remained, however. Though during the early 1950s the full extent of this personality clash had yet to emerge, it took Kreitman time to persuade his father-in-law to invest the capital necessary to install shop windows in place of shutters in Tesco stores so that the company 'was half way to becoming respectable'. It was a beginning, but by no means enough. After the hesitant initial venture into self-service at St Albans, and against accumulating evidence that the competition intended to invest heavily in the practice, the need was to expand rapidly into this new market.

At a board meeting in October 1950, Kreitman reported that four branches had been converted to the new system, and that in view of their success, the intention was to convert as many stores to self-service as soon as possible. Impressed by the improved profit margins achieved, Cohen agreed, and by May 1951 Tesco had thirty-five self-service units in operation. By 1955 four-fifths of all units had been converted.

J. D. Thomson, a one-time group inspector with the company, and later director of Tesco Supermarkets Ltd, remembers, 'They were exciting times. We were converting stores to self-service at the rate of almost one a week. The stores themselves varied from 500 square feet, tiny little places, to up to 2,000 square feet which, in those days, was very large. To begin with there was little money spent on the conversions. We just pulled the grocery and provision counters into the middle of the shops, then all the goods were stacked on top of them. As for the check-outs, they were set up near the door and customers came in and helped themselves.'

In more ways than one. Opponents of self-service within the company were not slow to point out the increased dangers of shop-lifting, for as long-time Tesco manager Harold Ketchell re-members, 'I could see people coming in and putting things in their bags and then just walking out. When I took over the Tolworth store [in south London] there was a lot of pilferage going on; we used to get as many as half a dozen a day there. Eventually I started making a few examples here and there, which would be covered in the local paper, and gradually the thieving stopped.'

However, the profits from self-service far outstripped the losses incurred, according to John Thomson: 'After conversion we'd be so busy on Friday evenings that the queue would start at the doorway and go all around the store. Often as not there would be two tills working like mad to get the people through, and as an inspector all I could do was relieve the cashiers so they could go and get a cup of tea. We'd often take £600 and more in an evening.'

On his visit to the States in 1939, Cohen had seen self-service in operation and enthused that 'the noise from the cash registers was music to any trader's ears'. Now they were ringing for him, and as cavalier with modesty as he was careless of the fact that, following the success of his pilot operation in Romford, Harold Wicker had already established a Self-Service Development Association, Cohen was quick to claim credit not only for introducing self-service into Tesco, but also for pioneering it in Britain as well. In his authorised biography, he is quoted as saying, 'This was to be the start of the consumer revolution, and our willingness to plunge into self-service when many others hesitated provided our credentials for championing the consumer cause after all those bleak years of control.'

The man was well on the way to becoming a legend – of his own making. Indeed, as Tony Di Angeli says, 'The idea that Jack was an innovator is ridiculous. The trouble was that whilst he was quick enough to spot an idea, and copy it, his godlike idea of himself then made him imagine he had thought of it first.'

Cohen the copier, Kreitman the innovator. Again, there were grounds for conflict, especially when Cohen claimed every innovation as his own, whilst denying responsibility for any mistakes. So whose company was it, anyway? His. Once the belief had been well founded, but it was to become increasingly destructive with the passage of time, though during the 1950s Cohen was saved from his own worst excesses due partly to the fact that mistakes were not as costly as they were later to become, partly to the fortuitous arrival of Edgar Collar in the summer of 1951.

Since the departure of Freake, Cohen had often ridden rough-shod over the board, coercing agreement where persuasion failed – though without achieving a significant improvement in results. His authorised biography suggests that he was working in adverse market conditions, but while other multiples were quick to benefit from the 'dash for freedom' of the early 1950s, Tesco continued to perform sluggishly. With the exception of Kreitman's drive towards self-service, the company appeared to have lost headway, deprived of any effective development plan to exploit the growth market which Cohen himself had anticipated for so long.

Since the end of the war he had been living for the moment when controls were finally abolished, yet when the time arrived Tesco was singularly unprepared to take advantage of it. He might talk big of customers 'yearning for something new' and the opportunities that this would provide for dynamic retailing, but in practice his own shortcomings, notably his contempt for long-term thinking allied to an authoritarian management style, continually placed his own ambitions at risk.

On the day before he died, in June 1963, Edgar Collar lunched in London with Tony di Angeli to explain in the clipped terms that were the hallmark of his personality how he had helped to bring Cohen to heel. Where, formerly, Cohen would go on holiday, cable back to Tesco some such message as 'Send £80,000, want to buy oranges', and the money would be despatched by return, the practice now was to lose the cable. After more than ten years as a main board director of Tesco, Collar had the measure of Cohen and his idiosyncratic ways. An accountant by profession, and joint managing director of Mores Stores, a London-based multiple, Collar had known Cohen for some years, but it was only with Freake's precipitate departure that he was approached to join Tesco.

As Laurie Don recalls: 'One day he received a call from Jack at Edmonton. He realised straight away why he had been summoned because when he arrived Mr Freake was waiting on the doorstep for a lift home, as his car had been taken from him. Freake was on his way out, and Edgar was to be his replacement. The Old Man had to have a foil to use against the family, Kreitman against Collar.'

Alternatively, Cohen may have come to realise what the loss of Freake implied, not least in terms of management capacity. Whatever the reason, and possibly suspecting that he was to be the cat's paw in the convoluted politics of Tesco House, Collar resisted Cohen's blandishments for nine months. He did not accept a place on the board until June 1951. In the decade ahead, he was to play a crucial role in rationalising the irrational by imposing firm management on the company which, in its turn, was to place a brake on certain (though by no mean all) of Cohen's wilder excesses.

Stan Prowse, a former warehouse manager with the company,

remembers, 'The financial wizard of Tesco was Edgar Collar. He was a man that Jack Cohen couldn't dictate to. He kept him and everyone else in their place.'

The memories remain, echoes and re-echoes of the 1950s. Kate Wilmer, who was to become an associate director of one of the Tesco subsidiary companies: 'Mr Collar was the man who set the company on its feet. He had a first-class brain, and could read a set of figures better than anyone I've ever known.'

John Allis, formerly manager of the company's shipping department: 'His expertise really started the company's post-war expansion. Mr Collar laid down the ground rules for larger stores, and kept a tight rein on finances.'

As economic with words as he was purposeful in action, Collar provided the natural counterbalance to Cohen, and not before time. Already beset by internecine disputes that were soon to poison family relationships, Tesco needed decisive management as never before, and in the four years after his arrival the evidence of Collar's influence became increasingly plain. It was all very well for Cohen to talk airily of expansion and to elaborate on his latest ideas, but they meant very little without the means to manage Cohen's dreams, without imposing some effective control on Tesco's highly individualistic management style.

Laurie Don: 'The Old Man got some things right, but was just as likely to get them wrong. He was never a very decisive man, he worked on instinct. Edgar got that under control. When he joined the board there was nobody who could read a balance sheet properly, and he was the one who first introduced branch accounts to identify such things as the profitability of each store, stock results and leakage. And it wasn't simply a matter of just reading the books, he knew what retailing was about as well.'

Slowly at first, but at accelerating pace, Tesco began to recover its trading momentum, and by 1955 the company's trading profits topped the figure achieved in 1948. The breaking of the £100,000 barrier was marked by the issue of one Preferred Ordinary share for every ten shares held, lifting the share capital of the holding company to £500,000 divided into 6,400,000 Preferred Ordinary and 3,600,000 Ordinary one-shilling shares. In addition, the capitalisation of reserves by a bonus handout increased the issued capital to £330,000, whilst with assets valued at £1,265,828 (excluding a valuation of £238,724 for buildings and freehold land) Tesco had moved into the millionaire league.

At the seventh annual meeting of the company, Cohen was bullish. There were plans in hand to develop Tesco's first super-market in a disused cinema at Maldon in Essex, whilst on 22 June 1955 a draft agreement for the purchase of Burnards was approved by the board. Operating nineteen discount stores in the London area, Burnards was a comparatively small trader, yet one that produced consistently good results and was managed by a highly professional team.

Jack Cohen had been friendly with Charles Berzin, the owner, for a number of years, and possibly because he was not a fit man, Berzin was happy to sell his interests to Tesco for £175,000 and a place on the board. Some weeks later, at a dinner at the Trocadero to celebrate the merger, it was revealed that Burnards' nineteen stores were taking more money than the entire Tesco group, which provided a shock as much as a stimulus to the parent company.

Daisy Hyams, by the mid-1950s a senior buyer with the company, is clear about the impact of the takeover on Tesco's trading strategy: 'I think we had a passage in our history when we weren't doing very well, and I think that taking over Burnards did change us and make us more competitive. They were really a very cut-price store, while we were selling at retail prices because we had got used to that during the war. By the time of the takeover, however, you could sell at what you liked, and Burnards had a policy that you never worked anything over 15%, regardless, and that did take us back to being very competitive.'

The comment is revealing. Historically, Tesco had been a major discounter but, suborned by the fixed price controls of the 1940s, it had failed to adapt to the deregulated markets of the 1950s. This failure had damaged both its profits and its image as a highly competitive trader. The Burnards takeover did more than simply tighten up Tesco's pricing policies, however. Of comparable import-ance, it added a new dimension of expertise to Edgar Collar's management team with the arrival of Arthur Thrush and Fred Turner (soon to be known affectionately as T 'n' T), whilst provid-ing the board with an insight into the acquisition business that was to play a key role in the company's future.

By the mid-1950s both a property and a takeover boom were

bove: An East London street market at the turn of the century

elow: An early twentieth-century photo of an East End Jewish school, of the
~~~nd at which the young Jack Cohen might well have taken religious instruction

Above: Avroam, Sime and their family, *circa* 1910. Jack Cohen is standing next to his mother

Left: 64535 2nd-class Air Mechanic Cohen, Jack, before his posting to the Middle East in 1917

Opposite page: Cissie and Jack Cohen on their wedding day in January 1924

Above left: Croydon market, one of Cohen's regular pitches, in the late 1920s

Above: Well Street marke Hackney, where Cohen began life as a costermonger

Below left: Sudbury Hill, 1937: the archetypal Tesco store of the pre-wa years. By 1939 the company had more than hundred stores of this kind trading in London and the Home Counties

Right: Jim Harrow, who first joined Cohen as a boy in the Croydon market, seen with the embryo Tesco transport fleet in 1932

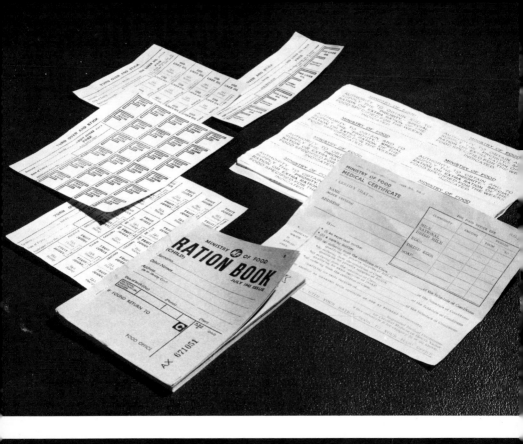

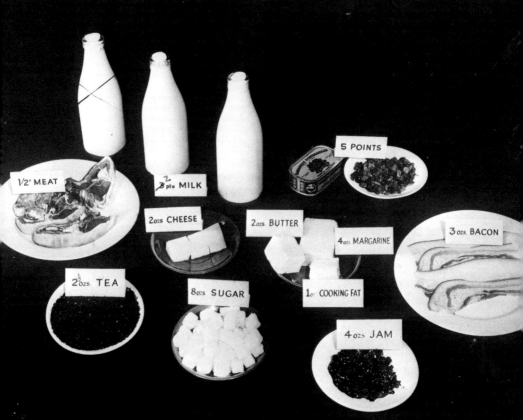

Opposite page:
Wartime rationing (above)
and the weekly wartime ration
for one person (below)

Right and below:
On the Home Front: queuing
for advice . . .

. . . and queuing for food

Above: The early 1950s saw an end to austerity: counter service in a typical post-war Tesco store

Left: The supermarketing revolutio begins: self-service at a Tesco store in the early 1950s

getting under way, the former triggered by a House of Commons announcement in November 1954 that building licences were to be dropped entirely; the latter, by the intensifying pressure on the resources of smaller companies to compete on capital terms with larger groups. Each was to have a powerful impact upon Tesco, although in the decade ahead the company was to expand more by acquisition than by in-house development.

A photo of the period captioned 'Undisputed victor of a friendly contest with other multi-millionaires at the Monopoly table' shows a delighted Jack Cohen munching on a king-size cigar and clutching an armful of paper money. As a pastime the game was highly rewarding, but as far as Tesco was concerned he was playing for real. Increasingly frustrated by the tight discipline of the new regime at Tesco House, it may well have been that Cohen found a new outlet for his dealings in playing the highly speculative acquisitions market. If he could not trade in goods, then he would trade in businesses, and within two years of the Burnards merger he was to clinch the takeover of Williamsons Ltd.

A motley of seventy stores and restaurants concentrated in London and the south-east, the company had recently been acquired by a group headed by David Behar, primarily with the intention of capitalising on its property assets. As for its trading profits, Williamsons was a disaster area: old-fashioned, ill-managed and extending credit to anyone of a creditable disposition, one Battle doctor having run an unpaid account of £2,000 for more than a year. Cohen, however, was undeterred, and the acquisition was to become as much a part of the legend of Tesco as of the man.

Robin Behar, son of David: 'My uncle, Jack Behar, bumped into Jack Cohen in the Turkish bath at the Royal Automobile Club. Jack was the black sheep of the family, a lovely chap, always game for a party, loved the girls, a leave-it-to-me-and-I'll-fix-it sort of a chap. Anyway, through the steam Jack Cohen said to Uncle Jack: "I see that David's bought some shops. What relation is he?" My uncle replied: "A nephew, so if you want to meet him, I'll fix it." And he did.'

It was the beginning of almost two years of tough negotiation, for Behar had never planned to sell off Williamsons as a chain, and he regarded Cohen's opening offers as totally unacceptable. Eventually, it was Edgar Collar who broke the deadlock, though even then

Hyman Kreitman had reservations about the deal. From a property standpoint, Williamsons might well be a useful asset, but as far as retailing was concerned, neither the stores nor the restaurants lent themselves naturally to self-service conversion. Cohen's strategy of growth by acquisition also placed serious constraints on Tesco's own capital development programme.

Cohen, however, was adamant, though even when the outline terms were agreed, Behar had doubts about whether to take cash for the company, or Tesco shares. In March 1957, Tesco issued 1,245,000 Preferred Ordinary shares of one shilling each, fully paid, as part of the purchase consideration for a controlling interest in Williamsons, and in due course a further 2,282,028 Preferred Ordinary shares were issued to buy the company outright.

Robin Behar: 'The paper offer was a bit risky. Tesco was a very small company, no one knew much about it, and everyone thought when you asked around that it was likely to be taken over by one of its main competitors, Victor Value. Against this was the fact that the Cohens had a reputation as terrific traders, although there was a question mark above their property side. As the Behars had been in the property business for four generations, it seemed a terrific match. My father took the paper, which was well worth having.'

With the takeover of Williamsons, David Behar joined the Tesco board, and Hyman Kreitman became joint managing director. The internal disputes intensified. Cohen was delighted with the acquisition, reporting, 'Your directors feel confident that after complete reorganisation, this purchase will prove to be the most valuable asset to your company', but others had different ideas, suspecting that Cohen may well have over-reached himself. The cost of the operation had been high, and to convert what had been a back-broken business into profit would cost even more. In his early days on the board, Behar must have wondered at what he found, for little attempt was made to disguise the hostility that now existed between Cohen and his son-in-law, whilst Edgar Collar and Charles Berzin could do little more than hold the ring between the two disputants.

Only one thing was certain: that if Tesco was to benefit from the acquisition of Williamsons, then an all-out effort would have to be made to revamp the company as quickly as possible. Certainly it could provide Tesco with invaluable High Street sites in places as far afield as Slough and Tunbridge Wells, but otherwise it was trapped in a time-warp, forty-nine of the properties having a small shop in the front and a café at the back where waitresses served tea and cakes to customers seated on red plush chairs. The whole enterprise was an anachronism, and with an intensity fused by the knowledge that Tesco could not afford to carry dead weight, the conversion programme began.

Before joining Tesco, Peter Goodwin had been the estates manager of Williamsons: 'Everything had to be ripped out of the old Williamsons, all the lovely old wood panelling of the restaurants and the red plush seats. Then the shelving and flooring and lighting people would move in, and everything would be chaotic to get them ready for opening. The floors were tiled in red Marley tiles, the Tesco red appeared on the ticket rows, there were red and white blinds above the provision counters, and even the lights were red to make the meat look better. It was one way of converting a company with a lot of good properties into a trading company.'

Individually, the transformation of Williamsons, the acquisition of Burnards, the conversion of Tesco's own properties to self-service, and the imposition of new management disciplines by Edgar Collar all played their part in improving the company's trading performance. When Cohen announced record trading profits of £586,361 for 1957 it seemed that Tesco's times of troubles were past, and with 185 stores now in service, the need was to develop not only a new head office but also new warehousing facilities. Two decades had passed since the opening of the Edmonton complex, then regarded as one of the most advanced in Britain, but now its facilities had been outstripped by the expansion of Tesco itself.

Since his first small venture into market gardening at Cheshunt, Cohen had always had an interest in the area, and in the mid-1950s he began to expand Tesco's holdings with the intention of re-locating the company's headquarters out of town. To Kreitman, the opportunity of designing an integrated system capable of adapting to the changing needs of the company was not to be missed. For all his deep-rooted suspicion of consultants, Cohen was persuaded to call in specialists capable of designing a warehousing system that would meet the future needs of the company. In 1957 Cohen unveiled the plans for the move, and early in 1959 the new complex was opened off the A10 in Hertfordshire.

Leonard Smith, who worked in the warehouse, joined Tesco in

the same year: 'It was a very well-planned system. The goods came in to be checked and stamped, ten or twelve delivery lorry-loads a day, and most of the goods were palletted. Four men unloaded them on to runners, and then on to conveyor belts. From the conveyors, the goods were unloaded on to racks, and because everything was racked you knew where everything was and the date on which it arrived.'

The key to the operation was turn-around time, for if the days of the two-box man had long gone, the need for high stock turnover remained. Cohen prowled the warehouse, chasing here, chivvying there, hustling all the time – 'Why is that still here, boy? Get it away soon.' The autocrat was in his element. This was where the action was, though there may have been more than that to his hyper-activity.

As a former warehouse manager at Cheshunt, Stan Prowse, says revealingly: 'We'd offload in the morning, and load up in the afternoon, so goods would be in the shops by Friday to sell by Saturday night in order to have the money in the till to pay for it on Monday and get the best discount. This shows how near the knuckle we were. We had to make profits all the time with goods in and out. Jack Cohen made sure of that.'

How near the knuckle Tesco was! The memory may be mislead-ing, an impression distorted by time, nonetheless it conflicts with the received wisdom not only that Tesco's finances were soundly based, but also that all was well at Tesco headquarters. Whether or not the company had over-extended itself as a result of the William-sons takeover, the fact remained that the pressure was still on to recover the cost of the venture, the more so as Tesco was now committed to an investment programme in supermarketing, under the direction of Hyman Kreitman.

Again, Cohen was later to claim a certain prescience for the development. 'As long ago as 1953, I anticipated that the develop-ment of the supermarket would gain pace, and throughout the next decade grow to almost unmanageable dimensions,' he said in 1971 – though it was more than three years after he had seen the future that Tesco opened its first store. In light of the assertion, the delay seems incomprehensible, not least, when a number of other multiples had already begun to experiment with the system, Sainsbury's having opened a 7,500-square-foot supermarket at Lewisham in 1955 – three months before Cohen was reporting to the AGM: 'I am watching the progress of supermarkets in this country with great interest having been to the United States on a number of occasions and studied this opportunity at first hand. I can assure you that the directors have this very much in mind and are alive to the possibilities for the future development in your company.'

Whatever the truth of the case, and whoever was responsible for initiating their development in the company, the issue was to become increasingly contentious in the years immediately ahead. In 1956, Tesco opened its first supermarket, though the distinction between self-service and supermarketing remained a fine one, turning largely on the size of units and lines that they carried. The problem for Kreitman was that whilst it was all very well for his father-in-law to talk up the supermarketing revolution, Tesco simply did not have stores of sufficient size to justify the claim, while Cohen's acquisition policy only aggravated the difficulties, restricting the funds available for development and lumbering the company with yet more inadequate stores.

Indeed, as late as 1958, Cohen himself accepted that 144 of 150 Tesco stores were running on self-service lines, many of them tiny units, incapable of any effective expansion. True, there was a scheme to extend the St Albans store by buying out the adjacent site, and true, there were plans for ten fully-fledged supermarkets on the drawing boards, but they would only come on line in the early 1960s, by which time the competition would be well entrenched in the market. What Kreitman wanted was action. All too often he only got words.

Cohen was masterly with them, always had been since his days in the market, but behind the patter there was an asperity, possibly made all the more cutting by his growing sense of alienation since the move into new Tesco House. The place was airy, spacious, well equipped, but the old intimacy had gone, the days when everyone knew everyone else and he could carry out his quality control experiments in his own office, then dump the remains down the lavatory. The buying and estates department had doubled in size, the staff of the shipping department under John Allis had quadrupled, whilst a new department dealing with transport had been established under Darkie Rose, long time in charge of the warehouse.

Where once Tesco had been his company, to dictate to as he liked, it was now growing too big for him. Where once he had managed by

his 'feel for the market', there were now emerging all those disciplines which he had despised for so long – 'marketing-
schmarketing', 'merchandising-schmerchandising'. Twelve years
had passed since he had floated Tesco as a public company, though
he had been careful to secure his hegemony; now it appeared that
control was slipping away from him – though not without a fight.

In 1959, Leslie Porter joined the company, initially as a consul-
tant on a fee of £200 a year, then as a full-time director drawing an
annual salary of £3,000. The husband of Cohen's younger daughter
Shirley, Porter had already established his reputation as a successful
businessman, first in the motor trade, subsequently as a textiles and
piece-goods importer. Independent-minded, and with a strong will
of his own, Porter had shown little previous inclination to join
Tesco, and his arrival in 1959 was significant for more reasons than
one. Practically, his experience in the textile business provided Tesco
with invaluable expertise at a time when Cohen was exploring the
possibility of introducing home 'n' wear lines into the larger stores;
but of equal significance, Porter's arrival may well have marked a
new development in Cohen's power game.

If there was a threat to his authority, then perhaps it was time to
introduce a new player on to the board, not so much to contain
Collar as to place a check on Kreitman. The ploy was an old one,
which he had worked before ('The Old Man had to have a foil to use
against the family, Kreitman against Collar'), and now it was to be
used again. In his authorised biography of Cohen, Maurice Corina
only touches on the subject; it was altogether too sensitive an issue
to be addressed directly, no more than hinting at the fact that the
Cohen–Kreitman relationship was close to breakdown: 'In every
growth business there is always a danger that the human element can
at any moment disrupt the continuity and confidence of top
management. People are different, and their individuality sometimes
clashes, perhaps disrupting corporate planning and policy-making.
Jack could not expect that Tesco would be any different from other
companies, but he was always keen to hear full-blooded argument,
which he regarded as essential for creative management. At the
highest level within Tesco, he and Hyman Kreitman never hesitated
to challenge each other. Sparks would fly when they were forging
some new policy.'

At first glance, the summary sounds innocent enough, but on

closer examination it reveals exactly what Corina was compelled to disguise. The human element, in practice the conflict between Cohen and Kreitman, was indeed disrupting the continuity and confidence of top management. The whole episode is still cloaked in silence, though it is clear that the fundamental differences in the personalities of the joint managing directors, leading in their turn to fundamental disagreements over management policies, would, eventually, trigger a head-on confrontation between the two men.

Each had their ambitions for Tesco, but both had different methods of achieving them, a difference that was neatly encapsulated by Cohen himself: 'I want something yesterday, he [Kreitman] is planning ten years ahead.' Even in the best of all possible worlds, the elements of the mix were hardly compatible. In Tesco House in the late 1950s, they proved fissile.

Schooled in the rough-and-tumble of the markets, and profoundly averse to intellectuals, Cohen demanded instant returns – or wanted to know the reason why. Deferred gratification was not his line of business, never had been, and even less so with time running against him. What he wanted was results, now. Kreitman was the antithesis of all that Cohen represented, the apotheosis of the new men who were sapping at his power, usurping his authority, appropriating his company. By late 1959, the relationship between the joint managing directors was at best strained, at worst acerbic – an untenable situation that was to have far-reaching consequences.

7. 'THIS AWFUL DRAGON'

(1959–65)

'The Marksian revolution had indeed
complemented the Beveridge revolution.
Both were in the logic of the times.'

Harry Hopkins
The New Look (1963)

The cartoon Supermac bestrode the election of 1959. Two years
before, in a speech at Bedford, Harold Macmillan had included a
sentence that was soon to become the catchphrase of the times: 'Let's
be frank about it, our people have never had it so good.' He was
right. Britain never had. The mood was expansive, a prelude to the
Swinging Sixties when everything seemed possible, and most things
were. But there was more to this *joie de vivre* than exuberance, for it
was fuelled by steady growth of consumer spending power, average
household incomes rising by more than 120%, from £16.6s.8d. to
£35.8s. in the ten years to 1970.

Seemingly, the bad old days had been relegated to the junk yard,
as antediluvian as Wilfred Brambell's rag-and-bone merchant in
Steptoe and Son. What was wanted was novelty, and consumers could
afford the cost of their expectations. The durable market boomed
(during the decade sales of washing machines, telephones, refrigerators doubled, trebled and quadrupled); package holidays 'took off',
whilst as Indian and Chinese restaurants burgeoned on the High
Streets of market towns where the staple take-away had long been
fish 'n' chips, food retailers began to explore new and exotic lines –
pastas and wines and cheeses with names as unpronounceable to the
tongue as their tastes were startling to the palate.

Of course, there were the jeremiahs who forecast that the good times could not last, and that if they did, they should not be allowed to, but for the majority the consumer society was what life was about – and, as always, the shop windows of Britain reflected their mood. It was the golden age of Carnaby Street and the mini skirt, of Biba and boutiques. Indeed, for retailers, it appeared that they had finally entered into their inheritance of Demand Unlimited.

Tesco was to be among its main beneficiaries. In the company's annual report for 1960, Cohen exuded confidence, and with reason, for Tesco was in good shape to take advantage of the forecast growth market. The board had been reinforced by the appointment of Arthur Thrush (a brilliant retailer, lately of Burnards) and Leslie Porter; there had been a consistent improvement in trading profits (up by almost £250,000 in the previous year); the capital reserves stood at £389,493; whilst in September 1960, Tesco had clinched the acquisition of John Irwin, Sons and Company.

A Merseyside-based group, with a network of 212 comparatively small stores in Lancashire, Cheshire and North Wales, Irwins was a trader of the old school (at the start of each board meeting, the chairman would say a prayer) that had failed to come to terms with post-war developments, knowing little about self-service and even less about supermarketing. What first sparked Cohen's interest in the group remains unclear, though it was consistent with his expansionist policies. With the takeover of Burnards and Williamsons, Tesco had achieved reasonable coverage in London and the south-east; now the plan was to expand northwards, and in the summer of 1959 he asked Ernie Fox (who had joined Tesco from Lipton's in 1935) to research Irwins in preparation for a bid. Fox's conclusion? That the company was likely to prove more of a liability than an asset.

Six months later, however, in March 1960, the *Daily Mail* carried a brief report that Tesco was again on the acquisition trail. The timing may have significance. Two years before, Kreitman had been given the task of supervising Tesco's supermarketing programme, yet here, once again, was Cohen dabbling with takeovers, this time against the advice of his own confidant. It was an impossible situation, for while Cohen might talk up supermarketing in public, in private he continued to frustrate Kreitman's brief, as David Behar was to learn with the opening of a Tesco supermarket on London's

Victoria Street. The store was not large, the cost of conversion not high, yet Cohen vociferously opposed the move, going so far as to warn Behar that his future with the company was at risk if the venture should go wrong.

The reaction was symptomatic of much else, not least of Cohen's ambivalence which Kreitman had to live with every day. For more than twelve years, he had been attempting to formulate a coherent development strategy for the company against the spoiling tactics of his father-in-law, but by 1960 he had had enough. In mid-summer he resigned his post as joint managing director and, to all intents and purposes, quit the company. The family don't talk about those days much any more, choosing to close ranks as much against memories as against strangers, whilst the story of events is confused as much by individual interpretation as by time. Whatever the facts, however, Kreitman's withdrawal coincided, almost exactly, with Tesco's renewed interest in Irwins.

Ernie Fox was deeply hurt by the decision: it ran counter to his best advice, and his fears that it would be impossible to up-grade many of Irwins stores were subsequently realised, at high cost to Tesco itself. Once nerved to the decision, however, there was no denying Cohen. The matter was discussed at the board meeting of 22 August, and there was a further, private meeting at Cohen's north London home before the final agreement was reached, at which Cohen played the devil's advocate to the scheme he himself had done so much to engineer. As ever, he was covering his tracks, determined to delegate responsibility should the deal go wrong.

On 1 September, the bid was made public, for the *Daily Mail* to report the following day that Norman James, the chairman of Irwins, had recommended that the offer of 1,536,491 Tesco one shilling shares, plus £1,126,986 in cash resources, was fair and reasonable. Sir Leslie Porter remembers the date vividly: 'Everyone was out of the office – Jack and Edgar Collar and the rest – and as I was the only one around, I signed the cheque for a million and more pounds. The bank phoned back to verify it because it only had one signature, but by that time Edgar had arrived back, so he counter-signed it, then sent off a confirmatory telegram. The cheque was returned later, because that was the practice in those days, and we had it framed and it's in the office still.'

Once the deal was struck, all hell broke loose at Tesco House.

Peter Goodwin, a former director of Tesco Estates: 'David Behar phoned me when I was at home, it was around seven in the evening, and said, "Sorry about this, but I've booked you on the midnight train to Liverpool and have got a reservation for you at the station hotel." I spent the next four days on a whirlwind tour looking at all the Irwin stores. It was almost a case of not getting out of the car. We would arrive outside another tiny store, take a quick look and then drive on to the next one. I really couldn't believe it. Nearly all were little corner shops, the sort of places where you sent Mary down for a half pound of lard and it went on the slate. I hate to think how much the bad debts were worth.'

And this was by no means the most serious of the problems. Superficially, Irwins may have appeared a good buy, the *Daily Express* proclaiming 'Boom Time for Tesco', but the acquisition was to have damaging consequences as far as the future of Tesco was concerned; on the one hand, masking its weakness in the development field; on the other, posing a continuing problem of management. As to the former, the finances of the takeover not only led to a further dilution of Cohen's holdings in the business, but also placed a further burden on Tesco's capital resources and, thus, a new restraint on its development programme at a time when other multiples, notably Sainsbury, were pursuing an intensive, in-house policy of developing supermarkets.

True, the takeover allowed Tesco to boast that it had 'gone national' (a recurrent phrase in Cohen's speeches), and that it was now operating almost 400 stores, but the claim disguised the reality that for all their value as property assets, a high proportion of these units were, at best, obsolescent, at worst, obsolete. Of course, so much is easily written in retrospect. Three decades later, with supermarkets having evolved into large stores, it is an armchair pastime to criticise a decision taken at a time when supermarketing was still in its infancy and acquisitions were widely regarded as a fashionable mode of expansion. Indeed, it was only in the late 1960s that the full implications of Tesco's strategy began to emerge, after a decade during which the company established itself as a pace-setter amongst multiple operators.

As to the question of managing a Merseyside-based group from the company headquarters at Cheshunt, that, too, appears to have commanded little consideration in the euphoria of the takeover bid.

Within half a decade, Tesco had doubled the size of its southern operation, and for all the administrative skills of Edgar Collar and the retail flair of Arthur Thrush, head office management was already over-stretched – yet now there were the manifold problems of Irwins to be resolved. As Mike Boxall, who joined Tesco in 1966 and was appointed company secretary in 1975, says, 'Size was the determining factor. Irwins was so big that the board simply could not envisage managing it from one spot. It was also important for the managers to feel that someone was overseeing them from near at hand.'

The solution seemed straightforward – allow the northern group full autonomy under the control of a newly recruited executive, James Grundy, who was soon to be joined by Ronald Bronstein in the role of company secretary. Eight years were to pass before the full implications of the decision emerged, but in the meantime Jack Cohen was already involved in his next deal.

He had known Isaac Klug, owner of Harrow Stores (Watford) Ltd, for a number of years, they were near neighbours in Finchley and frequently entertained each other. A patchwork of interests, Harrow Stores included three furniture shops (Warren and Beck) and a wholesalers (LMD Ltd), but majored on door-to-door credit sales. In his authorised biography of Cohen, Corina suggests that Cohen's interest in Klug may have had as much to do with recruiting new men for top management as with acquiring Harrow Stores itself. If the former was to prove a disappointment, then the latter turned out to be a costly affair.

It was not so much that little thought was given to how Tesco could go into furniture retailing without any effective transport (Mike Boxall: 'I suppose the assumption was that they could just whistle up a Tesco van to do the deliveries, or maybe a horse and cart!'), or even that Harrow Stores' hire-purchase debts stood at around £800,000. The real problem lay in what Sir Leslie Porter was to find on investigating the group's tally business – though only after the deal was struck.

In October 1960, less than a month after finalising the acquisition of Irwins, and apparently with little consultation and even less detailed examination of the business, Tesco purchased Harrow Stores and its subsidiaries for 1,985,577 Tesco one shilling shares. Only then did Sir Leslie discover just what they had bought:

'Harrow Stores worked on a 48% return, which meant that if something cost a pound, it was sold for £2.25 so that you could get a 50% profit after taking into account expenses, which were very heavy. The tallymen would collect the weekly payments, and if the lady wanted a coat they would sell her a blanket because that week it would be blankets that were on special commission.

'I went around with the men, and the things that went on in some of the houses was almost beyond belief. The women would throw their bundle of cards up in the air (Blundells, Sloanes, our own), and whichever came down first, that would be the one that would be paid that week. Quite often the tallymen would be invited in and the women would say, "Look, d'you want cash or shall we work it off upstairs?"'

Harrow were trading 'on tick' as far afield as Birmingham and Portsmouth, but whilst the properties out of which the group operated were generally well sited, the damage to Tesco's image was hard to assess. Although still operating at the lower end of the market, Tesco was attempting to refine its identity, but as Sir Leslie explains, the tallymen were quick to exploit the Tesco name to sell in their stock on the doorstep, with all that that entailed as far as the parent company was concerned.

Klug's time on the Tesco board was shortlived. On the day of his first meeting, Sir Leslie gave Klug a lift to Cheshunt, during which Klug lobbied for support for his latest venture – the takeover of United Drapery.

'I told Issy [Klug] we couldn't buy it because it was far too big. No, he said, he had looked at both companies and if Tesco were worth £10 million, then United Drapery were worth only £4 million. I wondered how he had worked this out, then realised that what he had done was to take our capitalised value (our shilling shares were then worth four or five shillings), but had taken the UD shares at par, ignoring the fact that United's shares had gone up about twenty times and were worth about a pound a share.'

Anxious to protect Klug from his own enthusiasm, Porter advised him not to raise the matter at the board, but Klug was undeterred. Under Any Other Business, he floated the proposal, and as Porter remembers, 'David Behar looked at him as if he was a maniac, and Edgar Collar asked to talk to me. Later I had a little chat with Issy, and by the next meeting he was out.' For a further year, Klug continued to manage Harrow Stores, then came a further revelation. Leslie Porter:

'Issy would go out and buy a discontinued line, say raincoats. The full retail price for them was maybe £20, but he'd pick them up for a fiver, and the normal wholesale price would be about £12. In Harrow Stores they sold them for the full retail price, but when Issy took them into stock at £20 there was a false profit. He hadn't done it intentionally, but the Harrow stock wasn't worth what we thought it was worth, and there had to be severe readjustments.'

In November 1961, the minutes of the Tesco board meeting reported that the trading position of Harrow Stores remained 'unsatisfactory' and that Mr I. Klug had tendered his resignation. The truth, however, was somewhat different. Cohen had pre-planned the resignation, and as Klug left Tesco House, Porter found that his own name was already on the door of Klug's old office, and a telegram of welcome was waiting for him on the desk!

Significantly, the *Financial Times* ran an article in December 1961, under the headline 'Split on Tesco Board', suggesting serious differences in management opinion 'as to how aggressive the company's expansion policy should be'. The leak was well informed. Twice in the previous fourteen months, Tesco had entered the acquisitions market, diffusing the family's shareholdings on both occasions, and whilst observers knew little of the internal problems created by the acquisition of Irwins and Harrow Stores, they could not be disguised from the board.

As forceful as ever, Cohen battled to dictate the policy of a company in which he and his family held a diminishing stake, and yet one over which he still appeared to exercise an almost arcane influence. It was all very well for the likes of Edgar Collar and David Behar and Arthur Thrush to attempt to curb his authority, but as long as he remained the Governor, then he would fight to ensure that his word was writ. In the week that the takeover of Harrow Stores was completed, Cohen celebrated his sixty-second birthday, and if he had learned only one thing from his four decades in business it was that no one respected a quitter – which was the last thing that he could be called.

Not that the problem was evident in the run-up to Christmas 1961. After more than two years of planning, negotiation and development, Tesco announced that the comedian Sid James would open its new flagship store in Leicester on 13 December. Built at a cost of £750,000, and with a trading area of some 16,000 square feet, four times the size of the average supermarket at the time, this was the shape of things to come as Hyman Kreitman envisaged it.

As the *Financial Times* of 10 December reported: 'The store will occupy most of the ground floor of a new multi-storey car park outside the main Leicester shopping area ... Besides the store, the complex will include a restaurant, a filling station (to be run by Total) and a five-minute car-wash. About half the store's selling area will be devoted to the sale of food displayed and sold on supermarket lines. In the remainder of the store the supermarket principle will be extended to cover a wide range of general merchandise including textiles and lighter electrical goods.'

But this was not all. For two months, the media had been trailing the story that Leicester would be opened as a discount store, the *Evening Standard* quoting Cohen in October as saying, 'This type of trading is still in its infancy here. People will have to be persuaded to accept it.' For himself, he had no doubts about the ethics of discounting. Through the 1920s and 1930s he had waged his own private war against price fixing, to the fury of certain suppliers, and while he had abandoned the practice during the wartime years, Burnards served as a salutary reminder that keen pricing was still the essence of mass retailing.

A Proprietary Articles Trade Association to fix retail prices had been established as early as 1896, and by the early 1920s the practice had become enshrined in law: 'Provided the original price charged by the producer is a fair and reasonable one ... the consumer is not unfairly prejudiced by the system of fixed retail prices.' As with Cohen, there had always been the sanction busters, though a subsequent series of pre-war rulings had effectively consolidated the manufacturers' position, which they reinforced by imposing a Stop List on rogue traders.

In the post-war years, the establishment of the Monopolies and Restrictive Practices Commission in 1948, followed by the 1956 passage of the Restrictive Trade Practices Act 'to prohibit the collective enforcement of conditions regulating the resale price of goods', provided an indication of a change of mood. By the mid-1950s, however, Resale Price Maintenance was so well entrenched, more than half of all consumer goods being price maintained, that manufacturers were prepared to fight a long and costly rearguard action through the courts to retain the practice.

As J. F. Pickering wrote, in his book *Resale Price Maintenance and Practice* (1966): 'The grocery trade was the first to show signs of a weakening of RPM after 1956. Opinions as to just how important the practice was in the trade differ widely. Undoubtedly there have always been traders who have cut prices, some of them without attracting manufacturer attention; others having done so less successfully found manufacturers cutting off supplies. At least two of the important supermarket chains of today, Tesco and Anthony Jackson Foodfare, started off as small cut price traders.'

Between 1956 and 1961, more than fifty injunctions were taken out against suppliers for price-cutting, but it was Cohen who took the issue out of the courts and into the headlines. By the early 1960s, Tesco was making occasional reductions on up to 4,000 lines, essentially a hit-and-run campaign that demanded rationalisation. Half a decade had passed since the Restrictive Trade Practices Act had entered the statute book, yet the manufacturers still continued to gerrymander, whilst the law scratched its wig and fudged its rulings. The situation was absurd, it demanded exposure.

The national press had always relished Cohen's bravado, but never more so than when he cast himself in the role of the housewife's friend with the opening at Leicester. All the old swash-and-buckle was there, Sid James to cut the tape, Cohen to patter up the crowd and the media: 'We are declaring all-out war on resale price maintenance. We are not attacking the small trader. It is the manufacturer we are after. We are fighting for the right of every believer in free retail enterprise to expect keen prices and greater choice.'

The manufacturers might object, but the customers loved it. Robin Behar remembers, 'By five o'clock everyone was exhausted, but there were still queues of people to get through the tills. Some of the tills had been closed and everything was pretty chaotic, when Jack said to me, "Come on, boy, you pack the bags and I'll run a till." And that's how it was. The chairman got on the till and I packed the bags until all the crowds were through.'

Within three days, more than 60,000 people passed through the Leicester check-outs. Tesco affirmed its commitment to opening further discount stores, and *The Grocer* reported, 'National publicity has turned Tesco into a sort of St George who is going to kill this awful dragon of RPM.' The battle between manufacturer and retailer was joined, with British Xylonite, manufacturers of Bex Bissell carpet shampoo appliances, threatening legal action if Tesco did not restore fixed prices on their goods.

Cohen was quick to turn the threat to his own advantage. The old price was restored, but with a poster-sized apology to customers:

BEX BISSELL SHAMPOO MASTER

Because the manufacturers have taken legal action to
maintain resale price

YOU HAVE TO PAY	67/6
THEY ONLY COST US	36/-
SHOWING 87.5% PROFIT EQUALS	31/6
OUR PRICE WAS ONLY 47/6, SAVING YOU	£1

This is what RPM means to you!

The media were delighted, but manufacturers were unabashed, and within the week Gor-ray, the skirt manufacturers, attacked from a new quarter. Tesco was selling four of their lines for ten shillings below the fixed price, to which Gor-ray countered by agreeing that retailers in the Leicester area could sell the same lines 'at whatever lower price they should decide upon until stocks run out' – the company offering to reimburse the difference between their cut-price tag and the normal selling price.

During the following month, a series of further skirmishes took place, with Tesco reaching a compromise agreement with Gor-ray, agreeing not to cut prices on at least two other manufacturers' lines, but re-asserting its right to determine its own pricing policies, and arguing that both manufacturers and customers would benefit from increased sales volumes at lower prices. By the middle of January 1962, however, the opposition had re-grouped, under cover of the law. On the 19th, Kayser Bondor went to the High Court to seek an injunction against Tesco for price-cutting on two of their products – nylons and briefs. The following day, the *Daily Mail* reported facetiously on one courtroom exchange:

'Mr Charles Lawson, QC, for Tesco, holding his court brief enquired, "There was some curiosity on my part at what a stretch brief was." Mr Strangman, QC: "I'm afraid I cannot gratify your curiosity." Mr Justice Cross: "There are many kinds of brief in this world, Mr Lawson." Mr Lawson: "So long as my learned friend is not stretching his brief too far, I don't mind."'

There was laughter in court, but it was short-lived. Too much was at stake for forensic double-talk. For almost two days the hearing continued, during which Kayser Bondor revealed that Tesco had obtained its goods through a subsidiary of Harrow Stores. Apparently, the practice was a variation on a well-tried theme. As Daisy Hyams recalls, 'We had always fought against RPM and, indeed, our supplies had sometimes been stopped by manufacturers for cutting prices. We were then obliged to obtain these goods secondhand from various wholesalers. As goods were coded, the suppliers soon discovered the source of our supplies and we continually had to seek new wholesalers.'

Although no records remain, was this a reason, if not the primary reason, for Cohen's deal with Issy Klug? In the autumn of 1960, was he already preparing his ground for an assault on RPM? Certainly Harrow offered Tesco an entrée to the non-food market, where price-fixing was a prevalent practice, whilst as J. F. Pickering wrote: 'A big problem facing many discount store operators is the difficulty of acquiring the ability to sell successfully products which they have never before handled ... Some operators overcome this by letting out parts of their stores to concessionaires, but Tesco have found this to be unsatisfactory and now acquire their "know-how" by taking over retail companies with experience in selling these particular goods.'

Whilst the extent of Harrow's know-how remained questionable in light of its trading losses, it was to serve a dual function for Tesco. For more than two years, the board had been considering diversifying into the non-food sector, the main constraints being the lack of internal expertise to manage such an operation, and the size limitations that the company's existing stores placed on handling durable lines. If the arrival of Leslie Porter to oversee a home 'n' wear operation and knock some sense into the nonsense that was Harrow Stores was to resolve the first problem, the opening of Leicester was to resolve the second. It was a combination that was to transform Tesco in the next half-decade, the expansion of the company's non-food business being paralleled by its growing investment in custom-built units such as Leicester.

More immediately, however, Harrow was to be used by Tesco as a stalking horse of RPM. In court on 19 January 1962, Kayser Bondor asserted that the disputed goods had been despatched to a subsidiary of Harrow Stores, though without the customary caution that 'the acceptance of this invoice is an undertaking that the goods entered therein will be offered for sale at the prices specified on the company's price list'. Tesco quibbled. No question, Harrow had been dealing with Kayser Bondor for more than four years; and no question, either, that the disputed goods had been received – but with inadequate documentation.

Mr Justice Cross was not impressed, and granted an interlocutory injunction against Tesco, considering that the issue was not whether RPM was desirable, but whether businessmen kept their word. When a company bought from manufacturers operating RPM policies, then it should abide by the conditions of such sales. That afternoon, the managing director of Kayser Bondor, David Fodeenday, welcomed the ruling, reiterating the old argument that 'price fixing protects the customer, for unless one has constant prices the goods must deteriorate because the price must go below the economic level'.

Momentarily it seemed that Tesco had lost out after all, even if the case had again exposed the ambiguities of the law. One reader of the *Daily Sketch* wrote, 'I think we should all be grateful to Mr Cohen and his company for taking on the big boys who profit at our expense. Now we know what RPM really stands for, Robbing the People Monstrously.' As far as manufacturers were concerned, however, it was still a case of laughing all the way to the bank, the Kayser Bondor decision simply nerving them to a new assault on sanction busting via the courts. The only likelihood of redress now lay with the government, as Cohen was to tell the *Financial Times*: 'We eagerly await action on the Board of Trade inquiry into RPM. Some manufacturers have made use of the existing law to maintain their hold on retail prices, but the history of the grocery trade in which Tesco have pioneered the virtual destruction of resale price maintenance has clearly shown that the general public is against this form of restriction.'

The words disguised the extent of Cohen's disappointment. After more than forty years of taking on 'the big boys', it seemed that they still had a price stranglehold on the trade. Unbeknown either to

Cohen or Tesco, a development was already in place which was to prove a death blow to price maintenance. As it was, there were other and more urgent matters to hand. At the Leicester opening, Cohen had promised to accelerate the company's supermarketing programme, implicitly accepting that Kreitman had been right after all. The future lay with new, purpose-built stores with ample car-parking to cater for an increasingly mobile public.

Within a year of the Leicester opening, more than thirty new supermarkets were planned for places as far afield as Folkestone and Gloucester, Poole and Nottingham, whilst pressure on the site-finders in the newly expanded estates department increased by the day. Peter Goodwin: 'In those days it was all done by trial and error. The joke was that we often used to plan on the back of a fag packet. Mr Turner and Mr Thrush were the grocery directors and they used to draw up in the car outside a shop that was to be redeveloped and say, "What are we going to do with this?" Once inside the store it would be, "I want this shop back 150 feet" and I'd reply, "Hang on a bit, that's a structural wall." Not that it made any difference. "That's your problem," they'd say. Those were exciting times.'

Exciting and risky, both. In the drive to obtain new sites, or to redevelop existing ones, the house rule was simple: if local planning authorities caused difficulties, develop and be damned. Robin Behar: 'Chichester was one of my father's sagas. Tesco had submitted about forty different schemes, but the council didn't know exactly what they wanted so they turned every one down. Eventually my father said, "Build it first, we'll answer for the consequences later" – and we did.'

David Behar could not have foreseen the delayed sequel to the adoption of such a cavalier policy, not that it seemed to matter at the time. Morale at Tesco House was high, the mood ebullient. Apparently the company had nowhere to go but up, not least as a result of the move into home 'n' wear. Whilst food sales were peaking out, sales of durables were booming. Powered by a combination of easy credit and low interest rates, and with incomes running above the level of inflation, consumer expenditure climbed consistently through the early 1960s – and Tesco was often hard pressed to keep pace with demand.

Leslie Porter: 'In Cheltenham we put in an escalator to connect the two floors – food and non-food – in an old Woolworths branch.

What was interesting was that the grocery turnover went up 20%, whilst in those days turnover on our food stores was increasing by only 10%. What we discovered was that if we were able to introduce something that everyone wants, all the other departments benefited, provided that you did not crimp them for space.'

Eighteen months after the opening of Leicester, Tesco announced a further expansion of its supermarketing programme, setting itself a goal of forty new store openings by 1965. The story anticipated the release of the company's figures for 1962, which showed a record turnover of £33 million for the year to produce a net, pre-tax profit of £1,699,231. Only one thing marred the occasion. The previous evening, Edgar Collar had died. Since joining the company twelve years before, he had been the quiet man who walked in Cohen's shadow, attempting to impose some order where there had been so little before.

Often it must have seemed to be an impossible task. Mike Boxall: 'The Old Man couldn't keep his fingers out of anything. He loved a situation where nothing was clear cut, and everyone tried to do everyone else's job because that was the way he had always done the thing. Give them a job, then start to dabble and make it difficult, that was Sir John's way.'

And this was the Governor whom Collar had attempted to manage – Slasher Jack as Cohen had come to be known. If, on seeing Freake's departure from Tesco that day in 1950, Collar had had reservations, he was subsequently to learn how well founded they had been. It was all very well to be regarded as Cohen's right-hand man, but it demanded nerve as much as tact, singlemindedness as much as talent to bring order out of the chaos that was the imbroglio of Tesco House in the 1950s. Arguably, it was Collar's steadying influence, a capacity to manage not only the conflict of interests, but also the clash of personalities that was a feature of the period, that provided the company with the discipline that was essential if Tesco was to become anything more than an extension of Cohen's dynamic yet wayward ambitions.

On the day after Collar's death, Peter Goodwin seriously began to consider quitting the company ('I couldn't get down to work without him, that's one of the reasons I left'); Tony di Angeli recalled his conversation of the previous day, and Cohen rang *The Grocer* to say that it was business as usual at Tesco. It was only in the annual report of the following year that he publicly expressed his regret at the loss of 'a colleague and friend whose loyalty, ability and devotion … have been of greatest value to us in the past twelve years'.

Within days of Collar's death, Kreitman returned to take over the vice-chairmanship of the company, to play a central role in what was soon to be seen as the most audacious gamble that Cohen, the gambler, had yet undertaken.

Trading stamps made their first appearance at Schuster's Department Store in Milwaukee, Wisconsin, in 1891. The stamps could be saved, and pasted in a book, customers being allowed one dollar in merchandise, or seventy cents in cash for a book of 500 stamps, representing purchases of $500. Five years later, Thomas Sperry developed the concept of trading stamps as an independent business, and sold in the idea to a group of New England retailers. The scheme was elegant in its simplicity: the newly formed company of Sperry and Hutchinson supplied retailers with the stamps, stamp books, premium catalogues and all the necessary merchandise for when customers handed in their books for redemption.

The scheme was an instant success, and by the outbreak of the First World War trading stamps given by retailers represented approximately 7% of total US retail sales. Forty years later, in 1954, US stamp purchases totalled $192 million, a growing element of this turnover being accounted for by supermarkets, whilst by 1962 almost half of all grocery sales in the States were covered by stamps. In fact, the late 1950s proved to be halcyon years for stamp-trading in the US. The *Progressive Grocer* reported in 1963: 'The steady increase in food store margins that had been evident since the mid-1950s eased off in 1962. The basic cause of the increased margins is the trading stamp that began its invasion of the food field in 1956 and reached a peak or a near peak in 1961 and 1962. In most stores the cost of stamps (2% to 3% of sales) has been added to retail prices, thus raising percent margins.'

While stamping may have been reaching saturation point in the States, however, Britain still remained a virtually untapped market, most retailers regarding the practice with unalloyed suspicion. A number of small companies had been in the business since before the war, though operating on shoestring margins, and when Richard

Tompkins established his Green Shield company in 1958 his first mail shot to potential customers generated only three replies. Discouraged as much by the fact that stamps absorbed approximately 2% of a retailer's turnover as by fears for the financial viability of certain stamp companies, no large multiple had entered the market. Cohen, among others, subscribed to the view of the National Chamber of Trade that stamps rarely generated the profits claimed for them.

Tompkins, however, was not to be deterred. The practice had never been effectively marketed in the UK before, and now the timing was right. During the 1950s, US evidence clearly indicated that, following the constraints of the immediate post-war years, a rising trend in income allied to a rise in consumer confidence had led to an explosion in demand for both durable goods and stamps. Indeed, the equation promised to be as profitable as it was straightforward: that where income exceeded expenditure, stamps provided an added selling point for retailers. It was a lesson the British had to learn, and Tompkins set about teaching them.

Fronted by a highly qualified sales team, Green Shield's first target was to penetrate the corner-shop market, and by early 1962, the company announced that it had some 8,000 shops using its stamps – less than 2% of total UK outlets but nonetheless a significant improvement on previous years. Cohen and Sperry and Hutchinson were quick to grasp the implications of the development. For the former it signalled what appeared to be an underlying shift in shopping practices; for the latter, it confirmed the potential of an underdeveloped market. Indeed, it may well have been Tompkins' success that first nerved S & H to reconnoitre the UK market. Impressed by what they found, they established the operational headquarters of the company in the West End. The great stamp war, as the *Daily Telegraph* was later to describe it, was on – to the consternation and alarm of the more conservatively minded multiple retailers.

For all their centrality to the economy, retailers have long been damned by a sense of social inferiority, the legacy of a stigma reaching back through Chesterton's *Ode to Grocers* ('that men may shun the awful shop') and Thackeray's *Vanity Fair* ('the selling of goods by retail is a shameful and infamous practice') to the time when Aristotle considered that trade was 'ignoble and inimical to virtue'. The notion may be absurd, but the prejudice remains, as the *Guardian* revealed in April 1989: 'Scene: The members' lobby on a Friday morning. Enter the Hon. Nicholas Soames, the young grandee, wearing astonishingly loud country tweeds.

'The Hon. Timothy Sainsbury, millionaire and junior defence minister: "Going ratting, Soames?"

'Soames: "I say, fancy being lectured about your gear by your grocer."'

The exchange precisely captures the conflict of interest that dogs every retailer. Requiring little start-up capital, it has always been a business for small entrepreneurs who, if successful, have done their best to live down their origins by living up to the adage that it is possible to get anywhere in trade, so long as one gets out of it. Tommy Lipton opened his first Glasgow store in 1871, and became a confidant of Edward VIII little more than two decades later. John Sainsbury opened his first shop in Drury Lane in 1869: his grandson sat in the House of Lords a century later. And Jack Cohen trundled a barrow into Well Street market in 1920 – and forty years later was to wonder what impact trading stamps would have on his own and his company's image.

The irony is inescapable, that it is social pressures as much as trading conditions that have motivated many of Britain's most successful retailers – and for Cohen, such pressures were intense. The braggadocio days of piling it high and selling it cheap were a thing of the past, replaced by a multi-million-pound company trading through more than 400 stores, and increasingly jealous of its image. Much had been achieved in the decade since Hyman Kreitman had persuaded Cohen to install shop fronts in place of roller blinds, and much still remained to be done, yet now there was the question of whether or not these little sticky things, stamps, would jeopardise all the rest.

Undoubtedly stamps were a gimmick, but a powerful one for all that, as had been proved by their successful deployment by independents and certain smaller multiples over the past five years. Whilst their share of the market continued to diminish, the rate of shrinkage itself had been checked. Research published by the Public Affairs Press in 1968 under the title *The Economics of Trading Stamps* indicated that stamps reinforced customer loyalty at a time of intensifying competition for trade on the High Street: 'With prices and services tending to be alike, the consumer continues to award her patronage impartially as long as a systematic attachment goes unrewarded. It is in such a situation that an introduction of trading stamps can be very effective for the retailer, provided the consumer responds to the system. Due to this deferred discount, a shopper may cease to be neutral about her supplier.'

The case was a persuasive one, but the doubts remained. Late in 1961, the National Association of Multiple Grocers had distributed a confidential memorandum to all its members, warning them off stamping, and along with such groups as Sainsbury, Allied Suppliers and International, Tesco had been a party to this unwritten agreement. Cohen told the *Daily Mail* that 'Trading stamps are a menace'. Either the majors remained united in their opposition to stamps, or there would be retail anarchy. But by the spring of 1963, US stamp operators were diligently testing the nerve of the subscribers to the agreement, probing for some weakness in their resolve. All that they needed was one sanction-buster, and the agreement would be exposed for what it was – worthless.

Cohen and the Tesco board recognised the danger. There could be no question that the benefits achieved from stamping would have to be set against the 2% levy charged by the stamp companies, and there could be no question, either, that the practice would have pricing and thus inflationary implications; nonetheless, one indisputable fact remained – that the first subscriber to break the agreement would gain an important if short-lived advantage over the competition. Through the summer and into the autumn of 1963, S & H and a pack of smaller operators kept up their sales pressure – a presentation here, a dinner party there – whilst the leading multiples nervously eyed the competition and wondered whose nerve would go first.

As late as 26 July, the Tesco board continued to reassert its opposition to stamps ('After lengthy discussion it was agreed that every effort be made to sign an agreement with other multiples to the effect that neither they nor we would take up stamps'), with the caveat that Hyman Kreitman be authorised 'to take whatever action he considered necessary in the event of another multiple deciding to take up stamp trading'.

It was a wise precaution, for unbeknown to the National Association, S & H were already close to their first breakthrough. In late

June, Garfield Weston had called a small press conference at his flagship store, Fortnum and Mason, to introduce the new chairman of his Fine Fare chain, George Metcalf. For all the capital pumped into it by Weston's parent company, the subsidiary was in deep trouble, which it was Metcalf's job to resolve. Six weeks later, on 21 August, the chairman of the Multiple Grocers' Association received a note from Metcalf informing him that Fine Fare intended to introduce S & H stamps on an experimental basis in selected stores from 21 November. The decision, Metcalf explained, was triggered by 'compelling evidence that a very substantial increase in price-cutting, promotional give-aways, and stamp-trading is occurring in the United Kingdom'.

The gentlemen's agreement had held for almost two years. Now it was in ruins, even if the association did not agree. Five days after the Fine Fare announcement, eighty of Britain's top retailers met behind closed doors at the Savoy to formulate their new policy on stamps. The meeting was unanimous in deprecating Fine Fare's decision, primarily because no dissenters were allowed to attend, and while it was agreed that any collective action against Garfield Weston's spread of companies could be construed as the work of a hostile cartel, a committee was appointed to mastermind the trade's response to Fine Fare's decision.

Once again, Cohen reaffirmed Tesco's position, but with a crucial qualification: 'We are opposed to trading stamps, but if Fine Fare opens up with them in a supermarket next to one of ours, then we shall probably have to adopt them too. We could try to fight with straight price-cutting, but I doubt whether that would be effective. Stamps make for added labour for the check-out girls at our cash desks, and they are always liable to be stolen or misused. But if this is the way to compete, we shall use them. I think that stamp companies will get rich in Britain.'

All the while, speculation mounted, whilst the controversy commanded media headlines. The issue was tearing the trade apart and the shopping public were fascinated by inside reports of the various machinations. Sainsbury and the Co-op were vehemently opposed to any form of stamping, Lord Sainsbury decrying the whole business as unseemly, and a Labour MP, John Stonehouse, president of the London Co-operative Society, demanding an enquiry into the practice from the President of the Board of Trade. Victor

Value dismissed the whole issue as 'a lot of panic', International remained enigmatic, whilst Fine Fare delighted in the whole furore, since the publicity it generated more than compensated for their 2% investment in stamps.

Indeed, it momentarily seemed that, amongst the larger multiples, they would have stamps to themselves, with all the advantages that that would entail. For almost two months the Savoy accord held and then, on Monday 14 October, Cohen's partner of the pre-war days, Michael Kaye, announced that he had instructed his Pricerite group of Home Counties stores to start issuing Green Shield stamps that morning. Only days before the company had proclaimed that it was totally opposed to stamping, and the bluff had worked. No-one expected the *volte face* when it came, creating a new crisis amongst the anti-stampers whose patchwork unity was fast falling apart. The question now was not so much one of retaining some semblance of credibility, more of who would go next?

Cohen heard the Pricerite news early that Monday morning, and while he and Kreitman agreed that the decision to go into stamps had been taken for them, there was a difference of opinion as to which company to opt for. Sperry and Hutchinson, the largest operator, were already committed to Fine Fare, and whilst Cohen favoured the King Korn stamp operation, Kreitman favoured Green Shield, as long as there was no conflict over franchise areas. Within forty-eight hours, Kreitman was in the Chicago offices of King Korn, to be disappointed by what he found. The company was not for Tesco, and from his hotel room he phoned William Beinecke, the chairman of S & H, to see whether there was any possibility of Tesco taking a share of their pink stamp franchise in the UK. The answer was straightforward: it would all depend on how George Metcalf viewed such a proposition. From Chicago, Kreitman flew to Toronto for a meeting with Metcalf, but for all the courtesies he received, the answer was unequivocal: Fine Fare was unwilling to deal.

Again, it appeared that the decision had been taken for Tesco. With Metcalf's rejection of a shared franchise, and Kreitman's negative report on King Korn, only one realistic alternative remained: Green Shield. What doubts Cohen may have had were quickly dispelled by Kreitman on his return from Toronto, and through the last weekend of October, Tesco's top management were in detailed negotiation with Tompkins and his advisers. The following morning, 28 October, a fortnight to the day since Michael Kaye had announced the Pricerite decision, the Tesco board finalised their trading agreement with Green Shield – and Fine Fare advanced the launch of Sperry and Hutchinson's pink stamps throughout their 553 stores.

By that evening, the stamp battle was joined on three fronts – on the High Street, at the headquarters of the Multiple Grocers' Association and in the offices of some of Britain's largest food manufacturers and suppliers. As to the first, Tesco were stunned by first-hand reports, later reinforced by media coverage, of the response to the Fine Fare initiative. Launched with all the razzamatazz of show biz, the retail circus quite literally came to town – teams of mini-skirted sales girls parading the High Streets selling in stamps, supported by day-glo posters that lauded their benefits. This was a new shopping experience, and now careless of his former reservations about the good name of retailing, Cohen committed Tesco to the offensive – on Tuesday, 29 October, the first Tesco store to trade in stamps opened its doors at Small Heath, Birmingham.

John Thomson: 'As chief inspector I was in charge of the opening, which was timed for nine o'clock. Building work and shop-fitting were all greatly behind schedule, and the store was in a turmoil of activity as we struggled to complete the many tasks that had to be done before we could allow Tommy Trinder to officially throw open the doors. At around half past six on Monday evening, our retail director, George Wood, arrived straight from a meeting at Cheshunt. Slapping me on the shoulder he said, "You're opening with stamps tomorrow." And open with stamps we did, with Jack Cohen and Tommy Trinder doing a cross-talk act on a hastily erected stage outside the front windows. This was the launch of stamp trading which was to carry us forward for many years.'

The following Sunday, as competition on the High Street continued to intensify, the *Sunday Express* reported from the battle front: 'Tesco, which launched its Green Shield stamp in twenty-two of its supermarkets last week, has had stamp-collecting housewives swarming around its counters.

'In Leicester yesterday, the giant Tesco store was besieged by thousands of battling housewives. Twelve women fainted. The staff were completely overwhelmed. Goods were knocked off the shelves and display stands.

'Finally manager John Eastoe cleared the shop and closed all the doors. After that women queuing were admitted twelve at a time. Mr Eastoe said, "I have never seen anything like it in my life. It was quite unbelievable and quite frightening."

'The Tesco manager in Peckham said, "We just can't move for the crowds of new customers", and it was the same in the company's newly opened Birmingham store: "We are doing fantastic business. Nothing can stop us now."'

Save, possibly, the anti-stamp lobby. Incensed by what they regarded as Tesco's backsliding, an influential group of multiples led by Lord Sainsbury, and including International, British Home Stores, United Dairies, Boots, Marks and Spencer and W. H. Smith, announced the formation of the Distributive Trade Alliance to resist any further incursions by stamp operators. Representing four-fifths of Britain's multiple grocers, and controlling more than 37,500 outlets between them, the alliance was not short of powerful supporters, especially in the manufacturing sector. What was it that Metcalf had written to the National Association of Multiple Grocers only a couple of months ago, that there was compelling evidence of the growth of discounting, stamp-trading and promotional price cuts throughout the UK?

Twelve months had passed since Kayser Bondor won their court battle with Tesco, yet in retrospect the victory proved to be a Pyrrhic one. Justice Cross may have found for the defendants, but the general public thought their case indefensible, and there was little sympathy for manufacturers when they began to move against Tesco, alleging that trading stamps were a covert method of discounting and, thus, in breach of RPM. Imperial Tobacco and Distillers were among the first to warn the company against giving stamps on their products, with the threat of withdrawing supplies, to be followed by groups as diverse as Cadbury and Thorn-EMI. Seemingly the entire manufacturing establishment was ganging up on the stamp-traders, whilst at Westminster the Distributive Trade Alliance pressed for the introduction of a bill to ensure that stamps carried their true face value and could be converted into cash.

Cohen, the old spoiler, was in his element. This was the very essence of his existence. For almost half a century he had been bucking the system, and if it was a fight that the manufacturers and multiples were after, then he would take it to them. An assiduously fostered rumour was abroad that stamps raised prices, so he slashed the cost of quarter-pound packs of tea by almost 50%. Fine Fare undercut Tesco on detergents, and Tesco countered by undercutting Fine Fare on sugar. Critics railed that the whole thing was an unbecoming mess, reflecting sadly on the reputation of Britain's retailers. Cohen retorted, 'Stamps seem to be what shoppers want, and we are here to serve them.'

In the heat of the controversy, his opponents appeared to have overlooked this point – but the shopping public had not. Ultimately, Cohen and Tesco and the other stamp traders appeared to be campaigning on their behalf. This mood was reinforced by the public's innate sympathy for the underdog. Indeed, the more the newly established Distributive Trade Alliance cried, 'Foul', the more the spectators to the contest retorted 'Play on', and through November, turnover at Tesco boomed whilst, of comparable significance, the Alliance and its allies were already beginning to lose ground at Westminster. Edward Heath, then President of the Board of Trade, said he could see no good reason for intervening in the stamp affair, and John Stonehouse tabled a private member's bill to abolish the practice of RPM.

By the turn of the year, the two issues, stamp-trading and RPM, were inextricably linked in the minds of the public and of Parliament. If the one remained, the other would go, and while a minimalist bill was tabled aimed at protecting consumers' interests from exploitation by stamp traders, a Cabinet meeting in mid-January 1964 was to approve Edward Heath's proposals for the abolition of RPM. Six months later, after a bitterly fought rearguard action by manufacturers, Heath's Resale Price Bill received the Royal Assent, for Cohen to reflect, 'The ending of resale price maintenance will be the green light for the most intensive retail development this country has seen.'

In his enthusiasm, he overlooked one fact: the law. Under Heath's bill, all price-fixers could register their products for investigation by a Restrictive Practices Court, whilst continuing to enforce their price lists until such a time as the court ruled on their cases. Manufacturers were quick to exploit the loophole, and although companies such as Gillette and Wilkinson soon abandoned price maintenance, they proved to be the exception rather than the rule.

Once more it seemed as if Cohen was to be frustrated by legal shenanigans. Thirty years had passed since Thomas Freake had issued his warning from old Tesco House ('Do not lend or sell Ovaltine or any other proprietary lines to any other trader whatsoever. Failure to comply with this request must definitely mean that we will have to stop your supplies as well as have our own supplies stopped'), yet it seemed that whilst everything had changed, everything remained the same.

The disenchantment must have been profound, though Cohen's fears were to be proved illusory. The newly elected Labour government reinforced Heath's Resale Price Act in January 1965, and from then on a diminishing number of diehard companies continued to press their cases via the Restrictive Practices Court – notably the Big Five sweet manufacturers, led by Cadbury and Mackintosh. What was widely regarded as the test case of existing legislation came to court in July 1967 and lasted for forty-three days, Justice Megaw finding in his summing up that RPM as applied to chocolates and sugar confectionery was illegal.

The long campaign was over, the decision providing legal sanction for wholesale transformation of the competitive structure of the grocery business by weeding out those inefficient independents and smaller multiples which for so long had been artificially sustained by fixed prices. After four decades of unrelenting opposition, Cohen had achieved his goal, and in so doing had played a significant role in revolutionising British retailing. Now in his mid-sixties, Cohen's success was the apotheosis of his career. The compliments he received from the likes of the new Prime Minister, Harold Wilson, even the knighthood he was given in 1969 for his services to retailing were insignificant compared to the public's recognition of what he had achieved on their behalf.

In retrospect, the story of the poor East End boy who made good must have appeared to Cohen to have a legendary quality – but always with the remembrance that it was a legend which he had had to carve out for himself. Nearly half a century had passed since he had first decided to go it alone, and now he was not only a widely admired public figure, but also the Governor of a company which, in the five years to 1966, had more than quadrupled its turnover to £88 million and raised its post-tax profits almost six-fold, to £3.3 million. But the exhilaration was short-lived, for the disillusion was about to begin.

8. 'THERE BEING NO FURTHER BUSINESS'

1965–9

'A distinctive condition, well described
as the "affluent society", undoubtedly
existed in the Britain of the 1960s.'

Arthur Marwick
British Society since 1945 (1982)

The consumer boom seemed to be inexhaustible. Careless of the fact
that Britain's performance as a trading nation, on which all the rest
depended, was in a state of near-precipitous decline (between 1955
and 1970, the UK's share of world markets fell by 9.3%), and
dismissive of early warnings that there might, indeed, be a limit to
growth, Britain continued to indulge in a breakneck shopping spree
through the second half of the 1960s. The cash was there (during the
decade, average weekly earnings rose by 94%), as were the goods.
Demand for the good life as represented by freezers and fridges,
phones and TV appeared insatiable, though the ultimate status
symbol remained the car – the number of licences issued rose by
more than a quarter to 11,802,000 in the five years to 1970.

There was a brief moment of concern in 1967 when the Wilson
government was forced to deflate due to a deteriorating overseas
trade balance, but for the rest, it appeared that the doomwatchers
had been proved comprehensively wrong. Where they read the
future darkly, instant gratification was the rule. Where they talked
up underlying trends, there was affluence as never before. Where
they ruminated on tomorrow, the trick was to live for today,
consumer expenditure rising by 76% to £27,000 million during the
decade.

In such conditions, it was hard for any retailer to go wrong, though that was little consolation for the smaller independents, who continued to lose ground to the multiples who, in their turn, were locked into intensifying competition. For food retailers such as Tesco and Sainsbury, however, one problem did loom large – accumulating evidence that expenditure on food had peaked in the late 1950s, to fall by almost four percentage points during the 1960s. Three broad options remained open: to increase one's share of the foodstuffs sector at the expense of the opposition; to diversify into non-foods, whilst continuing to compete for an enlarged share of the food sector; or to expand by acquisition.

Sainsbury were to pursue the first route, Tesco the other two – though with growing difficulty. In principle, the concept of keeping the company's options open was an admirable one; in practice it led to a strategy that was in conflict with itself. Exactly what *was* Tesco and what should it be? The answers were as varied as the temperament of those to whom the question was addressed – to one, a multiple grocer with a bit of home 'n' wear on the side; to another, a durable retailer with a nod in the direction of food; to a third, a property company with an interest in retailing; and to a fourth, a market predator with an eye for the quick takeover.

An exaggeration? Possibly, but not so far from the truth, for on the Tesco board of 1965 (see Appendix Seven) there were almost as many opinions as there were votes to cast. Eventually, such a diversity of goals was bound to take its toll, especially when compounded by the personal disputes that continued to wrack the board. At the time, however, Tesco's future problems remained disguised by its trading performance, Cohen declaring in the company's annual report that the company was trading more strongly than ever before. Apparently, the old adage that nothing succeeds like success was sound, for what could be more successful than a company whose share price had shown a twenty-fold increase in less than a decade?

Only one question remained – where would Tesco go from here? – and it seemed that Cohen and his team already had the answer. In November 1964, the company announced the first of three quick-fire takeovers: that of Charles Phillips, a chain of ninety-seven small, self-service outlets, run by 'Buddy' Weiner, a former GI. Phillips had been operating a Green Shield franchise for a number of years and, superficially, there could be no question about the logic of the move, for it helped to eliminate a clash of franchise interests. Others, however, had different ideas, based, in part, on the size constraints of the Phillips stores.

Laurie Don: 'Both Kreitman and David Behar opposed the deal, and it fell through once. A meeting was then held, from which both Kreitman and Behar were absent. The deal was struck without them, and we were told to announce it. Because we could not get hold of Kreitman, it was released to the press before he even heard of the decision. He was managing director at the time, and I remember thinking how odd it all was.'

Odd or intended, Cohen had once again outflanked his son-in-law, Tesco offering seventeen of its one shilling shares for every ten one shilling shares of Charles Phillips, and providing a place on the Board for Weiner and John Austin Wells. Whether or not the appointment of two former Phillips directors was a ploy on Cohen's part to further fragment control and thus limit Kreitman's authority remains unclear; if so, the move was to be offset in February 1965, with the takeover of Adsega, which led to a further, brief expansion of the board. Run by the two brothers Martin and Peter Green, Adsega operated forty-seven self-service outlets in the Manchester area, and was seen as a natural extension of Tesco's northern operation, based on the former Irwin chain.

Kreitman was keen on the deal. Adsega stores were keenly managed, well sited, and as Laurie Don recalls, 'The opportunity of getting thirty or forty stores of a reasonable size at one time was a good one.' The Greens, however, had other ideas. They showed little interest in Tesco's opening advances, and it was only after Kreitman had further talks with Martin Green at a trade cocktail party that the negotiations were re-opened. By February 1965, the deal was finalised, Tesco issuing 2,235,000 one shilling ordinary shares (at a market value of ten shillings) for Adsega, and further expanding the board to include Martin and Peter Green and Henry Seaburg.

Neither the Greens nor Buddy Weiner were to remain long with Tesco. In June 1965 James Grundy and Ronald Bronstein were appointed as directors of Adsega, with the remit of managing the company's expanded northern operation from a new 125,000-square-foot warehouse and office complex at Winsford, in Cheshire.

By then, however, Tesco had masterminded its third acquisition in almost as many months. Cadena Cafés Ltd was an old-established company based in Bristol, an operating mix of thirteen bakeries, twenty-five restaurants, and twenty-eight cake shops, mainly grouped in Hampshire, Gloucestershire and Oxfordshire. The proposed deal had considerable merits, not least by extending Tesco's operations into the Cotswolds and West Country, though as Robin Behar says 'In a property man's eyes, Cadena Cafés was as much a property asset as anything else. The sites were superb from a trading point of view, but first and foremost they were prime freehold properties, and that's what inspired my father to propose the deal. When eventually some of those sites were sold, they went for phenomenal prices. In fact, when the Southampton site was unloaded, it went for more than Tesco paid for the whole group.'

The acquisition was completed in March 1965, Tesco trading twenty-five of its ordinary shilling shares for two Cadena Ordinary £1 shares or, alternatively, offering twenty-six shillings cash for each 8% Preference share of £1 each. Although a secondary consideration, one positive advantage that resulted from the takeover was the expertise that Cadena was to bring the parent company in the management of in-store bakeries. But the immediate result of the deal was to reveal, yet again, the fundamental differences that beset the board. Undoubtedly the acquisition and development of good properties is central to the trading performance of any multiple, though such a function has always to be placed in the context of the overall objective of the company itself. Robin Behar: 'There must be a good marriage of the two. Obviously if the trading side is no good, then there is no company, but equally a retail side with a weak property division is very vulnerable.'

Tesco's problem in the second half of the 1960s was to separate the one from the other, and the continuing attempt to define its priorities was to lead to a growing confusion of purpose, with the company holding a spread of diverse properties, many of which bore no relationship to future trading needs.

This was not all. With each acquisition, the structure of Tesco management was becoming increasingly complex, a cobweb of interlocking subsidiaries which in theory reported to Cheshunt but which in practice tended to manage their own affairs. In principle, the delegation of management responsibilities via free-standing profit centres was estimable, providing that there was firm control from the centre, based upon a coherent development strategy – which is precisely what Tesco lacked.

For all Kreitman's attempts to pull together the various elements that made up the group, and provide them with a consistent policy, there was still Jack Cohen to contend with, and a considerable contention it was. After more than four decades in the business, much of the old spoiler still remained, though in one respect, at least, he had changed. It may have taken time to convince him of the full value of supermarketing, but once convinced, he was as anxious to claim the credit for their development as he was enthusiastic to promote them in Tesco itself.

The company's annual report for 1965 provided an insight into his mood: 'Whilst acquisitions have attracted most attention during the past year, we have continued to expand our chain of super-markets, and in the past twelve months twenty-five new super-markets have been opened. A further twenty-three supermarkets, at a rate of one every ten days, are scheduled to be opened before the end of the year, and a further rapid expansion is planned for 1966 and beyond.'

Indeed, against a self-imposed target of having a Tesco store in every major town in Britain, fifty-one new stores were opened in 1966 alone, many with all the flair and razzamatazz that was now becoming a feature as much of Cohen's as of the company's style. Promotions, gimmicks and glitz proliferated, and as the opening programme accelerated, so the razzamatazz intensified, a marketing free-for-all. The crowds and the media relished it, the more so when things went wrong, as when the circus reached Rayleigh, Essex, one grey spring day in 1969.

To promote Tesco's cut-price image, the company had taken to employing Sir Save-a-Lot, a knight dressed in medieval armour mounted on a white charger. The centrepiece of innumerable openings, but increasingly frustrated by having to play second lead to a shop, Sir Save-a-Lot momentarily lost his self-control. After a statutory tour of the town, he arrived at the new Tesco, cut the tape, then rode headlong into the store where his terrified charger reared at the sight of a biscuit display, dumped the unhappy knight into a pyramid of cornflake packets, then collapsed on its back amongst piles of Cadbury's chocolate rolls.

The impromptu act was too much for the crowd. They exploded into laughter whilst the manager, distraught at the thought that the horse might be seriously injured, complained to anyone willing to listen, 'We'll have to shoot the creature, and in front of the customers, too.' Finally Ian MacLaurin, now chairman of Tesco, but then a regional managing director, intervened. After phoning for a vet he nestled the horse's head in his lap, feeding it on chocolate biscuits until help arrived.

Even as slapstick, the incident proved good for business, one of a long procession of 'happenings' which brought life to the High Street and profits for Tesco. For ultimately this was what the whole shebang was about. The more conservative among the competition might deride all the glitz and the glitter, all the bombast and ballyhoo, but the company continued to pick up trade, as noted in the annual report of 1966: 'You may have read in the financial press that a table of relative growth has been compiled in respect of Britain's largest companies. It is gratifying to note that as a result Tesco has been rated top in this league of British industry.'

Tesco was on a high. The future might be out there, waiting, but the prevailing mood was to let it wait. As much by accident as design, the company had patched together a policy which, albeit temporarily, was producing unfailingly good results, any concern about the diminishing demand for foodstuffs being allayed on the one hand by the growing success of Tesco's own label brands; on the other, by the expansion of the home 'n' wear division.

Since the 1920s Cohen had been selling his own label products (Tesco tea and suet, Red Glow tinned salmon), and for more than thirty years Daisy Hyams had been charting their progress. The Dickensian office behind the old Clapton bus depot was long gone, for by the mid-1960s she was controller of Tesco's entire £3 million weekly food-buying operation.

Whilst Cohen himself might continue to indulge in his own buying forays, including a consignment of Polish cigarettes allegedly made up of lettuce leaves which, according to one of Tesco's present directors, Mike Darnell, 'reminded me of nothing more than the old herbal cigarettes which we smoked behind the lavatory at school', the entire purchasing operation was becoming increasingly sophisticated, not least in obtaining own label lines. Daisy Hyams: 'If you can place a large contract for a commodity and eliminate all marketing and advertising expenses, you are able to purchase at an advantageous price which you can then pass on to the customer. In short, you can cut out intermediary costs.'

Allied to the increase in the number of Tesco outlets (the book value of the company's freehold property portfolio more than doubled to £10,897,000 between 1965 and 1967), and the continuing popularity of Green Shield stamps, it proved to be a powerful antidote to the contraction in food expenditure, especially when reinforced by the company's move into the non-food sector. As distinct from the grocery sector, operating on the principle of high volumes and low margins, comparison shopping turns on high margins and low volumes, and with the market shift towards durable expenditure during the 1960s, Tesco's expansion into non-foods made a signficant contribution towards off-setting the downturn in the sale of foodstuffs.

In March 1966, Tesco opened a 16,000-square-foot store in Brixton, south London, half of the space being devoted to groceries and described by the *Financial Times* as 'one of the most modern and comfortable food shops in the country', the other to a home 'n' wear and furnishing department selling everything from toys and carpets to Tesco brand seeds. It was the shape of things to come. In the next half-decade, as the selling areas of new stores doubled from 4,000 to 8,000 square feet, and then doubled again, so the investment in durable lines increased, supported by the development of the company's own label, Delamare.

As Tesco expanded, so the pressure on management increased, which was one of the main reasons for the company's investment in an ICL 1300 computer. With a network of more than 600 stores, and with turnover topping the £100 million mark by the close of 1966, the case for introducing an advanced system was indisputable, though Cohen had his doubts. The notion aroused all his old antipathies: it was not so much the cost of the system, more what it presaged, which surfaced on the opening day for the installation. It had been a taxing occasion, and as Cohen was leaving the reception a journalist asked him for one final quote: 'What do you think of this enormous investment you've made?'

Cohen thought for a moment, then quietly replied, 'Computer comschmuters' before walking into his office.

In one respect he was right – systems are a tool of, rather than a substitute for, good management – though his reservations went deeper than that, deeper even than his tersely expressed reflection that Tesco could have opened two new stores for the price of the new installation. In half a century of trading he had seen many changes, but for him this new piece of hardware represented all that he could not comprehend, the ultimate challenge to the value systems on which he had built his company, and there is a certain piquancy about Robin Behar's recollection of a day when he and Cohen were walking past the new computer suite at old Tesco House: 'There was a fellow on loan to us from ICL, a systems analyst who had a lot of thinking to do. On the day in question he had his leg up on the desk, and Jack went marching in: "What do you think you're doing with your leg up in the air? Why don't you get out and do some work?"'

The two-box man was still Cohen's model, and the more the world changed about him, the more he came to rely on his contacts with store managers. Laurie Don reflects: 'I think he distrusted anyone who wasn't a manager. They were instantly recognisable as the traders he had always known.' By inclination a bottom-up, as opposed to a top-down manager, Cohen's approach generated devoted loyalty at the grass-roots level of the company, though his informal network was not always well received at Tesco House, where it was viewed with some suspicion as an alternative power base.

But although Cohen may have been coming to regard himself as an outsider, there was still one thing that he understood better than most: the need for a company, however large, to maintain its trading momentum, the more so in the highly competitive business of retailing. Once a company came to believe that it had nothing further to do but to rest on its achievements, once the original dynamism had gone, all that remained was for it to shut up shop. He could toll off the names of a number of multiples which, not so distantly, appeared to have a promising future, but had become little more than memories – and now there were troubles at Victor Value.

Established by Alex Cohen, no relation to Jack, the history of Victor Value had paralleled that of Tesco very closely, and in 1960 there had even been talks of a merger between the two groups. At the time, Victor Value was the larger company, and it was Alex

Cohen who proposed the deal. Sir Leslie Porter remembers that brief encounter well:

'Jack Cohen had had a serious operation for cancer, so the Victor Value team came out to Cheshunt. The Cohens, Alex the chairman and Maurie, the MD, came in, sat down and said, "Well Jack, it's going to be lovely. You will be president, Alex will be chairman, and Hyman, Leslie and Maurie will be joint managing directors. It'll be the greatest combination the City has ever seen in the grocery trade, and we'll cut Sainsbury's right out."'

At first sight, it appeared an attractive proposition, but less so when Alex Cohen began to press for sole control of the merged group, and entered into a wrangle over shareholdings. Sir Leslie Porter: 'The Old Man was incensed by this, and told Alex that his only interest in the deal was with the shareholders, then ordered me to throw them out of the building.' The talks were never resumed. Some months later, Victor Value absorbed Swettenhams, a Midlands retailer, followed by the takeover of the Anthony Jackson Foodfare group, controlled by Jack Cohen's nephew, Sidney Ingram, in 1965.

Largely a family-run business, and managed on what could best be described as highly idiosyncratic lines, Anthony Jackson's proved too much for Victor Value to digest, and by 1967 the company's share prices were falling, only to regain lost ground with rumours of a takeover bid. The full extent of the company's problems were revealed in the opening months of 1968. First it sold a leasehold warehouse in an attempt to ease its cash flow problems, then it dropped its King Korn stamp franchise to cut its overheads, and finally its figures for 1967 showed that there had been a sharp fall in pre-tax profits over the previous two years, from £664,998 in 1965 to £232,351 in 1967. No dividend was declared, and what had formerly only been market speculation now began to harden up with reports that three, if not four, companies were interested in pitching for Victor Value – Pricerite, Fine Fare, Great Universal Stores, and Tesco.

As Cohen contemplated the irony of how quickly circumstances had changed, and pondered all that that implied, Kreitman arranged a meeting with Alex Cohen's son, Neville, to discuss the possibility of reaching an agreement between the two parties. Time was of the essence, and to avoid fuelling market speculation, the venue chosen was a roadside lay-by. Kreitman's conclusion was straightforward: that Victor Value offered an exciting prospect, but that it would impose an enormous burden on Tesco's management resources. Within the week, and following a day-long meeting at the City offices of the merchant bankers Kleinwort Benson, the deal was finalised, Tesco bidding £8,500,000 for control of Victor Value.

As Alex Cohen and his board held a 54% stake in the company, the offer for the whole of the issued Victor Value capital was little more than a formality. Tesco offered two of its own one shilling shares (then valued at seventeen shillings) for three Victor Value Ordinary shares; one Tesco share for every three Victor Value 'A' shares (valued at five and eightpence), and sixteen shillings a share for the 5% Preference capital of £1 each.

By mid-summer, Tesco had completed its most significant acquisition to date, having added 217 stores to its existing chain, and lifted the company's total selling space to some 1.4 million square feet. Little more than a decade had passed since the company had been only one amongst the pack of smaller retailers fighting for a share of the market, but now, with 834 stores and a turnover nearing £200 million, it had established itself firmly in the league of top multiples – the only problem being to make the conglomerate work.

If Victor Value's demise stemmed from its inability to manage the acquisition of Anthony Jackson, then Tesco was now to be faced with much the same predicament. In an interview with the *Financial Times*, Cohen confessed, 'This is going to be a hell of a difficult job, which will take at least eighteen months, maybe two years before we get any rewards.' He was an optimist. Victor Value carried heavy liabilities, and the conversion of VV stores to the Tesco house style imposed a further massive burden on Arthur Thrush's retail team. But most importantly, the parent company had management problems enough of its own, without having to tackle anyone else's. Jim Pennell, at that time a buyer, and later a main board director, considers that the takeover 'very nearly brought Tesco to its knees'. Laurie Don adds: 'Victor Value proved a lot to bite off. Of course, it all sounded super, put in our own managers, convert the shops over four weekends, and then start giving Green Shield stamps, but the strain that put on the business was phenomenal. You don't take people out of an existing business to concentrate on a new one without it having some effect, otherwise you would have to ask: "What were they doing there in the first place?"'

More trenchantly, perhaps, it had to be asked what Victor Value's management had been doing? Sir Leslie Porter: 'I think that the Cohens had lost their grip. When we took over, we found that all the bosses, as well as other members of the family, were going into the branches near to where they lived and getting all their requirements from the shop without paying for them. Because they were doing it, the senior directors followed their example, then the managers followed suit, and so on down the line.'

Arthur Harvey, a longtime inspector with the group: 'I saw Victor Value grow and die. It died because the sons took over and did not put their backs into it. They would go into a shop not knowing what they were talking about, and the managers would laugh at them. They would stand and discuss cars and things, and that's when the troubles started. When all they could talk of was the lavish things they had to managers who were probably earning a small wage, it wasn't surprising that the managers began to think: "They've got enough money. How can I make a bit of profit for myself?" The shrinkage must have been appalling.'

As Ted Weaver, recruited from Scotland Yard in 1957 to head Tesco's security division, was soon to learn: 'On the morning after we had taken over Victor Value, Mr Kreitman called me into his office and told me that we had trouble on our hands. The company was heavily in the red, and he said that I'd better take the kid gloves off and go in heavy. Apparently, a number of managers were in possession of zeroing keys for the tills, and one night, as I was coming back through South Norwood, I had a remarkable piece of luck. I saw the shop light on, and the manager messing about with the till. This was around 9.30, and what he had done was to zero the till at 4.30, so that anything from then on was his own. That was just one of the ways Victor Value lost money.'

Tesco itself was no stranger to shrinkage, Jack Cohen himself having once operated on the principle of 'a penny for the manager, twopence for the profits', but the Victor Value situation represented something much more deep-rooted, a corrosive attitude that reached down from the top levels of the company to the girls on the check-out desks. The condition was symptomatic of the problems of the company as a whole, and the more Tesco executives explored the workings of the new acquisition, the more they recognised the need for a root-and-branch reform.

In contrast to previous practices, none of the former Victor Value directors were invited to join the Tesco board, whilst as far as their branch managers were concerned, a meeting was convened at the Festival Hall where there was no mincing of words. Either there was a radical improvement in their trading performance or … There was no need to spell out the alternative. Cohen was determined to make good his undertaking that Victor Value could be made to pay, though in the process even he was forced to recognise the need for some devolution of power within Tesco.

In May 1968 Laurie Don and Arthur Thrush had submitted proposals to the board for the reorganisation of the management structure of the trading groups within Tesco. A cat's cradle of virtually autonomous companies, the majority of which had evolved more by accident than design, the existing structure had served out its time. After a lengthy discussion, the proposals were referred back to the June meeting, but nothing further was heard of the plan, though it may well have been the trigger for Cohen's announcement on 6 June that Hyman Kreitman had been appointed joint chairman of the holding company, and that Arthur Thrush was to join Leslie Porter as an assistant managing director.

According to Corina's biography, Cohen had spent 'many lonely hours' contemplating this problem of management succession, but if he was finally to decide that it was time to give way to younger men, he was equally quick to add the caveat, 'But that doesn't mean I am going to relax in any way.' Four months later, on 6 October 1968, Cohen celebrated his seventieth birthday at the Dorchester Hotel.

The occasion was a nostalgic one, but if the disc jockey Alan Freeman's staging of *Jack Cohen: This is Your Life* was for many a prompt to memory, for others it had an altogether more immediate relevance. Corina considers that no one present could contemplate the thought that Cohen would soon have to move aside to make more room for members of his directorial and executive team. For almost half a century the man and the company he had created had been synonymous, for Cohen and Tesco to become a talisman of success. Surely the two were inseparable. Yet there were those who were as concerned with the future as the past, the putative heirs to the empire that Cohen had built.

Retailing is a tough business, none tougher, an everyday test of nerve and skill, demanding of its practitioners an implacable, ruthless quality if they are to survive in the imbroglio of Britain's high streets. To their customers, retailers may present a benign face, but it masks the reality that the business itself has no time and less tolerance for failures. Cohen had learned the lesson well, as his potential successors had learned it from him.

Now they gathered at the Dorchester, and whilst Alan Freeman itemised Cohen's achievements, his heirs pondered exactly what he had meant by his pledge to relinquish certain of his powers, and what could be done if he failed to accept that it was time to step aside. For all his manifold talents, the Governor was becoming something of a liability, out of touch with the times. And small wonder. He had first learned his skills in the markets of London's East End, to refine them in the immediate pre- and post-war years, but since then the industry had been in a state of accelerating change which even some of his young lions had found hard to comprehend.

The lights dimmed, the guests sang 'Happy Birthday' and raised their glasses to Cohen's seventy years, and while the majority wished him many more of them, a few wondered how many more there would be. Surely, Psalm 87 was right: 'The days of our age are threescore years and ten', whilst the rider was equally salutary, something about men being so strong that they might come to fourscore years, 'yet is their strength then but labour and sorrow'. That was the last thing anyone wanted, yet would Cohen bring it on himself? Only time and the Governor could tell, and three months later it appeared that Cohen did, indeed, intend to fulfil his promise 'to give the younger people their chance to show their ability'.

A board meeting of 28 January 1969 accepted a plan for the reformulation of the management structure of Tesco, with Sir John Cohen (knighted in the New Year's Honours list) remaining as joint chairman of the main operating company (Tesco Stores, Holdings, Ltd) with Hyman Kreitman; Tesco Stores Ltd would be the only direct subsidiary of the parent company; and all further power would be devolved to eight subsidiary companies, each of which would operate on a national basis, and all of which would have either their own chairman or managing directors and free-standing boards.

Sir John's name appeared on only one of them (Tesco Wholesale Ltd), and it seemed for the time being that the old order was giving way to the new.

This was fortuitous, for it seemed that Tesco's period of hyper-growth might well be coming to an end. Victor Value continued to be a serious liability (to help cover the costs of the takeover, Tesco had floated a rights issue on 7 November 1968, which further diluted the family shareholdings), whilst by the late 1960s the full impact of Tesco's earlier acquisitions began to emerge for the first time. The company might talk up its spread of 834 stores, and stress the extent of its investment in supermarketing, but in reality its in-house development programme continued to be dwarfed by the company's holdings of small and inadequate stores of the type Peter Goodwin had surveyed during his lightning tour of Merseyside following the Irwins deal of 1965.

And this was not all. According to Sir Leslie Porter, the prevailing policy was to minimise investments to maximise short-term returns, careless of the longer term consequences. The results were inevitable: 'If you look at some of the precincts where our shops were, you will see that because our property side was so frightened of the Old Man saying, "How can you pay that sort of rent?" that ours were not in the best position. The best position might come in at £2 a square foot, and the worst was £1, and while Sainsbury's would go for the best, Tesco would go for the worst. It was a cock-eyed policy. You have to speculate to accumulate, and quality is all important.'

Mike Darnell: 'We were very property-driven. If a site was a good deal property-wise we would tend to favour it, even though it might not be tremendously good as a retail site, and couldn't be developed into a good one. We were converting a lot of sites in the late 1960s which didn't give us a good image even after conversion ... In fact, we seemed to be opening space for the sake of opening it, not opening quality space which would stand us in good stead for the next ten years.'

And even this was not the only area in which Tesco was vulnerable. The company was also slow to respond to the development of a new generation of retailing: out-of-town superstores and hypermarkets. Definitions continue to bedevil the subject, to confuse exactly what is a supermarket, what a superstore and what a hypermarket, though the generally received opinion is that super-markets range in size between 4,000 and 20,000 square feet; superstores between 20,000 and 50,000 square feet, and that hypermarkets provide a minimum of 25,000 square foot selling area which, in practice, usually means a minimum of 50,000 square feet of gross floor space.

Here, however, a further qualification. As a Distributive Trades Economic Development Council paper of 1973 noted, super-markets are generally centrally located, as distinct from superstores and hypermarkets which favour peripheral locations, the latter providing one storey, self-service shopping, supported by adequate, flat car-parking facilities. As a concept, out-of-town shopping, specifically directed at car-borne customers, first emerged in the US in the early 1930s, the Country Club Plaza in Kansas opening in 1932. The idea was slow to gain acceptance, however, and as late as 1950 there were only eight out-of-town centres in North America. Fifteen years later, there were more than 8,000 which, between them, accounted for almost a third of total US retail sales.

In contrast, the French were the first to pioneer the concept of hypermarketing, Carrefour opening the first true out-of-town hypermarket at St Geneviève-des-Bois, near Paris, in 1963. Whilst the *hypermarché* was to become a feature of the Continental land-scape in the next half-decade, such developments met with intense resistance both from consumers and planners in the UK. Little more than two decades had passed since Lord Sainsbury had been abused by a judge's wife for expecting her to do her own shopping at one of the first small supermarkets opened by the company, yet now there was talk of units of ten or even twenty times this size. Multiples might argue the advantages of practising the economies of scale in retailing, and thus of the price savings achieved for shoppers, but as far as the shoppers themselves were concerned they could do no better than to echo the 1971 remark of a Consumer Council spokesman about 'the feelings of terror, of constriction in my heart, at the mention of anyone coming in with hypermarkets or similar things'.

The alarm was raised too late, for in 1969 Carrefour, in associ-ation with Wheatsheaf Distribution and Trading, had received planning permission for the development of a 100,000-square-foot store with parking space for 1,000 cars on an eleven-acre site at

Caerphilly, north of Cardiff. The enemy was already within, and in an attempt to rationalise what promised to be an increasingly contentious issue, the Department of the Environment and the Welsh Office published Development Control Policy Note 13 (*Out of Town Shops and Shopping Centres*), requiring all planning applications for stores of more than 50,000 square feet to be referred either to the Secretary of State for the Environment or the Secretary of State for Wales.

As A. J. May wrote in the *Architectural Journal* in 1976, 'There is no doubt about the significance of this policy. Many operators of out-of-town or edge-of-town superstores now deliberately keep the size of their developments below 50,000 square feet gross in an attempt to reduce the inevitable planning delay. All nine superstores currently under construction for Asda Superstores in England and Scotland, for example, are just below 50,000 square feet, gross.'

And if the policy itself was significant, so was the *Journal*'s passing reference to Asda. Whilst Carrefour was to obtain planning consents for three further hypermarkets (at Telford, Eastleigh and Minworth) in the early 1970s, it was Associated Dairies of Leeds who became the pacesetters in developing superstores. Historically, northern customers have always been more price conscious than those in the south, whilst northern planning authorities, hungry for development, generally proved considerably more sympathetic to the development of what the DoE had come to term 'large stores' than their southern counterparts.

But if this was where the future lay, Tesco virtually ignored the evidence, largely on the advice of its northern group. By the close of the 1960s, the profits of Tesco North had all but disappeared, yet Grundy and Bronstein continued to ignore the significance of what was happening around them, dismissing the rapid gains being achieved by Asda as a result of its large store development programme. Convinced that such units were only a temporary aberration, and reporting to Cheshunt that, as Sir Leslie Porter puts it, 'they could only put an economic rope around our necks', they pursued a policy of opening stores of little more than 4,000 square feet, maintaining that such units were the cornerstone of future profitability.

As directors of a virtually autonomous company, Grundy and

Bronstein's mistake was to have profound consequences for the whole of Tesco, not only disguising from Cheshunt the importance of what was happening in the north, but also colouring the main board's attitude towards large stores. Laurie Don: 'Asda had come on the scene and the people in the south had no idea of what was happening up north, because Grundy and Bronstein were kidding everyone that Asda's margins were so low that they wouldn't even survive. Head office wouldn't believe that people had been going shopping in what was virtually a warehouse. I said that we would have to tackle the problem, but in the south everyone on the board wanted to ignore it.'

The combination of what Mike Darnell describes as a property-orientated company, owning what Sir Leslie Porter calls a high proportion of inadequate stores, allied to what Laurie Don considers the board's failure to recognise the significance of what was occurring in the north was to prove punitive in the years immediately ahead. Twice before, with self-service and supermarketing, Tesco had been right only after the event. Now the mistake was repeated for a third time.

Whilst Grundy and Bronstein were at fault, however, ultimate responsibility lay with the main board, which was rapidly dividing against itself. The exact nature of the factions is hard to determine, for they were to become increasingly unstable as the troubles increased, exacerbated in part by Sir John Cohen's continued meddling, in part by the recognition that with Cohen's delayed but inevitable departure, there would be a fundamental shift in the management of the company. Clearly, the family would continue to dominate, for all that its holdings had fallen consistently to the point where, by 1969, they totalled no more than 5%, but there were others who had ambitions on power. Not least of them was Grundy.

Possibly the sole exception to the rule was Arthur Thrush. A director since 1960, he preferred to concentrate on the everyday running of the business rather than involve himself in the internecine feuding of the board. An outstanding retailer in his own right, 'AET' not only had a capacity for spotting young retail talent, but also for encouraging its progress through the company. Indeed, by the late 1960s, what might well be termed an alternative board was already in place – Thrush's team of store managers and young executives who owed their loyalty as much to their mentor as to the company that employed them.

Three years previously, in his annual report for 1966, Cohen had written about the company's continuing success in 'attracting to our organisation many young and able people from all walks of life', a point re-emphasised the following year: 'The new supermarket manager must be a businessman, a man who can organise, control staff and make decisions. Tesco are constantly searching for men of this calibre to train for management positions.' The reality was somewhat different, though in one case, at least, Cohen followed his own prescription.

In 1958, the present Tesco chairman, Sir Ian MacLaurin, was on tour with the Old Malvernians cricket team and staying at the Grand Hotel, Eastbourne: 'The team always had to dress for dinner, and I went down to the Canadian bar and Jack Cohen was there. It turned out that he regularly used to take his family holidays at the Grand, and he always used to say to us youngsters in dinner jackets, "Come and have a drink with me." In any case, I went across with my other chums, and he bought me a pint of bitter.

'Before we went in for dinner, he gave us all his card, and a few days later, more out of curiosity than anything else, I called his office and he invited me up to see him. The interview that followed was among the most bizarre I've ever known. I didn't really want to join Tesco, I had a perfectly good job already, just wanted to see what they were about, but it ended up with him saying, "What are you earning at the moment?" I told him £900 a year, at which he replied, "I'll tell you what, I'll pay you £900 for six months and if, after that, I like you and you like me, I'll make it a thousand and give you a company car." And it was the car that decided me!'

MacLaurin became Tesco's first management trainee, but whilst the theory was admirable, it bore no relationship whatsoever to the practice. Tesco had no training programme, and never had had: 'The idea was laughable. We had to train ourselves.' When David Malpas, appointed managing director of Tesco in 1983, joined the company from the John Lewis Partnership in 1966, much the same situation applied: 'I went for an interview with this fairly shady company called Tesco. I was interviewed by a man called George Wood [at that time a director of Tesco Stores], who held court on the upper floor of 236 King Street, Hammersmith, which at the time was one of our average-sized stores of 3,000 to 4,000 square feet. I could see from talking to George Wood that the company was holding a tiger by the tail, the business was racing away from them, and they really didn't know what they were going to do to control it.'

It was only in the early 1970s, under pressure from the government, that Tesco introduced a formal training programme, trainees in the 1960s being left to the whim of circumstance and the charge of Arthur Thrush. In the context of Tesco House at the time, Thrush's achievements were formidable, not least his skill in holding together and encouraging his protégés. Cohen's style might be inspirational, but what was needed was the everyday assurance that they were a part of a purposeful team working towards a coherent goal. Hearing word on the grapevine of the feuding at Cheshunt, there must have been times when they wondered what they were all about. Thrush managed not only to command their loyalty, but also to create a team of talent which, in the years ahead, was to transform the character of Tesco itself.

John Gildersleeve, himself a protégé first of Thrush and then of MacLaurin, and now a main board director: 'Arthur Thrush was a very significant player on the board when it was the outside versus the family. Many people have a great deal to thank him for. Ian, amongst others, was his protégé, and like AET he realised that whilst all the others were making their play for control of finance or the north or head office, it was all from a position of splendid isolation; they were only in it for themselves. Thrushy and Ian recognised that the way forward was with a team, and they started to build one.'

The notion may have been alien to the culture of Tesco, accustomed as it was to the creative tension of Cohen's management style, though even at Cheshunt there was growing concern that all was not well. Whilst both profits and turnover continued to rise, the pace of growth was slackening, with sales and assets beginning to fall away from the peak years of the mid-1960s. And as the first tentative signs of troubles emerged, so tensions in the boardroom rose, exacerbated now by the growing rivalry between the individual companies which made up Tesco Stores (Holdings) Ltd.

Leslie Porter: 'At board meetings, the budget would be discussed, and when things were getting sticky someone like George Wood, MD of Tesco Fresh Foods at the time, would say, "I've got three million I can give you", because he had got £3 million down in his bacon factory, and because he sold the product to the stores, who were his only customers, he could always overcharge them for it.'

This was not so much the economies of scale, as the economics of madness, a matter of balancing up the books against themselves which, whilst serving short-term ends, did nothing to resolve the fundamental weaknesses that beset the company, weaknesses which, in the last resort, were directly attributable to the main board. Apparently, the reorganisation of January 1969 had failed, and while Corina contends that the management consultants McKinsey and Co were called in 'to meet the anticipated challenge of the 1970s', it is significant that the prime objective of their brief was to *'realign the organisation to clarify management responsibilities and to strengthen management'*.

And not before time. As problems emerged, the board situation at Tesco was becoming increasingly envenomed. Kreitman, as cultivated as he was diffident, was no match for his father-in-law's bullying, but Leslie Porter was a different matter. As joint managing director, and chairman of Tesco Home 'n' Wear, he had no hesitation about squaring up to Sir John. The stories of the times are legion: of Arthur Thrush literally having to hold the ring between the two disputants; of the two men's continuing feud as to who should drive the latest marque of company Rolls; and later, of the day when, following luncheon, a scurry of directors heard a clash of steel behind them. Returning to the dining room, they found a duel in progress, Cohen and Porter having each taken a Wilkinson sword from the walls and entered into a clash of arms.

Black comedy, certainly, though there were few who laughed at the time. Altogether too much was at stake, and reading between the lines of McKinsey's report (see Appendix Three), there is an underlying sense of wonder at what they found. The doyen of management consultancies, having worked for such prestigious enterprises as the Bank of England and the BBC, their initial appraisal touched on such esoteric topics as 'Developing a Strategy for Optimising Department Mix' and 'An Analysis of Warehouse Throughput', but their key recommendations were tucked away in Appendix C – 'Role and Composition of the Holdings Board, Tesco Stores (Holdings) Ltd.'

As discreetly as possible, for such is the way with these things, they pointed out that the board itself must exercise more self control:

'At present the Board does not fulfil its functions in the most disciplined manner. This weakness arises for two main reasons. First, the distinction between the responsibilities of the Board, the Chairman, and the Chief Executive, is not at all clear, so that the Board tends to concern itself with issues that should be dealt with by the Chairman or the Chief Executive. Second, the Board does not conduct its meetings on a formal, systematic basis.

'We believe the Board can overcome these shortcomings and thereby improve its effectiveness by:

Concentrating at its meetings only on matters that are really its concern.

Formalising the preparation for and conduct of its meetings.'

In October 1969, the board accepted McKinsey's proposals. Central to all the rest was a recommendation to appoint a chief executive from outside the company to be responsible for the day-to-day management of the company's business who, in his turn, should be supported by three general managers, each of whom would be responsible for a specific facet of Tesco's operations. James Grundy was immediately appointed general manager of operations, and Laurie Don (relinquishing his post as company secretary) as general manager of finance and planning, whilst the third post (general manager of store development and expansion) remained open. On the same day, Leslie Porter was appointed deputy chairman, though the minutes made no mention of Cohen's future role.

The omission is significant, for exactly how was the founder of Tesco to be fitted into this new, streamlined management structure; exactly what place could be found for him in a company now planning for the future, rather than taking its remit from the past? As far as the family was concerned, he had hustled and baited Hyman Kreitman unmercifully for more than two decades, but Leslie Porter and the other directors were free agents, casting their votes where they would, though many with an eye on the main chance.

And yet sentiment, if nothing more, demanded that a place be found for Sir John. The man had given his life to making the company of which they were now the inheritors, and for all his intractability each of the six men who met around the boardroom table that October day of 1969 knew what they owed to him. The Governor might be awkward, autocratic, many things, but there was no denying what he had achieved in the half-century since he had invested his small gratuity in a barrow-load of stock. Yet the problem remained: how could Jack the Slasher, as he had been dubbed by Lord Trenchard, Chairman of T. Wall & Sons, be fitted into the new pattern of things?

The minutes of the board of 16 December 1969 provide the answer. Only one item was on the agenda: 'Sir John requested the board to confirm his duties as life president of the company.' The title sounded all very well, but what did it mean in practice? Was it a functional role, or merely a salve to his pride? Following what the minutes describe as a long discussion the matter was finally clarified: 'The board confirmed that he was responsible for public relations … and there being no further business, the meeting was closed.'

9. A TIME OF TROUBLES

1969–74

'Take the waiting out of wanting'

Access card advertisement (1973)

The Wilson government fell in June 1970, the victim of its own revisionism. Since 1967, when a balance of payments crisis had triggered the intervention of the International Monetary Fund, it had adopted a hardline economic policy, but the truth remained inescapable, as the new chancellor, Anthony Barber, was to note in his first budget in March 1971: 'For many years, under one government or another, the economic performance of our country has been poor – slow growth, recurring balance of payments weakness, faster than average inflation, a low rate of investment, a falling share of world exports and increasingly bad industrial relations.'

Warning that unless the position was reversed, Britain's standard of living would fall behind that of Western Europe, Barber called for a new economic realism – and within months had introduced a package of reflationary measures that included a cut in interest rates, a reduction in purchase tax and the abolition of restrictions on hire purchase. The cure was to prove worse than the condition. Whilst Barber's policy did little to stimulate growth, it inspired a credit-led boom which, in 'taking the waiting out of wanting' (as exhorted at the launch of Access cards), was further to exacerbate the UK's trade imbalance.

The provision of credit has always been a function of retailing, the French historian Fernand Braudel going so far as to maintain that it was a primary cause for the revival of trade in the late Middle Ages.

Six centuries on, during the inter-war years, Cohen himself was an agent of the practice, though it had changed much in the interim. Tick was no longer simply a tool for poorer people to obtain the essentials of life; by the eighteenth century it had become a rule of the Quality to maintain their wardrobes on credit, whilst in 1902, in the final volume of *Life and Labour in London*, Charles Booth was reporting: 'In many better-to-do neighbourhoods, the general prevalence of the credit system is noted. People not only buy their furniture, but also their clothing on credit, and even take a loan on a summer holiday. Everywhere ... the plan is to spend first and save afterwards to repay some form of loan.'

The copy writers and ad men of the early 1970s could hardly better Booth's description. Instant as distinct from deferred gratification was to become the essence of consumerism. What had once been the privilege of the few was now to be packaged, and marketed, and sold to the many, the ultimate commodity: credit. And careless of the small print, the public bought, though within two years of Barber unveiling his programme they were having to pay – interest rates rose from 5% in 1972 to 11.5% in July 1973.

The entire market was becoming increasingly unsettled, a situation that was to be further aggravated with the OPEC announcement in October 1973 of an embargo on Middle East oil supplies which was followed, in November, by the outbreak of the Arab–Israeli war. Seemingly, the whole world was being turned upside down, and with it the UK economy, debilitated as it already was.

If ever there was a time for purposeful management, it was during those 'stop-go' years, instead of which Tesco faced an impasse of its own making. Careless of McKinsey's strictures, Cohen was singularly unwilling to forego power or to regard the presidency as little more than a titular role: there was more to the implications than to the content of Kreitman's first annual statement to the company's shareholders in February 1970: 'I am happy to inform you that although Sir John has relinquished his office as joint chairman, he has not retired. He attends the office daily and participates in our policy discussions, playing an active part in the company's affairs.'

For the company's shareholders, who had come to regard Cohen as the very incarnation of retailing, it may have been reassuring news, but for Kreitman it had a more ominous significance. A quarter of a century had passed since he had first joined Tesco to pit his logic against his father-in-law's 'feel for the markets', and yet now, little more than two months after he had agreed that as life president his main function would be public relations, Cohen was again meddling in the company's affairs.

Seemingly, the Governor had nowhere to go but Cheshunt. To him, it was more a way of life than a workplace, and, during the 1970s, there was growing pathos about the sick and ageing man who haunted the corridors of Tesco House. Innately suspicious of his successors and incapable of abandoning his own creation, he deployed all his old skills – a smidgeon of persuasion here, an eruption of hectoring there – which were now mixed with a sense of compassion by those with whom he dealt. They had walked in his shadow for so long, it was hard to walk away from him now.

Although Tesco's entry into non-foods had, initially, proved profitable, there was growing evidence that the sector was becoming a liability, and not only because of the Chancellor's latest squeeze on credit. The paramount requirement for such diversification was space, yet with an average store size of 5,000 square feet, space was the one commodity that Tesco's acquisition programme had denied the company. McKinsey reported that the investment in home 'n' wear was at the expense of grocery retailing: 'Non-foods take up a lot of space but are the least profitable goods in the supermarket.' Central to all the rest was their argument that to examine the gross margins on non-foods divorced from the selling space allocated to the sector was misleading, and that whether in small or large supermarkets, non-food turnover per square foot was significantly lower than that of foodstuffs.

Indeed, compared with an overall group profit rate of 5.83%, profits of the southern home 'n' wear operation totalled little more than 3.2%. The figures are as revealing for what they include as for what they omit – the performance of the northern group. When Kreitman delivered his first annual report, Grundy and Bronstein had been operating what was, to all intents and purposes, a free-standing company based in Winsford, Cheshire, for almost four years – four years in which they had failed to respond effectively to the emergent challenge of superstores, and in which Tesco (North) had consistently failed to live up to both its promise and its profit targets.

An ambitious and self-assured man, who appeared to know every answer but the right one, Grundy had been a main board director since 1966, and following the McKinsey reshuffle had moved south to Cheshunt to become general manager of store operations, a post he was quick to exploit to browbeat certain of his own senior executives. Mike Darnell: 'The man was extraordinarily authoritarian. Periodically, one would receive directives from him that had to be obeyed unquestioningly. If they weren't, you didn't have a job. He carried these practices to such ludicrous extremes that he eventually communicated with executives by registered post to their home address. At the time, the thing became something of a joke, though it was enormously damaging to our motivation. We were living in an atmosphere of fear.'

Even in the snake-pit of Tesco House, accustomed as it was to long years of management feuding, it was a situation that could not last. In the late summer of 1970, Ian MacLaurin, then in charge of Tesco retail operations in the south, was reporting to Grundy, and his shadow, David Morrell.

'I had some good allies, but feelings were so bad that I seriously began to consider going it alone, and as a last resort, decided to test the situation to breaking point.

'Before going on holiday, and while out on a store visit with Morrell, I fed him with the story that I had sold my Tesco shares and was seriously thinking of resigning. It was all said in the strictest confidence, to see how far it would go.

'When I got back, HK [Kreitman] called me in and said he'd heard that I had been selling my shares and was thinking of leaving the company. So much for Morrell's trust. It proved exactly what I had suspected all along, and I told HK precisely what I thought.'

Within 24 hours, and following Arthur Thrush's urgent intervention, Grundy had been posted back to the north, where his operation came under intensifying scrutiny.

It was no longer simply the poor returns of Tesco (North) that signified. There was a growing realisation that such returns reflected the management hiatus that existed at Winsford. It seemed that everything that could go wrong was going wrong. Mike Darnell: 'Whether you started with the question of cost to operate, or the buying gross, or the resultant profit, it didn't matter – the stores weren't profitable. They were going downhill fast.'

Darnell himself was posted north to investigate the situation towards the close of 1970, to find that the control structure had all but broken down. There was virtually no management system, even less direction in individual stores, and a high and rising level of shrinkage. To cover such losses, it was discovered that there were two warehouse locations from which stock was moved from one store to another whenever there was a stock take, to ensure that stock levels would always be right. The practice of what Darnell now terms 'rotating stock' was symptomatic of the malaise that was undermining the entire northern operation.

Grundy and Bronstein had had their time. Now it was to end, precipitately. In June 1971, Kreitman called MacLaurin into his office to ask what could be done about the situation. The answer he received was unequivocal: MacLaurin would take his retail team up to Winsford and sort out the troubles. Following an emergency board meeting, MacLaurin was told to be at head office with his car at six the following morning as he, Leslie Porter and Arthur Thrush were going north.

Ian MacLaurin: 'Until we were half way there, AET wouldn't tell me what was going on, then he said that they were going to fire Grundy and that I was going to take over the whole retail side of the company. Anyway, we got to Winsford, and walked in on Grundy who was having a meeting with some of his fellows. It was Leslie who did the talking: "Well, Jim, shake hands with your colleagues, I'm sorry to say you have to retire through ill health." Then he told Grundy to clear his desk in half an hour, but to keep his car until the end of the month. That was the deal, and he was gone.'

By midday, Porter and Thrush were on their way south again, leaving MacLaurin in charge of a tense situation. Thrush had told the northern directors that MacLaurin was their new boss and 'I went down to lunch and they all sat around one table, and I sat by myself.' For the next eighteen months MacLaurin and his team slaved to recover the northern operation. If the task was tough, then the schedule they set for themselves was tougher, working twelve hours a day, six days a week. Even so, it was punctuated by moments of comedy.

Ian MacLaurin: 'That's when I first met people like David Malpas. George Wood had taken him on, and he was a real tearaway. I remember I was having a meeting in Leicester, when David turns up. He had an old Morris Oxford or something, and while he could get it going, he didn't seem to know how to stop it. I was walking across this pub car park in Leicester when Malpas roars in with this bloody thing, and aims it straight for me, his boss, just misses, then roars with laughter, and parks it. That's how I came to meet our present MD.'

Such light relief, however, was in short supply, for while Mac-Laurin and his team were slowly putting the north to rights, the boardroom factions at Cheshunt remained. Three months before Grundy's departure, Laurie Don had resigned. Pertinently, he was later to say that one of the reasons for the move was that 'at some point a rising executive in Tesco can go no further', which prompted the *Financial Times* to speculate whether, for all the management reshuffle, the real power in the company still lay with Cohen and Kreitman. The paper went on to say, 'Any sign of a break-up of Tesco's top management team is naturally disquieting for the City, particularly as memories linger of the investigation by McKinsey, the management consultants, a couple of years ago. That report recommended the search for a new chief executive outside – and though the post was advertised, nobody has been found to fill it.'

The concern was not limited to the City, and the departure of Bronstein and Grundy in the summer of 1971 fuelled such speculation, which was temporarily checked only when Leslie Porter took over as managing director in May 1972, telling *The Times*: 'There is a problem for any large public company when large family holders are actively involved. Obviously we have realised that in a business where things move so quickly, there is an advantage in having a managing director who understands the requirements from the word go. It seems that I suit the bill, and it is good to know that my brother-in-law, Hyman, and Sir John are behind me.'

Significantly, the report closed with a reference to Alfred Singer, recently recruited from Rank Xerox as finance director, and now to support Porter as deputy managing director: 'Singer has worked well with Kreitman and Porter and is a man to watch for the future. Just as pertinently, he has operated well under the ever-watchful eye of Sir John, who still goes to the office daily – and helps everyone out.'

Just how watchful Sir John actually was was revealed in a private broker's report of September 1972. During an interview with Alfred

Singer, Cohen put in a brief appearance, which prompted Singer to describe him as 'one of my greatest problems'. Eleven months later, Singer, too, had gone, to echo Laurie Don's remark: 'A question of family shareholdings is part of my reason for going.'

As he indicated, however, there was more to his resignation than a question of where control in Tesco lay. Beyond his role as finance director, Singer's chief concern was with strategic planning (in 1972, he was chairman of the UK Long Range Planning Society), an invidious role in view of Cohen's known hostility towards the subject. Indeed, as a confidential report on the company undertaken by a university research team was to conclude, 'Perhaps one reason for the absence of corporate planning of a formal kind lies in the unwillingness of the family to allow an outsider any autonomy in the process of strategy formulation ... All the resignations by senior executives appear to be connected with the realisation that power and career prospects of non-family executives have been limited in Tesco. They may also be partially reflective of the company's relatively poor performance in recent years and, in particular, its lack of a clear strategy for growth.'

In short, Tesco had lost its way, a confusion of policies simply reflecting the fundamental divide that existed within the board. *The Economist* noted in December 1971 that 'the trouble with assessing Tesco's current performance is, that it is so much of a hybrid', while the *Investors Chronicle* pondered whether the company had gone 'ex-growth'. Since 1969, the company's performance had become increasingly patchy. Apparently, the years of the 'Tesco miracle', as the *Sunday Express* described it, were over. Once, under Cohen, the company's purpose had been as clear as its identity, but now his authority was being whittled away, slowly but nonetheless inexorably, and with it the dynamism which, for so long, had been a feature of Tesco. Perhaps the old ways were best after all?

David Malpas: 'It was only when Sir John stopped thinking of himself as a barrow-boy, and released the reins a bit, or became ineffective as a barrow-boy, that the business really started to go wrong. He understood that what he wanted to do was "Pile it high, and sell it cheap", and that was a successful formula, and could have gone on being successful for a long time. Of course, we wouldn't be the business we are today, but we would still have been a profitable company if we had gone on doing what he did, and understood, and

wanted to do. By the early 1970s, however, the business seems to
have fallen into the hands of others, who were degrading the purity
of Cohen's formula.

'I couldn't say to what extent they were the perpetrators of this
change, from being a quite pure, organised business with a clear goal
and successful policy, to being a ramshackle and not terribly
successful organisation, with lots and lots of square footage but not
much in the way of sales, with lots of stock, and lots of pretty odd
merchandise as well sometimes. How it happened I don't know, but
happen it did.'

The situation had been more than two decades in the making,
compounded, as it was, of a patchwork of corrosive relationships
and an increasingly divergent view of Tesco's position in the market.
It may well have been that if Cohen's formula had not been
degraded, the company would have continued to trade profitably by
piling it high and selling it cheap, though the market itself was in a
process of radical change. The consumer of the early 1970s bore
little similarity to the housewives that Tesco's managers had served
when they ran up their shutters and laid out their wares on the
pavements of Burnt Oak and St Albans in the immediate post-war
years. It was not just that times had changed, so had expectations,
powered by the growth first of disposable income and then of
accessible credit.

The continuing success of the Kwik Save group indicated that a
considerable market still existed based on keen pricing and discounting, but this is not where Cohen's successors wanted to be. Asda had
won a 3% share of the market with only thirty stores, against Tesco's
6% with more than 800 units, but the new men at Tesco House had
a different vision from Cohen as to where the future lay. Powered as
much by personality differences as by divergent opinions, this was
the heartland of the conflict that had been long in the making, and
one which, in dividing the board against itself, was to rock Tesco
through the first half of the 1970s. As the conflict intensified, so the
company's performance deteriorated, and as the company's performance deteriorated, so the conflict intensified.

After half a century of trading, it appeared as if Tesco was
suffering from terminal disorientation. A growing number of problems wracked the board, but one was symptomatic of all the rest: the
profile of the company's development programme. Ultimately, a

store is much more than simply trading space. It represents the entire persona of a company, and by the early 1970s Tesco was damned not only by the inadequate units it had procured during its period of growth by acquisition and its policy of buying into second-class sites, but also by its cavalier treatment of local authorities during the development boom of the late 1960s, the time when Tesco had built first and answered questions afterwards.

Whilst Sainsbury, the market leader, cosseted its image, and Asda, the newcomer, adopted a highly aggressive development strategy, it seemed that in attempting to be all things to all customers, Tesco was being successful with none. And if there was, indeed, a conflict of identities, with an inadequate corner shop here and an ill-sited supermarket there, attempts to resolve the problem by rational-isation met with entrenched resistance from local councils with memories of the not-so-distant times when Tesco had ridden roughshod over their planning regulations.

Although the development boom did not burst until 1973, pressures for change in the existing development practices had been emerging since the mid-1960s. Critical of hit-and-run developers, and disenchanted by a system that gave them little voice in their own communities, the public were becoming increasingly vociferous in demanding a share in the planning process, as recommended by Arthur Skeffington, Parliamentary Secretary to the Ministry of Housing and Local Government, in *People and Plans* (1969): 'Planning is the prime example of the need for participation, for it affects everyone. People should be able to say what kind of commu-nity they want and how it should develop, and they should be able to do so in a way that is positive and first hand.'

The Skeffington report was endorsed by the Labour administra-tion, and subsequently consolidated by the Conservatives with the Structure Planning process in 1972, a system aimed at involving people in determining the economic, social and environmental future of their own counties. The days of the tearaway developer were numbered; Prime Minister Edward Heath stigmatised their practices as 'the unacceptable face of capitalism', and *Property Appointments* noted in 1973: 'Central and local government, not to mention the general public, are fed up with a situation in which planning authorities are placed in the position of being the poor relation, having to beg any bone the kind developer will throw to them. Now we are to have positive planning, to the benefit of communities, rather than to the profit of speculators.'

Local authorities began to recover a significant degree of planning power – at a time when Tesco was reviewing its development priorities. The coincidence was not propitious. As a director of planning, and the president elect of the Royal Town Planning Institute, Ewart Parkinson, said at the time, 'Many Councils regard Tesco as something of a retail cowboy, and while Sainsbury and Marks are always welcome if they are looking for anchor retailers, Tesco is rarely considered.'

The comment made ominous reading for a company that depended on its presence to maintain its turnover, and as the *Sunday Telegraph* reported in June 1972, 'The hoped-for expansion into hypermarkets is not going well. Tesco is having trouble obtaining planning permissions ... and its lobbying of the Secretary of State for the Environment, Mr Peter Walker, has brought little progress.'

And this was not all, for Parkinson added, 'In addition, a lot of Councils take exception to what they regard as the visual pollution of their high streets resulting from Tesco's abrasive trading style.'

Individually, Parkinson's indictment was serious enough. In combination, it precipitated a crisis in Tesco. Not only was the company being excluded from essential developments, but of equal importance, it appeared that its entire image was in question. Once the often bizarre mix of showbiz and razzamatazz, of day-glo posters and Sir Save-a-Lot had served well enough, but now it seemed that unless the company abandoned certain of its more flamboyant practices, prized as they were by Cohen, then its hopes of recovery were at risk.

The external dilemma that faced the board, of abandoning its traditional practices in pursuit of new markets, was aggravated, internally, by the capacity of the board to deceive itself, for as the development budget turned down, so volumes began to fall. David Malpas: 'Much of our performance was based on a lie, the lie being that trading was good, volumes were good and gross margins were good when they weren't. The truth was that prices were high and stock results were in permanent surplus so that we were producing high margins out of diminishing volumes.'

No doubt the situation incensed Cohen. It was not so much that his company appeared to be hell-bent on expunging its past, more that in the process it seemed that Tesco was no longer giving its customers a good deal. And in this he was right, for whilst Daisy Hyams was widely regarded as one of the shrewdest buyers in the business, the benefits of the deals she was doing were not being passed on through the stores.

David Malpas: 'Prices were rising all the time because the retail side of the business was increasing the price of the goods locally to produce the results demanded of them by head office. So we had the daft situation, which today seems incredible, of the board demanding results of stores which they knew couldn't be produced by any mechanism other than high prices and yet, at the same time, continuing to fool themselves that Tesco remained price competitive.'

Green Shield stamps did little to help. With the buoyant market of the 1960s backed by increased spending power, stamps had made a significant contribution to Tesco's sales appeal. As conditions deteriorated through the early 1970s, however, those 'little sticky things' became an increasing liability, and not only for the 'visual pollution' that offended planners.

Mike Darnell: 'We were held back on the price front because our number one weapon was stamps. Our reply to cut prices was to get more heavily involved with Green Shield, which did have an on-cost. Stamps may have had some meaning for the customer, but we couldn't seem to grasp the fact that they were showing diminishing returns for Tesco. The trouble was that it seemed that we had no other marketing tool to rely on until there was a radical re-think about the whole company.'

If Tesco was, indeed, living with a lie, then it was soon to be exposed. Where throughout the 1960s the advice of City analysts had been to buy Tesco stock, the old Tesco magic was fast wearing thin; now the word was to 'Hold' or 'Sell'. Serious problems, it was suggested, were emerging: problems of store size and location; problems of turnover and margins; problems of marketing and management.

In isolation, each was bad enough, but now they appeared to be living off one another, exacerbated by what the merchant bank Guinness Mahon termed 'a crisis of identity'. Much was heard of a new Tesco, but precisely what did it mean, and if the old format was obsolete, then what was to emerge in its place?

bove: Off-loading at St Peter's Street, St Albans, the first Tesco self-service store

elow: Part of the company's fast-expanding transport fleet in 1961

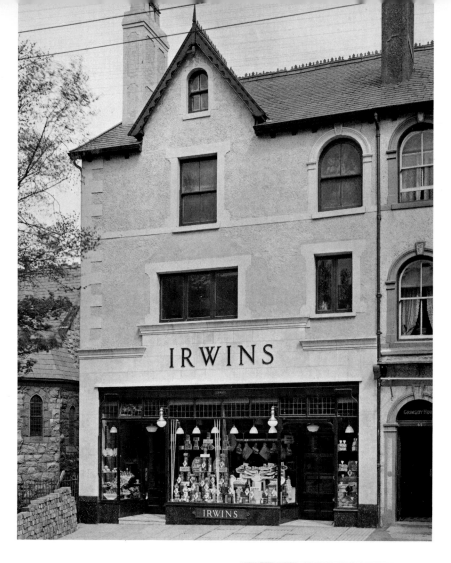

Tesco on the take-over trail: typical
stores run by Irwins (Liverpool) and
Burnards (Hendon, North London)

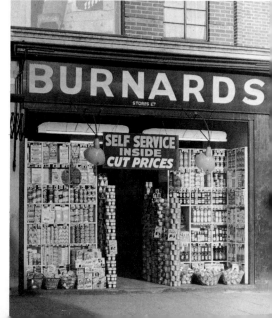

Right: Tesco goes to war on Resale Price Maintenance: a scene outside the company's Leicester store in December 1961

Below: The Green Shield era: a Tesco supermarket in Stoke-on-Trent promotes the benefits of those little sticky things – 'stamps' in the late 1960s

'For shoplifting in Tesco's the fine is normally £30. But for the next few weeks, this court is pleased to offer 3p off'

Cartoons by Mac in the *Daily Mail* and Giles in the *Daily Express* mark the ending of Green Shield's association with Tesco and the launch of Operation Checkout in June 1977

"It has been brought to my notice that you have offered 50 Green Shield stamps for our spin-bowler."

Above: The interior of a large Tesco store in the late 1970s, similar to the view that Sir John Cohen would have seen on his last store visit

Right: Sir John Cohen, who for almost half a century imposed his own persona on the company. He died in 1979

Among the people who have helped make T

Clockwise from left: Edgar Collar, Hyman
Kreitman, Arthur Thrush ('A.E.T'), Fred Tu

Clockwise from below: Daisy Hyams,
Sir Leslie Porter, Sir Ian MacLaurin,
David Malpas

Above: The Princess of Wales shopping at Tesco, Southport, following the launch of a new healthy eating booklet in September 1990

Left: The Tesco store in Hereford

Unless there were answers to such questions, and soon, there was a very real possibility that the retail empire that Cohen had created would collapse about him. Since the 1950s, the company's greatest problem had been to manage success, but those had been the years when retailers had never had it so good. Now, however, there was growing evidence that in a stagnant market, Tesco was vulnerable on a disturbing number of accounts, all of which ultimately turned on the quality of top management.

McKinsey, said by the more generous-minded to have been brought in to break the deadlock over future control, and by the more cynical to act as a placebo, had failed. The impasse remained. Four years had passed since Cohen had promised to 'give the younger people their chance', but in 1973 he was still playing his old game of divide and rule in a continuing effort to impose his will on the company.

Possibly, of course, Cohen was right. Possibly the old-style Tesco was better than the new, and it was his immediate successors who had it wrong. Only one thing is sure: that for all his undertakings to make way for younger men, Cohen's spoiling tactics during Kreitman's brief spell as chairman gave his immediate successor little chance of proving himself, and culminated in the farrago of the Square Meals venture, and the bitter recriminations that followed.

As with so much else, the story is confused by the contradictory interpretation of events. Why the company should have first become interested in the operations of this retail subsidiary of Brooke Bond Oxo remains unclear, though it may be that after five years of quiescence Cohen had again been bitten by the acquisition bug. Leslie Porter: 'Sir John came along to Kreitman one morning and said, "Look at this bloody advert in the paper [referring to Square Meals]. Brooke Bond can't be both manufacturers and retailers. You've got to buy it."'

And Tesco did. After a cursory examination of the Square Meal books in a hotel room on the outskirts of Luton, an offer was made and accepted by Brooke Bond. Whilst the Square Meal figures may have looked attractive, however, its *modus operandi* was altogether more questionable. Mike Boxall: 'It was a real Mickey Mouse set-up. The basis of the operation was that commission-only salesmen would tap on people's doors with the patter "Frozen foods are the in thing. Just sign this form and we'll get you a freezer, then you'll have some imitation money to come along to our premises and buy the frozen foods. It will all be done on credit, so don't worry, just sign this form." United Dominion Trust provided the cash for the purchase of the freezer, and the clients were given some Monopoly money, with which they could go along to the Square Meals premises and select their rather poor quality food. The whole thing was a mess, diabolical.'

Just how much of a mess was soon to emerge. Immediately the deal was completed, questions began to arise about the planning consents granted for the Square Meals outlets. They were licensed for wholesale rather than retail trading, and Tesco's estate director, Francis Krejsa, was soon to be inundated with enforcement notices demanding the shut-down of such units. 'The situation was absurd. We had bought into positions out of which it was impossible to trade.'

The fiasco symptomised, exactly, the management imbroglio at Tesco House. Kreitman held the chair, and Cohen the presidency, and yet the question remained: Who ruled? For all his protestations, it seemed that the Governor's remit continued to extend well beyond his special responsibilities for public relations, to the point where his son-in-law could no longer tolerate the discord.

Leslie Porter: 'Hyman called me to his home and said that he couldn't go on, he was going to give up the chair. I suppose that Square Meals was the final straw, so I looked through all the figures and decided to get rid of it. I knew Prideaux, the head of Brooke Bond, very well, and phoned him up and said that the whole thing was absolutely wrong, and that I wanted to see him.

'Jack insisted on coming along, and when he and David Behar and I got to the meeting, we got an admission from Prideaux that as long as we gave back everything that we had from Square Meals then it would be OK with him. Because Prideaux agreed to our terms, the Old Man said, "No, it's wrong. There must be something good in it if he wants it back" even though we had convinced him that there wasn't. The whole thing was impossible.'

The confusion was finally resolved, at a cost to the company of some £1.3 million when it could least afford it. In the half-decade to 1973, Tesco's sales increased two-and-a-half times, compared with a ten-fold increase between 1960 and 1969, and whilst during the Barber boom of 1972, post-tax profits staged a modest recovery from their low point of the previous two years, by 1973 profits were again deteriorating, to fall by almost 20% in the two years to 1975.

	1970	1971	1972	1973	1974	1975
			(£ millions)			
Sales	238	259	299	359	433	514
Net profit before tax	12.5	13.8	16.5	21.7	24.5	23.2
Net profit after tax	6.6	8.2	9.8	13.3	12.2	10.9

Small wonder that Kreitman was disenchanted, though as David Malpas now reflects, 'If only someone had been able to talk to the Old Man, he would have realised that the thing he had created was being destroyed by all the nonsense that was going on, but then I suppose he must have chosen the board at the time.'

And what Cohen asked of the board in general, but more particularly of his chosen successor, was that they should be surrogates of himself, subscribing to his opinions in order not only to perpetuate the image of the company he had created, but also the dynasty which he may well have hoped to found. The irony was that in pursuit of his goal, he came close to undoing exactly what he set out to achieve, securing the future of the company that he loved so fiercely, and for which he had given fifty years of his life.

On 20 September 1973, Kreitman, for so long Cohen's whipping-boy as much as his heir apparent, resigned as chairman of Tesco, though retaining his directorship. As so often during those troubled years, the brevity of his letter to Leslie Porter disguised considerably more than it revealed: 'I am writing to you not only as a member of the family, but also as the chief executive ... of the company. I have now decided after twenty-seven years with the company to give more time to my family and personal affairs; it is therefore after a great deal of thought and with regret that I tender my resignation as chairman of the company.'

10. THOSE LITTLE STICKY THINGS: STAMPS

1974–7

'A much-cited worldwide Gallup opinion survey
conducted in 1977 suggested that, on their own
valuation, the British people were amongst the
happiest in the world.'

Arthur Marwick, *British Society Since 1945* (1982)

To determine the who's who of Tesco was fast becoming a pastime
of retail-watchers in the City and the media by the close of 1973. In
little more than three years there had been two major board
reshuffles, each of which had triggered top level resignations, and
now Hyman Kreitman, too, had gone. The future did not augur
well, the more so as it appeared that the UK could be entering a
serious recession. By 1973, the Barber boom had spent itself, and
forecasts for the mid-1970s ranged from the cautious to the
catastrophic – a Hudson Institute report echoing Barber's 1971
gloomy appraisal of the economy almost word for word.

At such a time, in such a situation, the cardinal requirement was
for incisive management, yet seemingly that was exactly what Tesco
lacked. It was all very well for the company to talk up its prospects,
but critics suggested that the company would be better served if the
board talked more constructively amongst itself – though there
could be no denying that in Leslie Porter, Tesco had found a
chairman who would stand no nonsense from his father-in-law.
Since the 1960s, when he had reservations about joining the
company, Porter had made it clear that he would not be party to
Cohen's games. Much had changed in the meantime, but Porter's
resolve remained, and now he was in the chair. As shrewd and

uncompromising as his father-in-law, the two men were a mirror image of one another, a *Times* sketch of the former serving equally well for the latter: 'Stocky Mr Porter, usually seen chewing on a large cigar, is talkative, tough and a born salesman.'

In the years ahead, Porter was to need all the salesmanship he could muster as much to impose a new direction on Tesco as to maintain confidence in the company during its time of troubles. Initially, he split the management function between two new managing directors – his own protégé, Laurie Leigh, being responsible for non-foods, Ian MacLaurin for retailing and foodstuffs. Tragically, Leigh died of a heart attack within two years of taking office, leaving MacLaurin as the sole MD backed by the Young Turks assembled by Arthur Thrush.

Ian MacLaurin: 'I don't know exactly when it was that AET and I sat down to try and identify the next generation of Tesco management, sometime in the early seventies, I suppose. Anyway, we picked half a dozen or so names, and today four of them are on the main board – David Malpas, Dennis Tuffin, Mike Darnell and John Gildersleeve – whilst Brian Williams, Colin Goodfellow, John Smith, Alan Besbrode, John Bird and Clive Longley are senior directors of Tesco Stores Ltd.'

But if Thrush had a capacity for bringing on talent, what he came to regard as the third force in Tesco had still to prove themselves during the troubles of the mid-1970s – though the troubles weren't entirely of the company's making. The 1973 hike in oil prices, allied to the Arab–Israeli war, had highlighted the vulnerability of western economies to energy politics, and within months of Porter taking office the US Treasury Secretary, William Simon, was warning that America was facing the longest recession since the end of World War Two.

Already weakened by the Stop-Go policies of successive administrations, Simon's forecast had a nightmare ring for Britain. As the axiom had it, 'When America sneezes, Britain catches cold', and by the spring of 1974 it was becoming increasingly clear that economic conditions were deteriorating fast. The new Labour chancellor, Denis Healey, concluded, 'Britain entered 1974 in worse condition than nearly all her partners in the industrial world. Growth had come to a halt. Our balance of payments deficit was running at a rate of 4% of Gross National Product, and the Retail Price Index showed an increase of 10.6% on the previous year.'

For fifteen years, Britain had never had it so good, but now came the reckoning, with Healey pledged to squeeze inflation out of the system. The implications of the Chancellor's intent could not have come at a worse time for Tesco. It was not so much that the company needed time to recover from its own self-inflicted wounds, more a question of what would happen if there was low or even zero growth. For fifteen years, the company's expansion had been powered by a consistent increase in disposable income, but now, with a downturn in the market, Tesco looked suspiciously vulnerable; more hostile commentators pondered whether the company might fall victim to a takeover bid.

Improbable as it was, the rumour was reinforced with the release of Tesco's interim figures in the autumn of 1974, which revealed a 19.8% drop in pre-tax profits. The company, according to the *Telegraph*, was in deep trouble, and on rumours that the full figures would reveal a £20 million fall in profits, the brokers Grieveson Grant noted in their quarterly report of the retail industry, 'Tesco's interim was far worse than the market was expecting, and well down on our own more optimistic forecasts. Stripping out last year's Square Meals losses at £1.3 million, the figures represent a decline of 23%. With no indication of improvement in general economic conditions, Tesco shares should suffer a significant re-rating downwards.'

The good years, the tearaway years were over, and within months of succeeding to power in 1974, the newly constituted board was faced with two broad options – either to adopt a siege mentality in the hope that conditions would improve of their own accord, or to re-examine the entire trading strategy of the company in an effort to eliminate past mistakes and devise a new formula for growth. For all its complexities, the choice was as straightforward as that, the new men on the board arguing for root-and-branch change; the rump under Cohen defending the principles on which Tesco had been established.

Not that Tesco's practices any longer matched its principles, an in-house study revealing disturbing evidence about the company's price competitiveness with other multiples. If there was one tenet that Tesco held to be absolute, it was that it always offered amongst the keenest prices on the high street. Cohen had made this his article of faith, and even though the company no longer piled it high, the board believed implicitly that they still sold it cheap. By the mid-1970s, they knew better. Contrary to their own beliefs, Tesco was far from being the most competitive multiple, standing only fourteenth on a pricing scale published by independent analysts.

The findings sent a shockwave through the company. At the best of times, the revelation would have been alarming; combined with the fall in the value of real incomes, it mocked Tesco's proudest boast and threatened to leave the company in an increasingly exposed position, its pricing weaknesses becoming more apparent as consumers became more cost-conscious as their spending power declined. Patently, the over-riding need was for the company to recover its cost competitiveness, not only to sustain its trading image but also to compete in a static or even contracting market.

This was easier said than done, for much of the problem continued to turn on Tesco's buying strategy, which still bore Cohen's imprimatur. Daisy Hyams had done much to make the system more sophisticated, but at head office an open-door buying policy still remained in force. Mike Darnell: 'As far as the Governor was concerned, it was still the old style entrepreneurial activity that counted. There were open-buying days two days of the week, when anyone could come into the office, walk up to reception, ask to see a buyer, have something on offer, and a deal would be struck there and then for a product that might have no relevance whatsoever to our future marketing plans – and this at a time when Sainsbury was becoming very much a quality operator, both in terms of the service it offered and the quality of its products.'

The practice had its entertaining moments, as when Porter and Cohen entered into a bitter dispute as to the ownership of a pair of sample underpants, but that did nothing to disguise the damaging nature of the system. Half a century had passed since Slasher Jack had been his own best buyer, and the legacy remained, to be compounded by the fact that each of the company's stores not only did a certain amount of buying on its own account but also operated what, in effect, were its own price lists.

David Malpas: 'We had a price list that was in the way of being a suggested price list, and then branches did what they liked with it. It was all done on an *ad hoc* basis, branch by branch, so that you had the company's price list, then an organised, informal price list, then an even more informal one on top of that. It was all very odd, and while everyone pretended it wasn't happening, they all knew it was. Of course Daisy protested, and while those in charge of the retail side said nothing of the sort was happening, the results coming through from the stores clearly showed that it was.'

The whole haphazard structure made as much nonsense of logical marketing as it did of rational accounting. Indeed, if the one turned on individual impulse, then the other led to extensive shrinkage and, in consequence, to cosmetic stock-keeping on a massive scale. And this in a company whose turnover in 1974 exceeded £433 million – excluding shrinkage! David Malpas: 'The whole situation was prompted by fear, for no one ever dared to know how much shrinkage there really was. That was a dirty and horrifying word because under the barrow boy culture, to have short stock at the end of a trading day meant that you had been dishonest and you would get fired. As the only crime you could commit as a Tesco manager was to have short stock, the resulting falsification of stock returns led to the near ruination of the company.'

If Tesco was to have a viable future, the system demanded a radical re-structuring. The company could no longer afford a situation in which the parts deceived the whole and the whole deceived itself. Effective financial controls had to be introduced to impose some order on the existing chaos. Nationwide, Tesco was operating out of 830 stores and its 830 managers had each developed their own trading style. To make matters worse, the entire culture of the company still depended on bottom-up as opposed to a top-down management.

In the early years, the practice had offered significant advantages, providing a powerful incentive to individual initiative. No longer. The convention had long outgrown its usefulness, and the pressing need was for rationalisation, a task that would demand time and patience in equal proportions, not least when related to the realignment of the company's development strategy. Between 1973 and 1979, more than 200 stores of less than 5,000 square feet were to close their doors for the last time. This could not happen without opposition from Cohen, for as Ian MacLaurin was later to remark, 'They were next to the Old Man's heart, and as we couldn't get rid of them wholesale, we just closed a few down each week without telling him.'

To close stores, however, was the easier part of the problem, yet one which, if carried to its logical conclusion, would mean that Tesco would fall victim to its own disappearing trick – unless it could mount and sustain a large-store development programme as a matter of urgency. It was here that the real difficulty lay, because the company had little practical experience in managing superstores, and because of entrenched local government resistance to Tesco and all that the company represented.

By 1975, the company's development budget had fallen to £1.8 million, considerably less than the cost of developing a single large store, while the chief executive of one county council echoed Parkinson's earlier warning that Tesco was not welcome on his patch. Without a solution to the problem, without new store openings compensating for closures, there was a very real danger that the company would be trapped either with its timeworn image or without sufficient modern outlets to create a new one. In the autumn of 1975 Ian MacLaurin delivered the first of the company's Occasional Papers in a bid to re-establish Tesco's development credentials.

His argument was simple: if local authorities tended to neglect the importance of retailing when drawing up their plans, then retailers were equally culpable in not explaining their intentions to local authority planners. 'As one of Britain's largest industries, there must be a mutual benefit in retailers opening and sustaining a dialogue with central and local government to ensure that the public we both serve obtains the right shopping mix. This is in all our interests, for I am a firm believer in the maxim "Jaw, jaw; not war, war". I have the impression that, in the past, we have tended to indulge too often in confrontation. Perhaps, in future, we can learn the lessons of participation, to the benefit of all concerned.'

The response was immediate, *Supermarketing* carrying the head-line, 'Retail Planning: Tesco Fills the Gap', and in pursuit of its own principle of consultation, the company went to public enquiry only three times between 1976 and 1979, in contrast to mounting twelve generally unsuccessful appeals in the previous four years. The policy of disengagement was a calculated one, and slowly but surely under the unassuming direction of estates director Francis Krejsa, local authorities began to recover confidence in Tesco. Where, once, it had been regarded as a retail cowboy, it now came to be recognised as a pace-setter in retail planning, and within two years of the company's development budget bottoming out in 1977, it had risen twelve-fold to lay the foundations for a new generation of Tesco stores.

The approach, based on maintaining an open dialogue with local authorities by addressing issues of mutual concern (in the three years from 1975, Tesco was to publish six *Occasional Papers* devoted to subjects as varied as retail deprivation in the inner cities and the future of employment prospects in retailing), was symptomatic of a shift in the culture and the strategy of the company. Kreitman and Singer had both failed in their attempts to persuade Tesco, or rather, Jack Cohen, to 'think long', at punishing cost to the company, but now Porter and MacLaurin were to substitute analysis for intuition.

Porter laid the foundations for the new credo, reflecting on the dangers of short-termism at a meeting of the Marketing Society, to conclude that 'the future is out there, waiting', a policy that was to be amplified and extended by MacLaurin. Invited to address a conference of brokers in London in mid-1976, MacLaurin startled his audience by abandoning the usual practice of selling up Tesco in favour of a detailed analysis of emergent factors (political, economic and social) likely to shape the performance of retailing in the years ahead: 'Retailers cannot afford to be indifferent to the happenings at Westminster or Whitehall, oblivious to the legislative decisions of Brussels or Strasbourg, careless of the movements of the markets at home or abroad. All have their effect on our ability to trade cost-effectively, for we have to remember the shop is the reflection, not the determinant of the environment in which it operates. Occasionally we retailers may pretend otherwise, but in doing so we are only fooling ourselves, for how, in practice, is it possible for us to live in self-imposed isolation?'

Significantly in the light of his own experience, MacLaurin closed by laying stress on what he termed the Management Factor – 'the ultimate arbiter of success or failure in the decade ahead'. He left his audience at the Europa Hotel nonplussed. This was not what they had expected to hear. Marks or Sainsbury might reflect on the future with authority, but for Tesco to address the issue was unprecedented. For half a century the company had been noted more for its feel for the market than for its cerebral qualities, yet here was MacLaurin playing the thinking man's retailer.

Only one thing troubled his listeners. Whilst the words might be admirable, they were contradicted by the everyday reality of Tesco itself. For all of Porter and MacLaurin's rhetoric, the company remained lumbered with an obsolete image, far distant from the future now being conjured up by the new management team. Until the one could be reconciled with the other, their doubts about Tesco would remain, even if there were tentative indications that the company was beginning to tackle the whole question of its persona.

Within months of taking command, Porter and MacLaurin had opened up the tortured issue of Tesco's high street image. In commercial terms it was not only that the company was wedded to an aggressive visual style, but also that much of the competition continued to favour an equally abrasive approach in their attempts to win and to hold custom. Explicitly, the choices were as clear as they were antithetical – either to retain the existing format and risk future growth, or make a clear break with the past and risk existing custom – whilst, implicitly, the matter had altogether more emotive connotations. Indeed, the whole character of the company turned on the issue, for to argue that times had changed, and that it was time that Tesco changed with them, was to question the very essence of Tesco itself.

The dispute rumbled on for months, and the deadlock was only broken by accepting a compromise formula – that without any commitment, a study should be undertaken of the house style of the non-food sector. The implications were to prove far-reaching, though there was little indication as to where the reappraisal would lead when the board called in the American design group, Doody, in mid-1975. Completed by the late autumn, Doody's findings were to confirm the board's worst suspicions about the company: that Tesco was jeopardising a significant element of its custom by clinging to its ageing house style. The old guard might object, but the razzamatazz would have to go.

So much, however, was easier said than done. Whilst Doody's recommendation that Tesco adopt a new type style allied to a simplified red and white colour scheme posed few problems of implementation, it opened up the altogether more difficult question of the company's relationship with Green Shield. For more than a decade, the image of Tesco had been determined by the hard sell of stamps, the windows of its stores offering a blinding display of

day-glo posters that pulverised the senses, leaving customers punchy
with their pyrotechnics.

As the market turned down, so the displays became more frenetic,
more garish as Tesco played a Dutch auction with stamps. Mike
Darnell: 'As the years rolled on, stamps became less and less
significant, yet all the while they were becoming more and more
expensive to the business. We were probably buying them cheaply
from Green Shield, because we were always wanting to do deals, but
we were using more and more of them in the stores. We were giving
double stamps, treble stamps, quadruple stamps, two double stamp
days, double stamps all week, anything. It was always stamps,
stamps, stamps. I suppose we saturated the market, so that they
became meaningless to the customer who, by the 1970s, wanted
keen pricing rather than little bits of paper to stick in their books.'

Clearly, it was not only a matter of image, but also of commercial
hard sense that demanded a review of the company's stamping
strategy, not least when it had been revealed that '1974 was the first
comparatively poor year for Green Shield'. The Doody report was to
reinforce the half-formulated doubts about the validity of stamping
to Tesco but, as yet, nothing was clear, nothing was concrete. Once
the issue had been opened, however, it would not go away, and such
is the grapevine of retailing that rumours were soon circulating in
the trade that the company was increasingly unhappy with Green
Shield.

At first little more than speculation, Tesco was soon to exploit the
gullibility of the rumour-mongers by manufacturing their own
gossip – a half hint here, a calculated indiscretion there – as much to
confuse the opposition about its intentions as to mask the board's
activities in their dealings with Green Shield. Indeed, by the early
months of 1977, Tesco's campaign of disinformation had become so
successful that news of the company's intentions were rife in the
industry. The retail correspondent of the *Financial Times*, Elinor
Goodman, speculated, 'Few people expect Tesco to abandon stamps
altogether. A more likely course of action would be for the company
to renegotiate a new contract which would allow it to dispense with
stamps in situations where they are seen not to help the trade. Even
so, the decision cannot be an easy one. The two companies
weathered the stamp war together, and for many the names of Green
Shield and Tesco are synonymous.'

And all the while, behind a smokescreen of rumour and counter-rumour, the board continued to examine its options. As early as 1975, Leslie Porter had asked the company's public affairs consultants whether stamping was in breach of EEC regulations, whilst Ian MacLaurin was taking confidential soundings of his own senior executives' attitudes towards stamps, and the likely impact on the company if they should be dropped. His findings confirmed his own burgeoning suspicions that Green Shield were of rapidly diminishing value to Tesco, especially at a time of economic constraint.

And a growing number of letters reaching Tesco House fortified the conclusion. Leslie Porter: 'How would you expect people to react when they had saved 400 books for a TV set, then found that they needed a further 100 books if they were to obtain their gift. Inflation was biting hard at Green Shield, and with people having to save more for less, it was not surprising that there was a growing disenchantment with stamps.'

As evidence of the petrol companies confirmed. By the mid-1970s, an increasing number of filling stations were sanction-busting by offering customers a choice of stamps (and these, in growing numbers) or a reduction in pump prices – and against escalating fuel costs, more than 70% of customers were opting for price cuts. The message was clear, and less than eighteen months after Tesco's interim figures of 1974, and more than a year before the Green Shield contract was due for renewal, at least three different options were being canvassed at board level: of those who held that Tesco must remain in stamps; of those who held that, while stamps remained important as a trading tool, a new and much tougher contract would have to be negotiated with Green Shield; and of those who held that stamps would have to go.

The divide turned as much on the personalities involved as on commercial considerations and, initially, discussions centred on the rationale that Green Shield, aware of their clients' trading problems and with 35% of their business locked up with Tesco, would make significant concessions to the company in order to safeguard their contract. It was to prove wishful thinking. By June 1976, there were unconfirmed reports that Green Shield were exploring the possibility of finding a new client to replace Tesco. Whether true or not, the gambit was to prove counter-productive, tending to harden the position of the anti-stampers on the Tesco board.

Within the month, Tesco had dropped stamps and introduced deep price cuts at two of their smaller stores – at Crewe and at Fegg Hayes in Staffordshire. A test-bed as to the real value of Green Shield, the operation was mounted with maximum security under the resurrected trade name Adsega, but word of the experiment was soon circulating in the trade. Finance director Ralph Temple warned the board on 26 July of the need to inform Green Shield of the experiment 'to prevent antagonism of their learning it elsewhere'.

Much later, Ian MacLaurin was to say that Green Shield's response to the Adsega initiative was the first, though possibly the most damaging, error that the company made during the early stages of the contract renegotiation. The exercise not only tested Green Shield's nerve, thus providing Tesco with a powerful psychological weapon to deploy in their dealings with the company; it also provided an indication of how much Tesco itself could benefit if it were to drop stamps. If Cohen and his confederates had reservations about the Fegg Hayes and Crewe test market, they were to be laid within six weeks – turnover at both stores having increased substantially.

Such evidence was to prove invaluable to the anti-stamp lobby on the board. Where previously they had had to rely upon best-guessing, they now had the facts and figures to substantiate their case, and while the advocates of Green Shield still held their ground, their position was under constant attack – especially after a board meeting of 21 September 1976. The discussion lasted for much of the day, but at the close there was no longer any possibility of disguising the hostility of a hard core group to continuing to trade with Green Shield.

Although sceptical of head office's capacity to deliver on its promises, the majority of the company's regional managing directors agreed that Tesco should break with Green Shield, and it was with this in mind that MacLaurin proposed that Tesco 'move away from stamps' and explore, as a matter of urgency, alternative uses to which such a £20 million economy could be put. His case was supported by Ralph Temple, who revealed that on a like-for-like basis the company's turnover was not keeping pace with general trends in the industry, while Donald Harris, director of administration, listed the options available to achieve the additional turnover required to maintain or improve Tesco market share if stamps were to be abandoned.

Whilst the final outcome was inconclusive, there could be no escaping the fact that the case of those continuing to favour stamps was becoming increasingly untenable, the more so in view of Richard Tompkins' apparently inexplicable behaviour. A leaked report that he had no wish to renew the Tesco contract further steeled the anti-stamp lobby's resolve, and led to the company's negotiators being able to issue a take-it-or-leave-it-alone ultimatum to Green Shield. Four major concessions were demanded, each carefully drafted to test Green Shield's nerve as much as its goodwill.

First, and a direct extension of the Adsega precedent, MacLaurin was instructed to find ten further stores where Green Shield would allow Tesco to conduct non-stamp experiments. In return, the board accepted that Green Shield might ask for the transfer of their franchise to other multiples in selected areas. Little more than a face-saver, such a concession could not disguise the main thrust of Tesco's intentions, for if, by dropping stamps and introducing price cuts, such units were to show a significant increase in turnover, then it would further undermine Green Shield's position.

The second point was a direct extension of the first: a demand that Tesco should be allowed maximum flexibility in trading with or without stamps in no more than fifty stores or, alternatively, a selected number of units that cumulatively accounted for no more than 25% of the company's turnover. Here, however, there were to be no concessions to Green Shield's sensibilities – the clause on flexible trading was only to be agreed if Green Shield accepted that their new contract with Tesco would only operate on an annual basis.

And if this was not demanding enough, the third and fourth points of Tesco's ultimatum were equally bruising: that the company should receive a concession on the price of stamps in their larger stores, and that there should be no increase in the price of stamps during the contract period. As openers for a series of negotiations that were to run until the late spring of 1977, these were confrontational demands, an unequivocal indication that unless Green Shield were willing to compromise, then stamps were dispensable as far as Tesco was concerned.

Green Shield's brusque response to Tesco's terms played straight into the anti-stamp lobby's hands. Green Shield did not seem to care whether Tesco renewed the contract or not. In fact, during the run-up to the renewal Tompkins himself never met Tesco's negotiating team, leaving his colleagues Richard Goodman and Peter Pugsley to trade with MacLaurin and Hyams; while it was not until January 1977 that the company responded to Tesco's conditions, offering terms that MacLaurin was to describe to his board as 'absolutely valueless'.

On the question of flexibility, Green Shield offered no dispensations; on the proposal to provide price concessions in the larger Tesco stores, they countered with an offer of a 5% discount; no mention was made either of further test marketing or the proposition to freeze the price of stamps during the contract period. Indeed, only one concession emerged: that Tesco might drop stamps in their northern stores. As both sides knew, it was a meaningless gesture, not so much because stamps were fast losing their appeal in the cost-conscious north, but because of the impracticability of the whole concept. Just where did 'the north' (and price-cutting) begin; just where did 'the south' (and stamps) end? Tesco rejected the proposal with all the contempt they felt it deserved.

In hindsight, it is incredible that as late as February 1977, with only four months to go before the renewal of a £20 million contract that accounted for more than a third of their retail portfolio, Green Shield failed to recognise the dangers implicit in their negotiating strategy. For all the manoeuvring for position, it must have been increasingly clear that Tesco, and more especially MacLaurin, were deeply disenchanted with stamps, and had no wish to deal.

Yet Green Shield remained intractable. Only three tentative explanations are possible to account for such dogged confidence: that the company was, indeed, firming up a deal with a rival multiple; that it was relying on Cohen's devotion to stamps to bundle a new contract through the board; or that it was placing its faith in an Economist Intelligence Unit report into the future of stamp trading published in January 1977.

If the first, then Green Shield was soon to be rudely disabused. If the second, then it over-estimated Cohen's continuing influence on the Tesco board. If the third, then its faith was to prove misplaced. After a detailed examination of the current standing of trading stamps, the EIU concluded: 'It is likely that stamps are here to stay, at least at the level at which they are at the moment. They do, in fact, have a good chance of improving their penetration, not through new outlets, but through the use of stamps in the incentive business. Consequently, we may expect stamps to play a continuing role in our everyday lives, possibly even increasing their penetration among households because of their increased use of rewards, and increasingly sophisticated advertising techniques for stamps.'

On such assurances are strategies formulated, tactics devised and companies made or broken – as Green Shield was to learn. With the report to hand, the company's negotiators continued to maintain a hard line in the closing stage of their discussions with Tesco – for all the warnings of one of their own executives of Tesco's rapidly hardening attitude towards stamps. Peter Crossley had worked on the Tesco account for more than ten years, and his information was soundly based on his day-to-day contacts at Tesco House: 'From late 1976, I became increasingly aware that Tesco might not renew our contract. This wasn't founded simply on my own hunches, but on my dealing with the company's senior management. I was convinced that Green Shield was going to be dropped, but no one at head office seemed to give a damn for what I said.'

Whatever the reasons for such tardiness, Green Shield's credibility diminished as Tesco's confidence rose, the more so following a visit to the States by a small team led by MacLaurin. In ten days, they visited stores in three major centres which not only confirmed their own gut feeling about stamps, but also provided valuable information as to how to go about dropping them. By early February 1977, and with the growing conviction that a break with Green Shield was inevitable, MacLaurin had been instructed by the board to find an advertising agency capable of handling the job of 'relaunching Tesco'. Several names were canvassed, but McCann Erickson were selected unanimously.

In the weeks that followed, the agency was to play a seminal role in clarifying the board's often inchoate suspicions about itself, and in devising a strategy to obtain maximum impact for its client's objectives. In the winter of 1976/77, however, Mike Franklin, the main board director of McCann's in charge of the Tesco account, and his team in Howland Street, London, had little idea of where their venture might lead. All that was certain was that their client had a problem, as in-house research was soon to confirm. The time available until the June expiry of the Green Shield contract excluded any possibility of undertaking in-depth research, but a limited study was soon to confirm Tesco's fears about the interaction between stamps and the company's image.

In contrast to the Economist Intelligence Unit, McCann's findings validated Tesco's belief that in a depressed market stamps were an ineffective marketing tool, less than 5% of the sample admitting to being 'stamp mad'. Against this, the majority of those interviewed said that, at best, they regarded stamps as 'handy' and only saved casually, at worst as being a positive nuisance.

Equally significant, the survey indicated that few people would 'definitely leave Tesco' if the company withdrew from Green Shield, even the 'at risk' customers saying that they would prefer cut prices or special offers whilst, crucially in terms of what was to follow, evidence emerged that a high percentage of the upper and upper-middle income groups (accounting for 5 or 6% of the total market) said they never shopped at Tesco, in part because the company traded in stamps.

According to McCann's, the findings had a direct bearing on the public's perception of Tesco – that for all its 'friendly market trader feel', the company had a more working class image than it deserved due to the clutter within stores and their gimcrack appearance. Conversely, Tesco was widely regarded as being more price competitive than it actually was, a legacy of Cohen's success in selling the company as the keenest trader on the high street.

Combined, McCann's research led them to two closely related conclusions: 'First, that on *prices*, Tesco's image is better than reality. Second, that on *quality*, the reality is better than the perceived image.'

Given this, the agency argued that the marketing 'gap' was clear: for Tesco to develop a higher quality image, at more competitive prices. Such a dual approach, McCann's maintained, would provide an ideal platform for the relaunch of Tesco, provided always that the company could show a marked improvement in its physical appearance, and that it was able to convince the public that it offered 'consistent and reliable low prices'.

In mirroring the anti-stamp lobby's conclusions, the research not only sapped the opposition's confidence, but also fixed the board's mind on the company's priorities for the future. Practically, Tesco was already some way towards fulfilling the first part of McCann's brief. Commercially, the pricing recommendations were to pose an altogether more difficult problem. True, Tesco would have £20 million in hand if it were to drop Green Shield, but how far would this go, and how long would it last if, as stressed, price cuts were to be consistent and reliable?

Daisy Hyams, who had recently been chosen 'Woman of the Month' by the BBC for her contribution to the government's anti-inflation campaign, was the main board director in charge of Tesco buying operations in 1977. Ultimately, it would be her job to work out the implications of McCann's recommendations, and it would be her decisions that would determine whether, if stamps were to be dropped and deep price cuts introduced, Tesco's books would balance, or not.

Innately diffident, she was later to dismiss the problem as 'all just a part of the job', though others called it a nightmare. Effectively what was being asked of her team was to compute the profit and loss variables of a multi-million pound shopping list, embracing some 16,000 convenience and durable lines, all of which carried their own carefully calculated margins (a penny here, a halfpenny there), and then to do it all over again, this time excluding the Green Shield factor.

Ultimately, all the rest depended upon this: upon balancing out the risks involved in jettisoning stamps and producing a price-cutting formula which would ensure that, for all of McCann's recommendations, and for all the board's new found enthusiasm to go-it-alone, Tesco did not bankrupt itself. If the company were to drop stamps, if Tesco was to be 'relaunched' (a word that occurred with increasing frequency in the board minutes), then no one knew with any certainty what might happen, or how Tesco's suppliers and competitors might respond. In theory, all the evidence pointed in one direction, and as MacLaurin was to point out this might well be 'Tesco's last chance of having a future' – but at the last resort, all depended upon Daisy Hyams getting her sums right.

Not that Tesco expected to show a significant increase in profits in the first year of trading without stamps. That would have been too much to hope for while they were holding down prices as well. The sole object was to recapture market share (by mid-1977, discounters had lifted their take to 15% of the grocery sector) and to establish the company in a new trading position. Porter laboured the point through the first half of the year, well aware that while McCann's believed that the company would generate sufficient new business to compensate for the loss of stamp-savers, an altogether more pessimistic forecast suggested that the company would have to raise its turnover by 15% (amounting to £90 million a year) to achieve break-even point.

Such a calculation added a further dimension to Hyams' already complex equations, and reduced her room for manoeuvre even further. Now it was not simply the size of the price cuts that had to be right; such cuts had to generate sufficient new business to achieve the increased turnover demanded to offset the cost of the cuts themselves. Her initial solution had all the elegance of simplicity: to concentrate the cuts on the top hundred lines handled by Tesco, which accounted for more than 25% of the business.

Once formulated, however, new difficulties arose, not least the knock-on effects of such cuts on associated lines which, unless corrected, would create a serious imbalance in the company's entire pricing structure. Eventually, therefore, she proposed a readjustment in the pricing of more than 600 lines to maintain the necessary pricing equilibrium.

Even this was not all, however. Having identified the areas for price cutting, there was a comparable need to decide how deep such cuts should be, and how much trimming each brand could bear, related always to the trading balance to be achieved. The task took Hyams and her team five weeks to complete, before running the figures through the Tesco computer to establish the sales volumes likely to be generated at the marked-down prices and, consequently, the overall profit and loss of the programme.

As Hyams recalled later, 'Throughout the entire exercise we operated on very pessimistic forecasts, allowing that all the increases in turnover would come on the lines we had reduced though we knew, quite well, that there was bound to be a rub-off on other products.'

Events were to confirm the accuracy of her calculations (in the first half-year after Tesco dropped stamps, turnover and profit in the grocery sector consistently ran within 1% of her team's estimates), but in the spring of 1977 such figures still remained unquantifiable. Nonetheless, the confidence of Tesco directors in Hyams' expertise, and their consequent conviction that the company could safely make deep price cuts, nerved the board to harden up their plans for dropping Green Shield.

Not that Tesco or McCann's had any idea of how a relaunch should be conducted. The goal was clear, the problem was how to achieve it. With little more than two months to go before the renewal date of the Green Shield contract, the critical need was to find a vehicle to realise what, so far, was little more than an abstraction, and to find a formula which, as a confidential agency memorandum stressed, would be 'flexible and creative, and would be meaningful to Tesco's existing and potential customers'.

It was a slight enough brief but one which, by mid-April 1977, had been stripped down and analysed in detail by Mike Franklin's creative team. Eventually, the 'Check-out' concept was the result of an act of collective imagination, a combination of a number of individual themes which, encapsulated in a single word, offered at least three powerful marketing advantages: it had the modern ring demanded by Tesco; it challenged customers themselves to test-market the quality of Tesco products; and above all else, it played heavily on the price-consciousness of customers whilst reinforcing Tesco's reputation for competitive trading.

Although the board had minor reservations about the detail of the campaign when it was first presented by McCann's, there was unanimous approval for the overall theme:

Check-out at

TESCO

Prices that help keep the cost of living in check

McCann's recommendations for Tesco's new livery, red out of white in a typewriter face, virtually coincided with those of Doody's, and as far as both national advertising and in-house displays were concerned, the agency's stress was on simplicity, quality and cleanliness of style. If their clients were going to break with the past, and not just the past of Green Shield, then the break must be both final and absolute.

And as McCann's reinforced the board's confidence, so Green Shield sapped their own position. On 7 April, the Tesco negotiating team had presented the final draft terms for the renewal of the contract to Goodman, who made it clear that Tesco's demands were totally unacceptable, Pugsley remarking, 'Tesco needs Green Shield more than Green Shield needs Tesco.' If anything was required to firm up Tesco's resolve it was this, and a fortnight later the board met to consider what the minutes described as 'the most important decision the company would ever have to make regarding its trading philosophy – whether or not to break with stamps'.

For the last time, MacLaurin led the attack. Tesco, he pointed out, was continuing to lose market share, and they needed not only to devise a short-term solution to the company's problems, but also to take a longer view of its position into the 1980s. On both counts, to regain price competitiveness as much as to improve the company's image, it was essential to drop stamps – or write an epitaph for Tesco.

Four other directors supported him (Donald Harris, Francis Krejsa, Ralph Temple, and George Wood), and it was left to Hyman Kreitman to speak in defence of Green Shield. The Adsega evidence, he asserted, was inconclusive, whilst if stamps were retained, costs could be reduced by having fewer stamp days. Finally, echoing much that had gone before, he predicted that the company's profits would fall the following year 'regardless of whether stamps continue or not' – to which one cynic quietly retorted that this being the case, it would be better to drop stamps immediately and save £20 million.

When the vote came there was deadlock – five all. For a moment it seemed that the hiatus would continue; then MacLaurin produced a note from an absentee director, David Behar ('I can't stand the sticky little things. Get rid of them.') and cast his proxy vote. Cohen's long reign was effectively at an end. Even then, however, he could not resist one Parthian shot. The meeting over, the ageing autocrat stormed into MacLaurin's office where, according to one witness, he shook his managing director 'like a rabbit', all the while raging, 'It's all your idea, and you know what'll happen if it doesn't work out.'

MacLaurin had no need to reply. He knew quite well. Nineteen years had passed since he had first met the Governor at the Grand Hotel, Eastbourne – nineteen years in which he had learned something from Cohen himself of the power games played at Tesco House.

At midday on Sunday, 8 May, and having delayed notification until the last possible moment, Leslie Porter rang Richard Tompkins at his home to relay his board's decision (see Appendix Four). On hearing that Tesco did not intend to renew the agreement, Tompkins retorted that it made little difference as a break clause in the contract meant that the account still had a further twelve months to run. This was typical of the prevailing attitude at Green Shield: while Tesco had checked out the contract in detail to establish that they had no commitment to stamps after 7 June 1977, Green Shield continued to live with its contractual illusion to within a month of the date for renewal.

It was a risible ending to a partnership that had transformed the shopping habits of Britain; more than two decades later the *Guardian* was to recall the end of those wildcat years when British housewives had mainlined on stamps: 'Their [the Tesco board's] decision was to change the face of Britain's high streets. The most successful business partnership in post-war Britain was to be severed … for Tesco was the supermarket flagship, the jewel in the Green Shield crown. Despite head-to-head discussions between the estranged parties, the die was cast. Tesco wanted a new, up-market image and there was no going back. The domino effect was rapid, and the once great stamp empire crumbled like Flake.'

11. OPERATION CHECK-OUT

1977

'What would the pattern of shopping be
like in the UK today without Tesco?'

Grieveson Grant
brokers' report (1978)

On the evening of Saturday, 4 June 1977, Ian MacLaurin and David
Malpas met in the former's office. It was late. They were tired, but
satisfied that all that could be done had been done. In the previous
month, they had covered more than 12,000 miles selling in Check-
out to Tesco's staff. Now all they could do was wait, and having
poured two drinks, Malpas turned to MacLaurin and raised his
glass: 'Here's to Check-out, or we won't be here this time next week.'
It was a toast less to their own futures than to that of Tesco.

If a week is a long time in politics, then the Tesco board
compacted a lifetime into the twenty-eight days between Porter's
call to Tompkins and the relaunch of Tesco. Since late the previous
year, they had been discussing the issue behind closed doors, but
now the news was out, and on Monday, 9 May, full-page advertisements appeared in the *Daily Mail*, *Daily Express*, *Daily Mirror*,
and *Sun* headed by a statement from Cohen: 'Tesco has always done
what its customers want. That's why we are going to change our
trading policy.'

The irony of the affair escaped the media, who preferred to lead on
'the great falling out' (the *Mail*) between the two erstwhile trading
partners, the *Sun* under the banner headline 'Green Shield Shock',
and the *Mirror* with the broad pun 'Tesco Stamps on Green Shield'
featuring a surprised-looking Tompkins, who is reputed to have

said, 'I am convinced Tesco have made a terrible mistake. They were our biggest customer, but now they have bought themselves a black eye.'

Whatever Tompkins' opinion, the government were delighted at the news. For more than two years Labour had been waging war on inflation, and in the process of cutting the RPI from a runaway 24% in 1974 to 8% in 1977, had concentrated the public's mind on the need for economies in the shopping basket. By mid-1977, however, the Westminster initiative was becoming timeworn and the Tesco announcement was just what was needed to revive a flagging campaign. Conversely, the government's attack on inflation was to provide an unrivalled trailer for the launch of Check-out itself, in-store monitoring by Tesco showing that at the time of the break with Green Shield, consumers were more price-conscious than at any time since the war.

Leslie Porter: 'Our timing was right in more than one way. Obviously, the government's assault on inflation had made people keenly aware of shelf prices, whilst as to the launch date itself, 9 June, we couldn't have chosen a better time than the Silver Jubilee weekend if we'd wanted to. The whole country was going to be *en fête*, and provided our plans went well, Tesco would just ride along with the mood.'

The caveat was critical – providing the plans went well. Before the morning of 9 May, only a handful of Tesco's 35,000 staff had been privy to the board's dealings, but at eight o'clock that morning, as housewives tuned into the news of the company's break with Green Shield, MacLaurin opened a briefing session for 250 of his top managers at Cheshunt. Until that moment they had heard little but rumours. Now they were to hear it all: an explanation as to why stamps no longer had a place in the company; a breakdown of the plans for the forthcoming launch of Check-out; and an outline of Tesco's new trading philosophy.

The overall objective, MacLaurin explained, was three-fold: first, to increase turnover and market share; second, to generate and sustain an increase in customer loyalty; and third, to transform Tesco's former image and reposition the company in the market. In the short term the first goal was critical, not least in its ability to restore the bruised morale of Tesco staff, on which the second and third goals of the campaign would depend. Indeed, unless this could be achieved, unless Tesco's employees could be infected with the board's new-found enthusiasm, it remained questionable whether the company could manage the transformation it was demanding of itself.

The message was implicit in all that was said during that three-hour meeting for, innately, morale is the key to buoyant retailing. With it a store has purpose, dynamism; without it, there are troubles, and as Tesco lost headway in the early 1970s, so morale had slumped. It was not so much a question of figures, more that store managers and their staffs could see for themselves what was happening on the high streets. In the intensely competitive world of retailing, shopkeepers are acutely aware of the performance of the opposition – and during those dog days it was clear that Tesco was being out-performed by its rivals. Where formerly the company had been a pace-setter, it was in danger of becoming an also-ran, and as the opposition gained momentum, so morale in Tesco's stores fell.

As the main board director responsible for retailing, MacLaurin was deeply conscious of the problem: 'Check-out was aimed as much at our own people as at our customers. Unless we could generate new life in the business, and give our people on the ground a feeling that Tesco was really going somewhere, we would continue to be plagued by a host of problems, among them the loss of our best staff to the opposition.'

When the meeting finally broke up, there were no questions left to ask. All that remained were twenty-eight days in which to meta-morphose the image of Tesco, during which time senior executives from Cheshunt peddled the Check-out message throughout the UK, to receive a unanimously encouraging response. Leslie Porter: 'If Check-out achieved nothing more, it resurrected everyone's morale. Our staff began to feel that something was happening at last, that they were at the centre of events again, and this generated enormous excitement.'

Which was not to be wondered at. As the days counted down to 9 June, so the intensity of activity increased. At national level, McCann's continued to tease public curiosity about Tesco's plans, and whilst press speculation mounted as to exactly what the company was intending for its relaunch (the *Financial Times* reflec-ting that with gross margins at their lowest level since the war, there was not enough surplus in the grocery sector to fund deep price cuts for long), the opposition watched and waited, and Green Shield fought to recover lost ground.

Shocked out of its complacency at last, Green Shield spent the month before Check-out attempting to drum up new business. Richard Tompkins led the fight back personally, and by the end of May it seemed as if his efforts were producing positive results. From what Green Shield described as 'a queue of bidders', three groups had taken up options on the Green Shield franchise, notably International, who planned to offer stamps in 600 of their stores.

As *The Times* reported, 'International's managing director admits that competition in the high street will be intense. By offering discounts as well as stamps, the group hopes to raise turnover in stores which have just acquired Green Shield by 20 or 30%.'

International's hopes were to prove stillborn (by the early autumn, the company had dropped stamps from all but a hundred of its stores), though the media coverage generated by Green Shield's activities (on the day before the launch of Check-out, Tompkins scheduled £60,000 for saturation advertising) tended to focus mounting public interest on what Tesco was about. And by the first week of June it was about a lot. Allied to in-store briefings, detailed instructions had been issued to every manager as to what they should do between closing their stores on the evening of Saturday, 4 June, and reopening them on the morning of Thursday, 9 June.

In the intervening period – 'and the fact that it was Jubilee weekend was a godsend,' says David Malpas – every window had to be stripped of the old-style day-glo posters, and redressed in the new red and white house style; every interior had to be redressed with displays, markers and posters; and all affected stock had to be repriced. Virtually the entire Tesco staff, from the board down, were involved in the operation – and all behind whitewashed windows. The idea may have smacked of gimmickry, but it served two practical functions – it further intensified media interest in Tesco; and it provoked general curiosity (especially amongst the competition) as to exactly what was happening behind those blind frontages.

During the final phase, the tactic worked admirably, spies from Tesco's high street rivals going to extraordinary lengths to try and discover what was happening behind the whitewash. The final gambit of the relaunch also lived up to expectations: implying until the first week of June that Tesco would reopen on Wednesday, 8

June, but not reopening until the following day. It was a high-risk gamble (the loss of a single day's trade at the time amounting to some £2.5 million), but it was to pay off handsomely. It gave managers an extra twenty-four hours to refurbish their stores, and also provided Tesco House with an insight into how the competition (caught unprepared by Tesco's move) were reacting to the company's initiative.

By lunchtime on the 8th, they knew, Tesco managers monitoring price cuts on the high street and ringing in to Cheshunt with their reports. Generally, the response was unremarkable. Even at this eleventh hour, the competition remained sceptical about what Tesco could do, the company's teaser advertisements immediately before the launch merely reinforcing such doubts.

Over the three days of the Jubilee weekend, Tesco mounted an advertising blitz in the national press, on radio and TV, though without revealing anything about the company's pricing intentions, merely prompting attention with the message: 'From Thursday, 9 June, Tesco give you something you want more than stamps – Check-out.' It wasn't until the close of normal business on the 8th that the company released its first sixty-second commercial featuring a wide range of price cuts on promoted lines. By then, it was too late for the competition to respond.

Mike Franklin of McCann's: 'The opposition had expected Tesco to go on the 8th, and had prepared their promotional and price-cutting plans accordingly. As it was, they were left competing against themselves without any idea of what Tesco was going to do. In effect, they were price cutting against an unknown quantity, and this gave Tesco a terrific advantage.'

It was not until the morning of the 9th, however, that Tesco learned precisely what it had achieved. In the meantime, behind the sightless windows of stores throughout the UK, the company's staff counted down the final hours to the launch of Operation Check-out. Four days had passed since they had closed their doors on the past, but the future remained an unknown territory.

One of the first calls received at Tesco House that Thursday morning came from Pontypridd. The manager was worried. The crowds in the store were so large that he had been forced to close the doors. Seemingly, Check-out was developing a life force of its own, and by midday the Cheshunt switchboard was being inundated with calls from stores throughout the country reporting a state of near siege – twenty-five-yard queues forming at High Wycombe; customers in Crawley and Stevenage and Swansea emptying the trolleys of staff trying to refill the emptied shelves; turnover in Preston increasing by more than 200% by the end of the day, until the store was running out of supplies.

Throughout the UK, from Perth to Truro, the story was much the same: a stampede of custom that made a nonsense of all Tesco's previous projections, a buying mania that had lifted turnover to unprecedented heights. By the close of business Check-out had more than justified itself, but while the media reported on the 'High Noon in the High Streets' (the *Sun*) as 'shoppers stormed the cut price shelves' (the *Mirror*), the question remained: Would the business hold up, or was Thursday, 9 June no more than a momentary aberration?

Incredulous at the amount of new business they had generated, even the Tesco board doubted whether it would be possible to maintain such an increased volume in trade. As far as the press was concerned, their tone remained bullish, but Porter later admitted, 'We were astounded by that first day of Check-out. It was hard to imagine that it was more than a temporary phenomenon, and that we wouldn't be back to business as usual by the weekend.'

But reinforced as much by word of mouth as by intensified advertising (during the last three weeks of June Tesco spent £1.5 million on press and TV exposure), the business did, indeed, hold up – though there was mounting media scepticism about how long the company could continue to maintain its price cuts. As the popular dailies vied with one another for stories about Operation Check-out, reporting that families could save between £1 and £2 a week by shopping at Tesco, the *Financial Times* pondered, 'Will the cost of the company's initiative prove too high for it to sustain?'

The trade echoed the question, concluding that Tesco's stated intention of holding down prices at 'a reliable and consistent level' was at best unattainable, at worst suicidal, and that with gross margins already depressed, the company would soon be forced to return to its former price structure. Summarising the situation, Reeves Smith, chief executive of the Food and Drink Federation, concluded that any price war must, of necessity, be short-lived, as neither suppliers nor multiples could afford to maintain 'dramatic price cuts for many weeks'.

For all the brouhaha, the received wisdom was that Tesco was fighting a phoney war, a conviction that was to lull the competition into a delayed reaction and to encourage the City to believe that Tesco remained a 'weak hold'. In a detailed analysis of the situation published only eleven days after the launch of Check-out, brokers Grieveson Grant came to two related conclusions – that with the ending of stamps, Tesco had some limited room for manoeuvre; and that with other multiples reacting flexibly, it would be increasingly difficult for the company to pick up the extra business that it sought. To summarise: 'It is one thing to persuade customers to purchase well-advertised, heavily price-cut special items. It is another to convince them to change their shopping patterns, yet this is exactly what Tesco has to do to achieve a sharp improvement in profit growth.'

Grieveson Grant overlooked only one thing: Tesco's staying power. While others were to lose their nerve, this was not the case at Cheshunt, and the directors' confidence was soon to prove well founded. Five days after the publication of the brokers' report, the board received a provisional summary of the results achieved in the opening phase of Check-out. Even the board was dumbfounded. On discounted grocery lines, first figures suggested that turnover on pet foods had increased by 91%, on canned meats by 86%, on detergents by 75%, on coffee by 73%, on baked beans by 61%, and on margarine by 55% – each product group providing an increase in turnover of £1 million or more. Overall, the summary indicated that turnover based on prices had risen by more than 30% (allowing for price-cutting), and on volume by 43%.

The Audits of Great Britain figures for July confirmed Tesco's figures, revealing the full extent of the company's success in its drive to achieve improved market share. During the four-week period from 10 June, Tesco's sales rose from 7.9% to 10.8% of the total market, overtaking Sainsbury and making Tesco Britain's second largest retailer after the Co-op. Virtually every other major competitor lost ground heavily to the Check-out initiative, Sainsbury (particularly badly hit by a strike at two of its main depots) from 9% to 8.2%, Asda from 5.6% to 5.4%, International from 3.2% to 3%.

Small wonder that Porter was reported as saying with unaccustomed modesty that 'the board's decision to cease trading stamps appears to have been a correct one judging from initial results'. Now there could be no question that Tesco should maintain its pressure on both the price-cutting and promotional fronts, the more so as the opposition continued to haver. Although International were now into stamps, and Sainsbury and Kwik Save had increased their advertising budgets, the industry's overall response to Check-out remained dilatory, a situation Tesco was quick to exploit, reflecting MacLaurin's belief that, 'Once we had the steam behind us, it became more difficult for the opposition to catch up.'

With growing confidence came growing aggression, to the point where, by the early autumn, the company had declared a price war on its two major coffee suppliers – Maxwell House and Nestlé. Since July 1975, the shelf price of coffee had risen by 350%, the price of a four-ounce jar of Nescafé rocketing by fifty pence in June 1977 alone. Four months later, Tesco announced that it was refusing to stock the leading brands of coffee at their new higher prices. Within the month Nescafé and Maxwell House had dropped the prices of their four-ounce jars by twenty-four pence, followed by a further price cut in January 1978.

It was a coup in the best Cohen tradition, for in promoting its new image as the housewife's friend, Tesco had succeeded in disguising its own problems; the *Financial Times* reported: 'Behind the news that Tesco will not buy any more Maxwell House or Nescafé until the manufacturers bring their prices down is a shortage of stock. This has resulted in at least one branch manager nipping around the corner to another supermarket and buying his supplies straight off the opposition's shelves.'

The cause of Tesco's problem was largely attributable to its own success. Check-out had generated so much new business that the company was running out of the cheaper brands of coffee (in the three months to September, turnover was up by more than 70%) faster than its competitors. By confronting its suppliers with the ultimatum 'Cut prices, or else … ' Tesco converted what would otherwise have been a difficult situation into a *tour de force* which reinforced not only its new image with consumers, but also the board's conviction that it did, indeed, have its strategy right. Once, and not so long ago, Tesco would have backed away from such a confrontation with two of its major suppliers. By the close of 1977 the company had again tested its nerve, and found it sound.

The company had good reason to be confident. A confidential survey published by AGB on 12 November indicated that Tesco had increased its household penetration by 17.9% since June; that the average expenditure in Tesco stores had risen by 23.9%; that the proportion of shoppers' expenditure taken by Tesco had grown by 24%, and that there had been a 20% increase in 'loyal buyers' (that is, the number of customers spending more than half of their grocery budget at Tesco) in the previous four months.

After the initial success of generating new volume, it seemed that Tesco's second objective was already being realised – the need to hold the new market share captured at the launch of Check-out. Four months of consistent and reliable price-cutting, allied to heavy advertising, had firmly established the company's new image in the public's mind. There could no longer be any doubts about the nature of the transformation that had taken place at Tesco, and finally convinced that the company could, indeed, maintain deep price cuts over an extended period, the competition at last began to respond to the Check-out initiative. Since dropping Green Shield in the majority of its stores, International had been promoting a 'Plain and Simple' discount campaign, but it was Sainsbury that Tesco followed with keenest interest.

Together with Marks and Spencer, the century-old company had long been regarded by Tesco as the benchmark of fine retailing. Yet through the autumn and into the winter Sainsbury failed to respond positively to the Check-out initiative, at growing cost to its own market share which, by November, was 2.6% below that of Tesco. Ian MacLaurin: 'We were surprised that Sainsbury were so slow to react. They are altogether too good traders to let us get away with anything for long, and as time went on and the market gap between our two companies continued to widen, we became more and more intrigued by what they were going to do to hit back at us.'

When the answer came, it was something of an anti-climax. In January 1978, Sainsbury announced its 'Discount 78' campaign, which closely resembled the promotional and price-cutting package launched by Tesco six months previously. However, if the latter's object was to win new custom by moving up-market whilst remaining price-competitive, the former's goal was to ensure that their up-market image did not act as a price deterrent to new custom. As Roy Griffiths, then deputy chairman of Sainsbury, was later to explain at a conference of retailers: 'The major programme we mounted under the heading "Discount 78" helped us to overcome what had been a problem for some time, particularly when opening up in any new territory – i.e. that the quality image that the stores generally presented militated against the reputation for low prices which had been widely appreciated in the areas where we had been trading for any length of time. In short, we looked pricey to new customers, whereas in fact for long years we had a leading position in price amongst high street retailers.'

Within a month of the launch of 'Discount 78', Sainsbury's market share had increased by two percentage points, and twelve months after the launch of Check-out, Sainsbury's sales were 1.9% higher than when the price war began – though Tesco still held a small trading edge, its market share having risen by 4.5% (to 12.5%) since that Jubilee weekend of 1977.

As in every war, there were winners and losers, and if the winners were to be Britain's eighteen million housewives, the losers were to bracket the entire industry. Sir Leslie Porter: 'Because we wanted Check-out to be successful, I think we went too low on prices and pulled the whole trade down with us. I remember I met Jimmy Goldsmith, of Cavenham's, at the Dorchester about a month after we'd dropped stamps, and he gave me such a punch in the tummy that it nearly killed me. When I asked him what he was on about, he said angrily: "Seven million pounds it's cost me since you've come out of stamps."'

While the multiples and their suppliers had sufficient reserves to weather the price war, however, the smaller independent grocers were not so fortunate. Prevented from dealing in volume turnover, and thus restricted in their bargaining power with manufacturers and distributors, their market share fell by 3% in the twelve months to June 1978, while independent groups such as Mace, and the retail food interests of groups such as Debenhams and British Home Stores also lost market share.

But even as Tesco indulged in a modest anniversary celebration of its achievements, a new generation of sceptics was emerging to ponder whether Check-out had been of any real benefit to the company and whether, for all the evidence, it could continue to hold its newly won custom. From the outset, Porter had stressed that 'we will put the first year's profits at risk and go for turnover, market share being more important than profit in the first phase of Check-out' – though analysts soon forgot his caution when Tesco published its preliminary figures in June 1978. Turnover had risen by a thumping 36%, but pre-tax profits had fallen by 5% (£1.5 million) during the year.

The Jeremiahs had a field day. Was the remedy to Tesco's problems proving worse than the malaise itself? How long could the company continue to discount? In cutting prices, had it cut its own throat? The sense of anticipation was almost palpable, as if the City and the media were only holding their breaths for the latest batch of bad news. When the news came, however, they were to do a precipitate *volte face*.

In February 1979, Tesco's interim results forecast a £37.6 million profit for the year, and as if washed out by some instant detergent, all the old scepticism vanished with the assurance that the board was 'highly satisfied with current trading performance, and anticipates that the budgeted profit will be exceeded, ensuring that this will be a year of record profitability'. This was the stuff of which financial confidence was made, and the opinion was unanimous that Tesco had, indeed, succeeded in metamorphosing itself.

Grieveson Grant: 'What would the pattern of food retailing be like in the UK today without Tesco! It has been at the forefront of developments in food retailing since the Second World War. The supermarket revolution owed much to the group, as did the high street price war. Tesco's dropping of Green Shield trading stamps was a major factor in the intensification of this price competition, allowing Tesco to introduce a strategy through Operation Check-out that resulted in sharp increases in sales, in market share, and in due course, market profitability.

'With improving margins and planned further expansion into higher margin non-foods and into the large superstore type of development, we consider the prospects for Tesco as good. A clear victor in the price war, it has regained and held its marketing initiative at a time of intensive competition. We consider the shares a *buy*.'

The recommendation was hard-won. Since 1974, Grieveson Grant had been among Tesco's foremost critics: four bruising years during which Porter had not only succeeded in retaining investor confidence in face of market hostility, but also in providing his team at Tesco House with the breathing space essential to rethink and to implement a new strategy for the ailing company. Indeed, for the first time in more than forty years, the word 'team' was to become acceptable to the Tesco culture. Until then, it had been little more than a talisman, demanding lip service to disguise the divide-and-rule policies that were central to the Cohen era. Now, however, a new management style was emerging based on the principle of collective responsibility.

This was Arthur Thrush's legacy, though he was no longer present to lay claim to the achievement, having retired in 1973 due to ill health. Nonetheless, the credit was his. While the board had been locked in its struggle for power, careless of the nature of succession, he had succeeded in creating a new generation of management which held that no man was bigger than the company itself. Unquantifiable as it was intangible and thus, possibly, so long alien to Tesco, the practice was to take time to mature. Arguably, however, Check-out was its first proving ground, and may well have been its most enduring achievement.

Ian MacLaurin: 'For the first time in Tesco's history, people began to realise the real value of co-operation. Without it, in fact, I doubt whether Check-out would have been the success that it was. It wasn't just a case of Leslie [Porter] fielding the flak, but also that he allowed the lads to get on with the job of trying to put the company to rights. Of course, getting our profit and loss right counted for a helluva lot, but I think that the most constructive thing we learned was the importance of teamwork; that with it Tesco was unstoppable, but without it ... '

He shrugged, and the sentence remained unfinished, an unspoken reflection on what might have been.

12. CHECK-OUT – AND AFTER

$$1977\text{--}80$$

'The improvement of intuition
is a highly technical matter.'

Daniel Bell
The Coming of Post-Industrial Society (1973)

The miracle was that Tesco survived the success of Check-out. A small miracle, possibly, and a paradoxical one besides, for in highlighting the company's potential, the campaign exposed the weaknesses that bedevilled the entire organisation. Superficially, it ranked among Britain's leading traders, employing some 40,000 men and women in more than 700 stores which, in 1977, generated a turnover of £600 million. The reality, however, was very different, as Check-out revealed.

Oscar Wilde once remarked that nothing fails like success, and in the year following the launch of Check-out the adage came to haunt the Tesco board. Seemingly, there was no halting the company, but while Leslie Porter talked up the prospects for the future, there could be no disguising the immediate, internal crisis caused by the success of the operation. Undoubtedly, the media hype was all very gratifying, but without being able to manage the new business on the ground, it could dwindle as fast as it had grown.

Sir Leslie: 'We had calculated for a 20% increase in turnover, and never imagined that we would almost double that figure. The thing was unprecedented, and that was the trouble. We simply weren't geared up to handle the explosion of new business, and this threw the weaknesses of the company into sharp relief. If we'd got our figures right, we could have coped. As it was ...'

In virtually every operational sector – distribution, buying, marketing, personnel, finance – Tesco was still trading with primitive systems at the launch of Check-out, while the management structure still bore the impress of Jack Cohen. Entrenched at the branch level, and reified by tradition, his penchant for bottom-up management had once served well enough, and there is still a trace of incredulity about Mike Darnell's memories of that once-upon-a-time era: 'Most managers had a cave-age mentality. They all had their own little cave where they could tuck themselves away and make their own little decisions, careless of their impact on the company as a whole.'

Dennis Tuffin, since 1985 a main board director, echoes the sentiment, whilst varying the metaphor: 'Above the managers there were the marauding war lords, the regional managing directors', and as one of Ian MacLaurin's four RMDs during the mid-seventies, he should know: 'I suppose you could say that before 1977 we ran four virtually separate armies. Our store managers were our shock troops, and while we were always aware that the top brass was back there, somewhere, we didn't have a central strategy. All we got from HQ was a few guns and a bit of ammo. Then we had to fight it out for ourselves.'

Seemingly, the buck stopped nowhere, and it was this *laissez-faire* approach by management that Porter and MacLaurin had to change. Compared to this, the trauma of dropping Green Shield was as nothing, for what was demanded of line managers and board alike was a root-and-branch change as much of their attitudes as of their trading practices. In fact, what had begun as little more than a suspicion of the value of stamping had led to a top-down reappraisal of the ethos of the entire company by the second half of 1977.

In the words of the old hucksters, everything had to go, for once begun, the process was inexorable, the examination of individual facets of the business only producing new questions to which answers had to be found if the company was to capitalise on Check-out. One requirement, however, was paramount: the need to concentrate power in order to make sense of the nonsense which had prevailed for too long. All the rest depended upon this. The notion, however, struck at the very heart of the Cohen ethos. It would take time to win the hearts and minds of the old Tesco guard – and time was not on the company's side, as the mounting crisis in its everyday operation revealed.

Taken unprepared, Check-out was threatening to overwhelm its creator. Conceived in response to the company's failing performance, it seemed that the initiative had taken on a life of its own, dictating the entire being of the company and dwarfing its ageing systems with its insatiable demands. Tesco was undoubtedly doing good business; the problem was how to manage it out of outdated shops and with a distribution system that was close to breaking point.

As to the former, it would take time to develop a new generation of stores capable of handling volume turnover cost-effectively. Sir Ian MacLaurin: 'The wage percentage of actually getting the goods into our sub-standard stores, many of them with one or two storeys, went through the roof. They were not designed for the turnover generated by Check-out, and we were just piling goods in and storing them anywhere, then trying to get them down to the shop floor. It was chaos, and the cost was astronomical. What we needed were modern, large stores, but you can't develop those kind of units overnight.'

As to the latter, distribution demanded immediate attention: 'Ultimately our business is about getting our goods to our stores in sufficient quantities to meet our customers' demands. Without being able to do that efficiently, we aren't in business, and Check-out stretched our resources to the limit. Eighty per cent of all our supplies were coming direct from manufacturers, and unless we'd sorted out our distribution problems there was a very real danger that we would have become a laughing stock for promoting cuts on lines that we couldn't even deliver. It was a close-run thing.'

How close is now a matter of legend: of outside suppliers having to wait for up to twenty-four hours to deliver at Tesco's distribution centres; of stock checks being conducted in the open air; of Tesco's four obsolescent warehouses, and the company's transport fleet working to a round-the-clock, seven-day schedule. And as the problems lived off one another, and as customers waited for the emptied shelves to be refilled, so the tailbacks lengthened around the stores, delays of five and six hours becoming commonplace.

Possibly for the first time in its history, the company recognised that it was as much in the business of distribution as of retailing, and that without a speedy resolution to the problems posed by the former, Check-out could well negate all that it had set out to achieve.

What was needed, and urgently, was a shake-out of the entire operation, and as suppliers struggled to restock the company's beleaguered stores, and managers struggled to cope with escalating demand, the board set about laying the foundations of a distribution system capable not only of relieving the short-term pressures but also of catering for future growth.

The statistics behind the crisis were straightforward. In April 1977, Tesco's grocery warehouses were handling some 1.75 million units monthly; by late June, that figure had risen to 2.4 million units – and with turnover continuing to accelerate, Francis Krejsa and his estates department were under orders to locate and open a new distribution centre within twelve weeks. Three weeks later, and having covered more than 4,000 miles in the Midlands area, Krejsa's team had drawn up and signed contracts for a new 100,000-square-foot warehouse at Bletchley, Buckinghamshire, which was operational by early September. Temporarily, the opening relieved pressure on Tesco's other depots, but the gain was only marginal.

In the three months following the launch of Check-out, Tesco's warehouses were operating at 94% capacity, which allowed no room whatsoever for expansion. Bletchley improved the situation to the point where, by the autumn, Tesco's five depots were working to 83% capacity. Against growth projections, however, this was still above tolerable limits, hence the demand for the development of at least two more mechanised depots. Within eighteen months, the target had been achieved, with the opening of a 175,000-square-foot unit at Crick, Northamptonshire, and of a further 126,000-square-foot depot at Milton Keynes, Buckinghamshire.

But this was only a beginning. In fact, like men who had seen the future, and found that it did not work, the board found that the near failure of a key facet of the business concentrated their minds wonderfully on a range of associated problems. And what they found, according to MacLaurin, was 'a real pig's breakfast', not least, of Tesco's buying practices. Whilst the consolidated price structure imposed pre-Check-out had done much to curb the private enterprise of individual managers, the explosion in demand post-Check-out had encouraged its re-emergence: 'I have this vastly increased turnover, so now I am going to have fourteen to the dozen from you, and fifteen to the dozen from you, and thank you very much and good day.'

It was good business as long as it lasted, but it did not last for long. Within days of 9 June, MacLaurin had written to all the company's suppliers, and instructed Daisy Hyams and her buying team that there were to be no more outside deals. Since time immemorial, or so it seemed, Hyams and her number two, Jim Pennell, had been frustrated in their attempts to impose some discipline on the buying function. It was an impossible task. The delegation of power down to the smallest store had consistently mocked their best intentions, a situation compounded by the fact that Cheshunt's own buying operation still bore the imprimatur of Cohen's cavalier practices which were no match for the hard sell of the company's suppliers.

David Malpas: 'The salesmen used to come in and say, "Taste this bean and that bean" and they would go through a bit of a performance with our buyers, and seem to let them make up their minds about the one they really liked. But with such big contracts at stake, these teams of salesmen used to spend weeks planning a visit to Cheshunt. They attended planning meetings and briefing meetings, and would rehearse their sales pitch to perfection. Every possible technique that could be used was used – flattery, cajolery, everything – reinforced by the fact that they knew they were dealing with a very unsophisticated buying operation, whilst they were at the sharp end of a very sophisticated selling operation.'

Individually the problems were bad enough. Collectively they were a formula for chaos, no one knowing exactly what stocks were being held by whom, or where. Jim Pennell: 'We had inadequate stock control systems throughout the business. Until Check-out, managers really looked after themselves, and pretty well stocked what they liked. They were always doing deals on the side, and this played hell with our buying and stock control policies. How could we be expected to rationalise a system when there were 700 or so mini-Cohens outside our control?'

It was time that the past moved over, and under the aegis of the newly established Ways and Means Committee it did. Following a pilot operation in the range rationalisation at the company's Maldon store in Essex, the committee, headed by David Malpas and Jim Pennell, began the exhaustive job of rationalising the entire Tesco range. Initially, managers treated the intentions and the title of the committee as something of a joke (David Malpas: 'Ways and Means was the least charismatic name we could think of, so we thought we'd call ourselves that!'), though not for long. Private enterprise was out, centralised buying was in, with all that entailed for Tesco suppliers and its own line management.

Jim Pennell: 'It wasn't easy. There was such a wide argument about what should be stocked and what shouldn't, that it could only be done by meetings. David started them and he'd begin by saying, "OK, this week we'll talk about beans or soups or whatever." Eventually we'd agree on a short list of so many own label, so many Crosse and Blackwell, and so many of Heinz or HP or whichever brand was the most profitable.'

The result was to stand the old buying practices on their head. Where, previously, the reps had sold into Tesco, Tesco's buying team now dictated their own terms to suppliers.

'Once we'd got a policy thrashed out, it meant that our buyers could go along to HP or whoever and say, "We're looking for the best deal, and it's very important to us. We're going along with our own label and Crosse and Blackwell anyway, but the other brand could be you. Please yourself", and we'd do a deal around that. It took a year to work through our shopping list, but that was the start of the controlled range, and looking back on it I wonder how the devil we'd negotiated when we had no control at all over what the stores were going to stock.'

The answer lies in the history of the deals that Jack Cohen pulled since the days when he first signed up the T. E. Stockwell concession and negotiated the purchase of 500 cases of 'Extra thick, creamy Snowflake'. For half a century, Tesco had traded like its mentor – sharp, certainly; ruthless, often; undisciplined, always – but with the coming of range rationalisation an era came to an end and with it, if coincidentally at first, an increased investment in own label. More than thirteen years had passed since Leslie Porter had begun to develop Tesco's own line of non-food products, but as far as foodstuffs were concerned the company still remained under-represented.

Check-out exposed this weakness, and whilst initially triggered by the need to secure supplies under its own control, the decision to expand into own label was to have far-reaching repercussions. David Malpas: 'To some extent you could say that our own label growth was stimulated by the failure of manufacturers to invest in new products during the inflationary years of the 1970s, and that this created the opportunity for retailers to develop their brands within their own stores independently of the manufacturers. As I say, to some extent this was true, but what really happened was that when we were going through this process of rationalisation, we recognised that here was a tremendous opportunity, because there was no reason why we should spend our time deciding between this brand and that brand, when we could use our own. We couldn't do it before because no one had any control over whether the stuff would be stocked in the branches, but all of a sudden we realised that we had this property, and that we ought to make use of it, and establish our own criteria for quality control.'

During the 1980s, quality control was to become the yardstick of Tesco itself, but during the late 1970s, the company's most urgent problem was trying to sell in its new image out of inadequate and ageing stores. Kreitman had been the first to identify this credibility gap, but it was MacLaurin who took Tesco's case for the development of large stores to the public.

Although long running, the superstore controversy remained a hot one. Since the early 1970s, the issue had wracked both the planning profession and the retail industry, as evidenced by the Glasgow Hypermarket Conference of 1971. In his opening remarks the chairman expressed the hope that the conference 'would enable each of us ... to get a reasonably informed prospect, rather than retrospect, of whether there is a place and if so, what place, for hypermarkets in our pattern of shopping'.

His optimism was unfounded, the subsequent discussion merely confirming the rival factions in their prejudices. A Chamber of Commerce spokesman inveighed against the 'monstrosity' of such schemes; a developer contended that US and Continental evidence had proved their worth; and a Consumer Council spokeswoman conjured up a feeling of 'terror, constriction in my heart, at the mention of anyone coming in with hypermarkets or similar things'.

Half a decade later, with only a handful of large stores having received planning consent, MacLaurin was to adopt a high profile in campaigning for their approval: 'Retailing is in a state of constant change, from the market stall and corner shop, via self-service, to the supermarket. In their time, each met with resistance, yet all eventually gained public acceptance. And I suspect that this is how it will be with what the Department of the Environment are now pleased to call "large stores". Arguably, such units offer significant advantages to the shopping public, not only by eliminating much of the drudgery of convenience shopping, but also by providing quantifiable savings in the shopping basket.'

Although motivated by Tesco's interest, MacLaurin's crusade, involving submissions to both central and local government and the publication of a stream of papers and articles on the subject, was to play an important role in sapping the antagonism of planning authorities to large stores, culminating in the 1977 publication of a Department of the Environment Policy Note which accepted that while such units provided price cuts of up to 10% on foodstuffs, they did not have their long-feared impact on smaller traders in their vicinity.

Although accepted in theory, the practice remained to be realised. Whilst MacLaurin's determination to open dialogue with planners had done much to exorcise old memories, the company only had one large store operational in 1977 (at Irlam, in Lancashire), though there were twenty-eight more on the drawing boards. Francis Krejsa: 'Before Check-out we didn't spend money, it was all about cutting corners, and acquisition decisions were usually made by the chairman, and maybe one of the retail directors, but certainly not on the basis of any sophisticated calculations. Things only started to move when Leslie Porter became chairman, but we had a clear picture of the type of store we needed – single-storey units, with flat car-parking – and in 1979 our development budget exceeded £10 million for the first time.'

The figure shrinks into insignificance compared to the cost of the company's current development programme, but at the time nothing indicated more clearly not only Tesco's growing acceptance by local authorities, but also its commitment to the future. Where formerly short-termism had been the rule, the board under Porter had already set its sights on the 1980s – 'the "Information Technology" decade' as MacLaurin was to call it – to contemplate that 'where retailers formerly traded in goods, today they trade in information'.

Now the notion may be commonplace. Then it commanded the headlines ('Technology the key to the future of retailing' said the *Financial Times*), an indication as much of Tesco's burgeoning reputation as the thinking retailer, as its awareness of the consequences of the ubiquitous 'chip'. As far as the company was concerned, in fact, one thing was becoming increasingly clear: that without the extensive application of advanced systems, the management of large stores would be questionable, if not impossible. In a 1981 paper delivered to a committee of Euro-MPs in Strasbourg, Dr Donald Harris, Tesco's director of computing, pondered the coincidence that the rapid evolution of retailing during the post-war years had been paralleled by the development of increasingly sophisticated systems, from the manual cash register to the micro-chip. He concluded, 'Consider for a moment the phenomenon of the large store, which may carry as many as 16,000 different lines on its shelves, and may handle a turnover of hundreds of thousands of pounds a week – then multiply such figures by the number of stores we have in the group, and you will get some idea of the problems of managing what is so often and so deceptively termed the quiet revolution of retailing.

'Increasingly, such problems turn on the management of information; on handling the extraordinary mass of data carried by the volume business that is retailing today – data on social and economic trends that determine location; data on personnel structures in a rapidly changing employment environment that itself is the product of technological change; and above all else, data about data, about stock control and cash flow and all the rest of the humdrum paper work that is central to the effective management of business.'

During the 1970s, Tesco invested some £100 million in advanced systems, and by the close of the decade the forecast was that the figure would be more than doubled in the decade ahead. Small wonder that Porter continued to emphasise that Tesco would have to forego short-term profit in order to maximise longer-term gains. Not so distantly, the notion would have been unthinkable: to invest in the future was not Cohen's style. The board of the late 1970s, however, knew better, and were quick to appreciate that unless they ploughed back the profits generated by Check-out, they would jeopardise the achievements of the operation itself. June 1977 had exposed the manifold and fundamental weaknesses of the company. Such a situation could not be allowed to occur again.

What applied in general, applied in particular to Tesco's staff. Check-out had done much for their morale, but much still remained to be done. Never tired of referring to retailing as 'a people business',

MacLaurin had recognised from the outset that while providing managers with the support services they needed if they were to run their stores effectively, the new, centralised discipline would lead to resistance at store level. So much was inevitable, for in changing the public's perception of Tesco, Check-out changed the company's perception of itself.

Ian MacLaurin: 'To rationalise it was essential to centralise, a notion that was totally foreign to most of our managers, who had modelled themselves on Jack Cohen. You can't say they were a rabble, because they worked damned hard, but they'd learned their business in a different school, without any discipline. In hindsight, I suppose you could say that our biggest investment after we'd launched Check-out was in our people, and one can't underestimate the enormous job that Dennis [Tuffin] and his team did in teaching them the new rules.'

Not that Tuffin and his team had nothing to sell. The profits generated by Check-out more than compensated for the loss of individual perks, whilst as Dennis Tuffin now says: 'In effect, Cheshunt took over the whole operational role of the company and made it as simple as it could. It provided our people with clear directions on what to display, what to sell, on store layouts, and range rationalisation, everything. Before that it had all been down to store level, but after Check-out the centre provided its managers with the service they needed to run their own stores properly. Ian [MacLaurin] was the architect of the change, and in the end he succeeded.'

Though not painlessly. Jim Pennell: 'It required a lot of bloody-mindedness on Ian's part to see that the job was done. He was happy enough to delegate responsibility, but for two or three years after Check-out he had to lead from the front, to bring on the new team needed to manage the change.'

Distribution, pricing, buying, stock control, development, personnel – once the cat's cradle began to unravel, there could be no going back, no leaving any loose ends which, in the future, could snarl up the works again. When the board voted for Check-out in the early summer of 1977, they can have had little idea where their decision would lead. Then it had simply been a matter of recovering turnover and repositioning Tesco in the market. By the close of the year, virtually every aspect of the business was under review.

Tackling issues piecemeal could only perpetuate the mistakes of the past.

Eighteen months after the launch of Check-out, David Churchill, then retail correspondent of the *Financial Times*, was to reflect on all that this implied: 'As I see it, Check-out was the acid test of a new breed of management. No one really believed that Tesco was capable of acting so consistently and so forcibly, and this scepticism goes a long way to explaining the dilatory response by other retailers to the Tesco initiative. Quite simply, they thought that the company was going to kill itself, and just hung around to see when it would happen. In the event, the success of Check-out and all that followed was a measure of the quality of the new generation of management that had emerged at Cheshunt.'

Significantly, the comment coincided with a note being posted throughout the Tesco group:

GROUP TRAINING – STATEMENT OF POLICY

1. That all new starters will receive off-the-job induction training supervised by a qualified instructor, individually tailored to the specific requirements of each new starter;
2. That all new starters, as appropriate to their requirements, and the requirements of the company, will be trained until they reach a level of efficiency acceptable to the company;
3. That appropriate training will be given to all categories of staff before, or immediately following, promotion;
4. That all employees under the age of eighteen be entitled to a full day release, and that all other employees will be encouraged to undertake courses relevant to the development of their careers.

Once it had been little more than a conceit, lip service to an ideal; now the instructions went out under Porter and MacLaurin's signatures, one more indication of the extent of the company's break with the past. Ian MacLaurin: 'The Old Man may have talked about recruitment and training, but then he always had a vivid imagination. The reality was that until the late seventies, the whole thing was really a lucky dip – if you got any training you were lucky, if not you were dropped straight in the deep end. That was no way to build a company of professionals, and Check-out taught us the need for professionals if we were going to manage the company into the '80s and beyond.'

Whether in public or in private, this was to be the touchstone of his policy – that Tesco was building as much for tomorrow as today – to be iterated and reiterated in innumerable memoranda and papers. In 1976 a conference of London brokers had wondered at the ambition, sceptical of its realisation. By the close of the 1970s, they wondered no longer, for there was growing evidence of the reconciliation between the company's public declarations and its internal methodology. While much still remained to be done, as Porter and MacLaurin were quick to admit, there was no gainsaying the difference that three years, and Check-out, had made.

Where, once, the company had been struggling for existence, Churchill's 'new breed of management' was already reshaping Tesco; where once the company had been something of an also-ran, it was now a retail pacesetter which, in transforming itself, had shaken the entire industry out of the complacent belief that there was no limit to having it so good. For the impact of Check-out reached far beyond Tesco, and not merely as far as the immediate response of the competition was concerned.

In the summer of 1979, Mike Franklin, who had master-minded the Check-out operation for McCann's, considered: 'Until June 1977 the industry was inclined to be very flabby. Four years of continuous inflation, of not knowing how prices would stand from day to day, led first to confusion, and then to the attitude: "To hell with it, we'll just pass on the price rises to the customers and let them sort it out." Check-out put a stop to all that. It checked the industry in its tracks and made it start to think about exactly where it was going and what it was doing. The result was a perceptible tightening-up of attitudes, of trying to rationalise what, for too long, had been irrational.'

Brian Moore, at that time executive editor of *Supermarketing*, agreed: 'The industry had had it too good for too long, and had come to believe that there was no limit to growth. Check-out gave it pause for thought, which led to an overall improvement in the level of retail efficiency, and a shake-up in thinking about what the various sectors of the industry were about. Eventually it would have happened anyway, but Check-out highlighted the situation vividly, and demanded an effective response.'

Just how effective the response was to prove was revealed by retailing's contribution to the government's campaign to contain inflation. In the two years from June 1977, the RPI fell sharply from its previous record levels (from 16.5% in 1975/76, to 11.2% in 1977/78), and while a range of other factors obviously contributed to this achievement, the price war launched by Tesco played a significant role in curbing price rises in the shopping basket.

In itself, the achievement was not unique. Fourteen years before, Cohen had done something similar during his protracted onslaught on Resale Price Maintenance, though with one important difference. Whilst the RPM campaign had been prompted by Cohen's gut reaction to what he had long regarded as a restrictive trading practice, Check-out was based on much more than simply cutting prices and waiting for the profits to roll in. From the outset, Leslie Porter had made that clear, confident that Ian MacLaurin and his team could implement the counter revolution that was to transform Tesco.

In 1973, Professor Daniel Bell had published his bestseller *The Coming of Post-Industrial Society*. Half a decade later, MacLaurin was to take the work as his text for a paper delivered at a retail conference in Zurich, to echo Bell's seemingly paradoxical apophthegm: 'The improvement of intuition is a highly technical matter.' For all his qualities, this was something that Cohen never understood, which was the difference that Check-out made.

13. TOWARDS 2000

1980–90

'No consumer society can exist or expand
without a belief in modernity.'

Neil McKendrick, John Brewer, J. H. Plumb
The Birth of a Consumer Society (1982)

The British share a love–hate relationship with their retailers. There is nothing they like more than to browse around the shops, but as for shopkeepers ... as for shopkeepers, Shakespeare had it right when he wrote that lying becomes none but tradesmen. And so the prejudice is recycled, as absurd as it is deep-rooted, a peculiarly Anglo-Saxon combination of petty bourgeois snobbery allied to nostalgia for a past that never was.

Yet the attitude is as ingrained as the illusion is indelible and if, little more than half a lifetime ago, the critic McQueen Pope was raging against 'the upstarts of trade', then two centuries past Henry Fielding was deploring the tendency of shopkeepers 'to step out from behind their counters and become gentlemen', and so on, back to the time when Aristotle laid down his interdict against trade, and forward to the day when Ian MacLaurin's mother wondered whether he had done the right thing by joining Tesco for 'Surely, they're grocers?'

Apparently the stigma is as ineradicable as its consequences have been pernicious, an insidiously conservative attitude, hostile as much to commerce and industry as to enterprise and innovation. The combination is a powerful one, of prejudice reinforced by moral sanction, as evinced by the recent history of British retailing. More than a century has passed since the French pioneered the department store; more than half a century since the Americans explored the potential first of self-service, then of supermarketing, and later still, of the large store – each of the latter developments meeting with the entrenched resistance of those arbiters of taste, the English middle class, who, in applying the past to the present, trust that the future will not change.

Tesco itself has not always been exempt from this illusion. During its sixty-year history there have been moments when it seemed as if the company was irreparably trapped in a time warp, always a dangerous condition but never more so than during periods of accelerating social, economic and technological change. In the four decades to 1990, the standard of living for the majority of Britain's population rose further and faster than ever before, the result of a revolution in personal expectations far removed from the stricken world of Cohen's apprenticeship.

Indeed, his contempt for this new world, and for the men who managed it, may well have been triggered by fear of what he did not understand, and a longing to retreat into a past that he had controlled so well. That it no longer existed made little difference. To him it remained ineluctable, in contrast to the future that Porter and MacLaurin insisted in talking up.

Even before Check-out, strategic planning was taking its place in the vocabulary of Tesco House, though it sometimes remained difficult to practise what the board was coming hesitantly to pronounce. Old habits die hard and, as if in some terminal spasm, the company mounted two quick take-over bids in the late 1970s – first of 3 Guys in Ireland, then of Cartier, a small Kent-based retailer. Cartier was soon to be integrated into the Tesco structure, but 3 Guys proved more problematic, and was finally sold off in March 1986.

Only one month before, Tesco had made a final break with Victor Value, selling the limited-range Victor Value discount operation to Bejam for £20 million. In the case of both 3 Guys and Victor Value, the aim was straightforward: to concentrate the company's mind solely on its core business of food retailing. As for the rest, all the marginalia that had been acquired down the years, they had no place in the strategy of Tesco House. Since the turn of the 1980s, in fact, the entire thrust of the company had been for clarity of both purpose and image – not least, in the development sector.

While the company's large store programme had made some

headway in the late 1970s, there was still much ground to be made up. Undoubtedly, Francis Krejsa's considered handling of the development programme, allied to MacLaurin's determination to 'open and maintain a constructive dialogue with planners', had done much to overcome local authority hostility, but the legacy of small and antediluvian stores continued to militate against the company's ambition to refurbish its image. At the launch of Check-out, a minimum of three and a maximum of six years had to be allowed between obtaining an outline planning consent and opening a new store. In the meantime …

Ted McFadyen, a long-time authority on British retailing, and for seventeen years editor of *Retail and Distribution Management*: 'Of all the factors that have most affected the grocery sector in the past ten years, possibly the most important has been the move to edge-of-town or out-of-town retailing, and all the things that are consequent upon location. Tesco's major handicap right into the late seventies was the inadequate nature of the stores out of which it was trading.

'It was a punishing liability, and arguably the company's most notable success over the past decade or so has been the key role it has played in formulating a new locational strategy, and then developing a generation of edge-of-town and out-of-town stores to cater for a new shopping public. For a company handicapped as it was, it was a formidable achievement, for it literally transformed the retail landscape.'

And in the process, it transformed Tesco. Between 1977 and 1983, the company closed 371 supermarkets, averaging 3,700 square feet, and opened 97 new stores, averaging 30,000 square feet. Equally important, as noted by the brokers Capel Curie Myers in their review of August 1983, the company's newly established Site Research Unit was bringing a new degree of sophistication to its development programme, further reducing speculative developments by focusing on 'the assessment of local economies and the viability of particular trading sites'.

The good old days, bad old days when Cohen would see a shop in the morning and negotiate its purchase by the afternoon had long gone, and as the store opening programme continued to gather pace (in the five years to 1990, Tesco's development budget totalled £1.3 billion), so its image continued to change.

Some weeks before he died in 1979, Cohen had visited one of the first of the company's new generation of large stores, and had wondered at what he saw. It was an augury of the future, for in less than a decade Tesco had effectively exorcised its past, its new store programme providing it with the means to transform its entire persona.

Sir Ian MacLaurin: 'Ultimately, the physical proportions of a shop determine its trading character. This is not to question the importance of smaller units. We have argued, forcibly, on a large number of occasions that they will continue to play an important role in the shopping hierarchy, not least as far as comparison shopping is concerned. Convenience shopping, however, is another matter.

'In fact, the two demand a totally different approach. What people really enjoy is comparison shopping, being able to browse around in their own time to choose a new dress or suit or a present for their children, while what they want of the convenience sector is for us to take the drudgery out of their weekly shop by providing them with an efficient, modern environment where they know they are obtaining quality goods at competitive prices.'

The formula has served as well for Tesco as for its 8.5 million weekly customers, and not only by upgrading the physical appearance of the company. The rundown and the shabby may have been replaced, but without a comparable improvement in the systems, the service and the stock provided, first impressions would have been negated, and much of the old image remained. As it was, the expanded footage generated by the new store programme provided a platform for Tesco to develop the new in-store image demanded by MacLaurin and his team – in terms of systems, first with article numbering, more recently with electronic points of sale; in terms of service, first with the emphasis on in-house training, more recently with the rapid expansion of the graduate recruitment scheme; in terms of stock ... but this is a story in itself.

When David Malpas and Jim Pennell first set out to rationalise the Tesco range in the aftermath of Check-out, they can have had little idea that their venture would end by helping to transform not only the culture of British retailing, but also Britain's eating habits. In 1978, less than a fifth of Tesco's foodstuff turnover was accounted for by own label, in contrast with its main, targeted competitor, Sainsbury, whose own brands accounted for 56% of their business.

As David Malpas later said, this was a major 'property' for exploitation provided that Tesco never settled for the second best:

'We decided from the start that we would apply a criterion of quality to our own labels. We wouldn't settle for the cheapest bean or the poorest chocolate or the worst soup, and this meant establishing our own benchmarks, on the basis that our own label must compare satisfactorily with the brand leader – and that where there wasn't a brand leader, we would set a benchmark for ourselves.'

For half a century, Tesco had traded with the most rudimentary quality-control techniques. Now all that was to change. As Tesco's turnover in own label rose, up by almost 15% in the five years to 1983, and as its team of food technologists expanded, so the company devoted increasing attention to the state of the art in the food business – a development paralleled by the public's growing concern for healthy eating.

There had been 'food fads' before, notably during the late 1920s, when 'the balanced diet' became *de rigueur* for those able to afford it, but this was something different. In the years between, affluence had become the rule, and by the mid-1970s evidence was already emerging that a growing number of people were beginning to ask increasingly awkward questions about what they ate and why.

This was no temporary phenomenon, an indulgence of cranks, rather a deep-rooted concern with the whole issue of the impact of food upon health. The more penetrating the questions, however, the more ambiguous the replies. At times it seemed that the entire food chain (producers, manufacturers, retailers) was locked in a conspiracy of silence against the consumer – orchestrated by the Ministry of Agriculture, Fisheries and Food. For all its protestations of concern, little substantive information was forthcoming, and matters finally came to a head in 1983 when it was widely rumoured that a report of the National Advisory Committee on Nutrition Education (NACNE) might well be suppressed, reinforcing a growing suspicion that the relationship between MAFF, the Department of Health and the food industry was too close for comfort. Powerful vested interests were at work, determined that the public's right to know should be subject to their approval.

Tesco was to play a crucial role in breaking the impasse. Five years had passed since David Malpas and Jim Pennell's first meeting, five years in which the company's commitment to quality control, allied to the rapid expansion of its food technology division, had transformed Tesco's philosophy towards food retailing. Where once Cohen had been his own food taster, flushing the leftovers down the lavatory; where once, and more recently, the Ways and Means Committee had had to establish its own quality benchmarks, without knowing for certain whether they were realisable, it was now becoming increasingly clear that the company had the capacity to impose its standards on the industry at large.

Seemingly, the hiatus over the NACNE report had done little to convince Whitehall of the public's right to know, least of all as far as nutrition labelling was concerned. True, the issue was a complex one (just what information should be carried on labels, and how could it be best presented?), but there was a growing suspicion that certain parties to the discussion were exploiting the difficulties to delay reaching any positive decisions.

On 9 January 1985, Tesco put an end to the farce when David Malpas launched the 'Healthy Eating' campaign. Frustrated by the talking shop of Whitehall, and convinced of the quality of its products, the company had begun to explore the question of nutrition labelling more than a year before. Market research clearly indicated the growth in public demand for more comprehensive information about what they were being sold – and if the government would not act, then Tesco would.

In a radio interview on the morning of the 9th, David Malpas outlined the thinking behind the programme ('People need to have more information about the foodstuffs they're buying, and to be told why they should change their eating habits'); the content of the programme itself (labelling Tesco's own lines with extended information on their contents; distributing information leaflets on the importance of healthy eating, and carrying specially designed logos on foodstuffs with proven health benefits); and its longer term objectives: 'We're pretty big people in the food industry, and what we hope to do is influence other manufacturers to follow our lead and say, "Look, we're putting more information on packs" so that the whole industry does it, and not just have it as a Tesco initiative.'

For a diminishing band of sceptics cursed with long memories, the initiative appeared as fanciful as it was impudent. Tesco might be many things, but an arbiter of quality, never. And even if realisable, where would it end, this pandering to public opinion – or had people become so churlish as to forget that they should be truly grateful for what they received? Apparently not, for in acknowledging that it was Tesco's lead in adopting nutrition labelling that broke the deadlock, critics such as Dr Tim Lang, Director of the London Food Commission, were quick to point out that providing clear and simple information about food products not only made good moral, but also good business sense.

Even as the opposition set off in belated pursuit of Tesco's lead, however, the board was laying the groundwork for its next initiative. As Ian MacLaurin was to write later: 'The inherent risk of success is that all too often it can induce complacency' – a corrosive condition that had brought the company close to ruin little more than a decade before. It was a mistake that Tesco would not be allowed to repeat – memories of the past were still too close, too astringent for that.

Sir Leslie Porter, who handed over the chairmanship to Ian MacLaurin at the company's Annual General Meeting in 1985, had been right – the future *was* out there, waiting, and the key to success lay in trying to anticipate the shape of tomorrow's world. While always mindful of G. K. Chesterton's advice in *The Napoleon of Notting Hill* about the dangers of playing the game of 'Cheat the Prophet' ('The players listen very carefully and respectfully to all the clever men have to say ... then go and do something else'), increasing stress was nonetheless laid on the need to pre-empt, rather than simply react to the rapidly changing environment of the 1980s.

Following the launch of the Healthy Eating campaign, there could be no question about Tesco's primacy in the field (see Appendix Six). Indeed, the Tesco initiative not only indicated what could be done, given positive thinking, but had also helped to raise public awareness, and stimulate public debate on the question of food and health – an issue that was becoming inextricably linked with the burgeoning green movement. Since the 1960s environmentalists such as René Dubois and Barbara Ward had been warning of the growing vulnerability of Planet Earth, whilst by the early 1970s strategic planners were forecasting that there might, indeed, be a limit to growth. Another decade was to pass, however, before their messages began to penetrate the public's consciousness, for yesterday's Cassandras to become today's gurus.

Doomwatching was no longer out of fashion, and as reports multiplied of the growing threats to the global ecosystem, and governments came to recognise the need for an effective, co-ordinated response, so an increasing number of people began to 'think green'. Ian MacLaurin has always maintained that retailing cannot be divorced from the environment in which it trades, a contention that was forcibly confirmed with the emergence of environmental consciousness during the second half of the 1980s. Dr Richard Pugh, technical director of Tesco: 'There are now so many people who are potentially some form of green consumer – not extreme greens who are anti-consumption, anti-nuclear power, anti-supermarkets, anti-everything – but a paler shade of green, who are pleased to learn that there is something that they can do as individuals, and who Tesco can help to do their bit.'

Disarming in themselves, the words disguise the lead that Tesco was to give and the contribution it was to make towards the emergence of the green consumer in the years following the launch of Healthy Eating. Where previously the issue had been largely confined to small, articulate groups who had been dismissed by the majority for preaching up their fears, Tesco helped to focus the attention not only of the retail sector, but also of the public at large on the impact of the industry on the environment as a whole. For in this, at least, the sceptics had been right, that once begun, there could be no turning back, and as the programme evolved, a natural if not always a seamless progression, it slowly gained a life force of its own.

Dr Pugh: 'Ten years ago, the choice of additive-free products wasn't part of any retailer's vocabulary; five years ago, healthy eating wasn't even on the agenda, and as little as three years ago most people still regarded green politics as something of a fringe issue, though it tied in consistently with everything that Tesco had been doing up to then. That's why I went to the board at Christmas 1988, and suggested that we treat environmentalism in the same way as we had treated Healthy Eating, and add it to our list of reasons why people shop where they do … so that we could be seen as the pro-active retailer on the green issue, as we had been with diet and health.'

So it was that, four years to the day after David Malpas had launched Tesco's Healthy Eating campaign, Richard Pugh unveiled plans for the greening of Tesco. Majoring on the introduction of thirteen new logos designed to co-ordinate information across the spectrum of 'environmentally friendly products', the *Financial Times* wrote: 'Consumers will be able to drive into the company's super-stores, fill up with lead-free petrol, deposit bottles or plastic containers for recycling, and go shopping for ecologically pure products'.

The Times applauded: 'The Tesco decision takes the [environmental] movement a giant step forward ... The emphasis which Tesco is to place on the environmental qualities of its produce will make the mass market inescapably conscious of the cause. Other supermarket chains claim to be already well advanced on the same path. But the new comprehensive labelling policy of Tesco would seem to go further than anyone else has so far ventured.'

Certainly further than David Malpas or Jim Pennell can ever have envisaged that first day they sat down to examine the problems of range rationalisation in the aftermath of Check-out '77. The *Times's* plaudit, however, was only one amongst the many (in October 1989 the company was awarded a five-star rating in the prestigious Green Consumer shopping guide), that reflected as much on the changing culture of the company as on its changing performance.

The statistics are easily quantified, but as David Reid, Tesco's director of finance since 1985, is quick to point out, there is more to the figures than is revealed on a balance sheet: 'There's no question that the company's performance has been impressive, but figures alone tend to disguise the change that has taken place in the whole character of the company. As a case in point, some years ago, one of the main board directors hired a private detective to keep an eye on his deputy, because he thought the man wasn't up to the job. That couldn't happen now, it would be completely out of character. Today we're a team of professionals, and the change in the culture that that implies has had a profound impact on the performance of the entire company.'

And if the 'greening of Tesco' reflected this shift at one level, so the acquisition of Hillards, a Yorkshire-based retail group, in the spring of 1987 did at another. Indeed, for students of retailing, it provides a graphic illustration of just how extensive the changes in Tesco have been. In the two decades to 1970, the company had grown as much by acquisition as by organic expansion, buccaneering forays inspired as much by Cohen's predatory nature as by sound business practices. The results may have gratified his rapine instincts, though each posed problems of varying degrees of intensity to the parent company.

The Hillards operation was to lay the past, and confirm that Tesco had finally reached maturity. Contrasted with the hit-and-run practices of the 1960s, the acquisition was mounted with text-book precision based on a careful appraisal of the market, matched by what the *Guardian* described as a 'lesson in takeover tactics'. David Reid: 'A small, multi-disciplinary team spent six months analysing every aspect of Hillards' performance. At first there were considerable doubts about its potential, but the more work we did, the more positive we became. In 1987, the company was forecasting a profit of some £10 million. We estimated that we could triple this figure within two or three years.'

It was only when this detailed undercover study was complete that bid plans began to be finalised, in consultation with the Tesco bankers, County, and brokers, UBS Phillips and Drew. Anticipating that the bid would be hard-fought, a strategy was devised that would not only enable Tesco to lift the level of its offer but also continually to refine its major selling platform, based on contrasting the vulnerability of Hillards ('The competition will not allow Hillards the time to reposition itself in the market ... We do not believe that Hillards will be able to compete effectively on its own'), against the innate strengths of Tesco ('Tesco has one of the strongest retail brands in the country ... This will secure the future of Hillards business.')

In the weeks following the launch of the offer in March, a four-man team from Tesco House made thirty presentations to City institutions. As foreseen, Hillards, a public company, but with the family still holding a 30% shareholding, fought doggedly to retain its autonomy. But by the first week of May, having raised its offer to 342.6p in cash for each Hillards Ordinary share, Tesco held 54% of the company's stock.

David Reid: 'It is the only hostile bid in the grocery business ever to have been won, and in the end it was the research effort that we had put into planning the takeover that resulted in our success. It was not only that it provided us with a clear indication of the potential of the company' (and as forecast, profits had tripled by 1990) 'but also that it supplied us with the essential background material needed to make our case.'

The outcome would have delighted Cohen. Hillards added a further forty-four stores in prime sites in south Yorkshire and the east Midlands where previously Tesco had been under-represented. But the methodology would have confounded him. The sheer professionalism of the exercise indicated the metamorphosis that had taken place within Tesco, which City editors finally and fulsomely recognised with the publication of the company's half-year report in September 1990. In the face of longstanding press suspicion that the new Tesco was not quite what it seemed, rather a figment of marketing hype, there could be no gainsaying media coverage of the figures which showed a 19% increase in turnover to £2.8 billion, dividends per share up by 21%, and the fifth consecutive year in which pre-tax profits showed a 25% compound growth rate.

The headlines were celebratory – 'Tesco passes the retail test with flying colours' (*The Times*), 'Vino Tesco is the toast for fine food shoppers' (*Daily Express*), 'Tesco a hard rival to counter' (*The Independent*), 'Tesco cashes in on quality' (*Daily Telegraph*) – but it was Roger Cowe of the *Guardian* who captured the essence of the change:

'A decade ago, Tesco was the modern equivalent of a music-hall joke. But now it is Tesco which is laughing – all the way to the bank. The headline figures for the first half of the year exaggerate Tesco's performance because of property profits, but the underlying trend still shows rising sales and rising margins.

'It was only at the end of the seventies that Tesco began discarding the "stack it high, sell it cheap" philosophy on which the chain had been built ... Then Tesco discovered what much of British industry has been learning: that people are often prepared to pay for better quality, are often concerned more with service than with price, and that there's often more profit in worrying about quality and service than in bribing customers with low prices ... The transformation of Tesco is a remarkable success story.'

The sense of pride in the company was almost palpable. The past had finally been laid. Yet the Tesco board know better than most that success is a fickle commodity, and even as the figures were being published, MacLaurin was pondering the relevance of the achievements of the eighties to the demands of the decade that lies ahead:

'I suppose the most important thing is to distinguish between a company that is simply large, and one that is excellent. The former applied once, but no longer. Inevitably, it takes time to turn a company the size of Tesco around, and not just in image terms. Ultimately, I suppose the whole thing has turned on transforming our own people's outlook towards the firm. Without this, Tesco would have remained much what it was – large, certainly; excellent, well … '

An interrogatory pause, and then: 'In fact, you could say that we've all been on long learning curve, and are still at it today. Which is why I'm confident about the future. I don't think any successful company can have room for closed minds, least of all in retailing. I've always said that we're in the people business, and in the past ten years we've come to realise that our own people are our most valuable resource, all 83,000 of them, and, not least, our board. If there are any tributes to be handed out, they should go to David Malpas and Dennis Tuffin, Mike Darnell, John Gildersleeve, David Reid, and more recently, Mike Wemms, together with our non-executive directors, led by Victor Benjamin. They're the ones who have managed the turn around, and made Tesco what it is today, a company motivated by excellence … '

Again the pause, then almost as an aside: 'But even excellence isn't immutable. It's changing all the time.'

So much for the metamorphosis of culture. Although the most intangible of the commodities in which Tesco trades, it remains the arbiter of the company's performance. Once there could be no question about the value system that motivated Tesco – Cohen saw to that. And no question, either, that without his single-minded dedication to the company, Tesco would long since have joined that forgotten company of traders who set out their stalls in the years immediately following the First World War – to perish in the ruthless business that is retailing.

But ruthless as it still is, the culture of the business is changing, and it is arguable that Tesco is as much the precursor as the product of such change. Again, the superficialities are there for all to see – the sophisticated stores, the quality merchandise, the advanced systems, the skilled management – all parts of an image of Tesco far removed from the rambunctious days of piling it high and selling it cheap. Even these are only a reflection of the fundamental change that has taken place in the company's attitude towards itself in the past decade which, in its turn, has had an impact on the industry at large.

It was not so much that Tesco shook retailing out of its apathy with the launch of Check-out; that it played a seminal role in transforming the public's attitude towards large stores; or even that the company's healthy eating and environmental initiatives played a conspicuous part in concentrating the mind of retailers on issues which, until then, too many of them had preferred to ignore – it was all this, and much more. Never notable either for its capacity for thinking long, or for its regard for anything other than its immediate returns, Tesco had compelled the industry to consider both.

What in the mid-1970s may have been little more than fine words have, in the years between, been given substance, for Tesco to become recognised as 'the thinking retailer' – though MacLaurin is the first to disclaim any notion of prescience. In an interview in *The Times* in September 1988, he said, 'there are no absolutes in the game of strategic planning, but as Tesco has learned, this does nothing to diminish its importance. In fact, without the capacity to interpret the shifts that are taking place in the world around us, all the internal changes we have made (the development of new stores, the selection and training of staff, the application of advanced systems, the creation of a new identity) would have been placed in jeopardy.'

Indeed, as Tesco have indicated, profits and social considerations are not necessarily incompatible. On the contrary, even when measured by the bottom line, the dynamic that 'Tesco cares' as much for the future as the present has contributed, significantly, to the emergence of the company as the UK's foremost retailer.

For MacLaurin, knighted for his services to industry in 1989, the shift is simply epitomised: 'Where once it was a case of all against the rest, today Tesco is a team.' As with culture, Slasher Jack would have made short shrift of the word. An individualist to the end, and as cavalier with personal feelings as he was robust in his business dealings, it is perhaps no coincidence that the new culture only emerged to become the motivating force in Tesco following his death in 1979.

Arguably it is only in the past decade that Tesco has come of age, developing a corporate identity that provides it with both the team and the dynamic to do business in the future that is waiting out there. Culture, an intangible commodity? Perhaps not, after all, for in its sixty-year history, the word has been transformed in the lexicon of Tesco and, in the process, has transformed Tesco itself.

APPENDIX ONE

Offer Document, 1947

A copy of this Offer for Sale has been delivered to the Registrar of Companies for Registration.

Application will be made forthwith to the Council of The Stock Exchange, London, for quotation for the whole of the issued Share Capital of the Company.

The List of Applications will open at 10 a.m. on Friday, 19th December, 1947, and will close on the same day.

TESCO STORES (HOLDINGS) LIMITED

(Incorporated under the Companies Act, 1929.)

SHARE CAPITAL
Authorised, Issued and Fully Paid.
£300,000 in 1,200,000 Shares of 5s. each.

Neither the Company nor any of its Subsidiary or Sub-Subsidiary Companies have any Debentures, Mortgages or Loan Capital outstanding.

OFFER FOR SALE OF
250,000 Shares of 5s. each at 15s. per Share
PAYABLE IN FULL ON APPLICATION.
Applications must be for a minimum of 50 Shares or multiples of 50 Shares.

Directors:
JOHN EDWARD COHEN, 27, Chessington Avenue, London, N.3, *Chairman*.
(Chairman and Managing Director, Tesco Stores Limited and J. E. Cohen & Co. Limited.)
THOMAS EDGAR FREAKE, 15, Pasture Close, North Wembley, Middlesex.
(Assistant Managing Director, Tesco Stores Limited.)
HYMAN KREITMAN, 16, Lytton Close, London, N.2 (Executive Director, Tesco Stores Limited and
J. E. Cohen & Co. Limited).
ARTHUR ALBERT CARPENTER, 30, Newington Green, London, N.16 (Director and Secretary,
Tesco Stores Limited and J. E. Cohen & Co. Limited).

Auditors:
FRANK A. COOPER & CO., 21, Copthall Avenue, London, E.C.2, *Accountants and Auditors*.
HOGG, BULLIMORE & CO., River Plate House, Finsbury Circus, London, E.C.2, *Chartered
Accountants*.

Bankers:
MIDLAND BANK LIMITED, Old Town Hall, Mare Street, Hackney, London, E.8.

Brokers:
ARTHUR AMAN & CO., 19, Great Winchester Street, London, E.C.2, and The Stock Exchange,
London.

Solicitors:
EDWARD MONTAGUE LAZARUS & SON, 10, Queen Street, Mayfair, London, W.1.
SLAUGHTER AND MAY, 18, Austin Friars, London, E.C.2.

Secretary and Registered Office:
HENRY JOHN HEDGES, F.C.C.S., Tesco House, Angel Road, Edmonton, London, N.18.
Registrars and Transfer Office:
COPTHALL REGISTRARS LIMITED, 21, Copthall Avenue, London, E.C.2.

MIDLAND BANK LIMITED, New Issue Department, Poultry, London, E.C.2, are authorised as Bankers for and on behalf of the Vendor, Mr. John Edward Cohen, to receive applications for the purchase from him of the 250,000 Shares now offered for sale.

Applications from employees of and suppliers to the Operating Companies, if made on the special forms provided, will receive preferential consideration.

Letters of Acceptance will be renounceable and the Shares will be registered free of stamp duty and registration fees in the names of the ultimate purchasers provided that Letters of Acceptance, with the Registration Application Forms duly completed, are lodged with Midland Bank Limited, New Issue Department, Poultry, London, E.C.2, not later than 6th February, 1948.

Acceptances of applications will be conditional upon the Council of The Stock Exchange, London, granting quotation not later than 12th January, 1948, for the whole of the issued Share Capital of the Company. Moneys paid in respect of such applications will be returned if quotation is not granted on or before such date and, in the meantime, will be retained in a separate account.

PARTICULARS

HISTORY.—The Company was incorporated in England as a Private Company on 27th November, 1947 (converted into a Public Company on 12th December, 1947), with the objects set out in its Memorandum of Association and in particular with the object of acquiring the whole of the issued Share Capitals of Tesco Stores Limited and J. E. Cohen & Co. Limited, which companies respectively own the whole of the issued Share Capitals of Railway Nurseries (Cheshunt) Limited and Edmonton Packers Limited.

The following are particulars of the four above-named Companies which are all Private Companies:-

(1) Tesco Stores Limited, which was incorporated in England on 28th January, 1932, and has an issued Share Capital of £1,425 divided into 1,425 fully paid Shares of £1 each, carries on the business of retail grocers and provision stores. This company is the owner of the widely known Trade Mark "Tesco."

(2) J. E. Cohen & Co. Limited, which was incorporated in England on 24th January, 1933, and has an issued Share Capital of £10,000 divided into 10,000 fully paid Shares of £1 each, operates a wholesale grocery business and supplies Tesco Stores Limited and the trade generally.

(3) Edmonton Packers Limited, which was incorporated in England on 3rd February, 1939, and has an issued Share Capital of £1,000 divided into 1,000 fully paid Shares of £1 each, carries on the business of food manufacturers and packers, the turnover of which for the current year will exceed £130,000.

(4) Railway Nurseries (Cheshunt) Limited, which was incorporated in England on 12th November, 1942, and has an issued Share Capital of £9,750 divided into 9,750 fully paid Shares of £1 each, carries on the business of Nurserymen at present consisting of the growing of cucumbers and tomatoes, which latter are supplied to the Tomato (Primary Distributors) Association Limited for sale to the trade generally.

Tesco Stores Limited was formed to take over the business originally started by Mr. J. E. Cohen shortly after he was demobilised from the forces at the end of the first world war and its progress constitutes one of the outstanding successes of the grocery trade. From very small beginnings the business greatly expanded and, up to the outbreak of the second world war, Tesco Stores Limited was steadily acquiring new branches from which to operate its business. During the war years expansion was necessarily restricted, but Tesco Stores Limited now operates over 100 retail branches mainly in London and the Home Counties, and new branches are being acquired from time to time as and when opportunities are presented; the number of its registered customers is now approximately 100,000. By the beginning of 1939 the business of Tesco Stores Limited and of J. E. Cohen & Co. Limited had grown to such an extent that it was felt desirable to create a separate organisation for the manufacture and packing (hitherto undertaken by J. E. Cohen & Co. Limited) of the group's own lines of food products, the majority of which are marketed under the name "Banquet," and Edmonton Packers Limited was accordingly formed for this purpose. The continued development of the group led, in 1942, to the formation of the fourth operating company, Railway Nurseries (Cheshunt) Limited, with the ultimate object (not at present fully attainable owing to continued food controls) of enabling the group to grow and market directly its own nursery produce.

APPENDIX TWO
Trading Performance, 1938–46

J. E. COHEN AND CO. LTD

	£ Gross Profit	£ Net Profit
31 December 1938	37,919–17–7	12,624–18–10
31 December 1939	51,198–18–3	30,929–19–1
31 December 1940	53,724–12–8	24,601–10–9
31 December 1941	60,177–19–6	29,913–8–6
31 December 1942	73,946–1–8	39,309–7–6
31 December 1943	62,511–11–6	30,540–15–3
31 December 1944	54,518–7–0	24,279–16–10
31 December 1945	59,713–16–6	27,287–8–1
31 December 1946	67,896–5–11	34,216–3–10

TESCO STORES LTD

	£ Gross Profit	£ Net Profit
31 December 1938	105,600–3–11	19,211–18–8
31 December 1939	125,383–4–0	27,760–14–8
31 December 1940	130,276–4–0	31,622–17–11
31 December 1941	131,767–1–8	33,347–12–5
31 December 1942	123,355–15–7	22,632–10–3
31 December 1943	132,934–8–7	31,121–11–4
31 December 1944	130,364–19–2	24,215–11–1
31 December 1945	145,806–4–11	32,216–12–10
31 December 1946	163,507–14–3	33,424–17–4

APPENDIX THREE
McKinsey Report, 1970

Sir John Cohen, President   March 9, 1970
Tesco (Holdings) Limited
Tesco House
Delamare Road
Cheshunt
Herts

Dear Sir John:

I enclose a memorandum <u>Role and Composition of the Holdings Board </u>which develops our conclusions and recommendations on the role and composition of the Holdings Board. Specifically, we are suggesting three changes which we think can make the Holdings Board more effective in carrying out its role of providing guidelines for the future growth and development of Tesco. These are that the Holdings Board should:

- Exercise more self discipline in interpreting its role and conducting its meetings

- Assign to a Chief Executive's Committee (which would become the chief operating committee on appointment of a new Chief Executive) responsibility for day-to-day operating performance

- Include additional outside directors to provide fresh viewpoints and advice.

Once you have had a chance to read and digest the enclosed memorandum, I should like to get together to discuss your reaction and, specifically, if you agree that these are areas which are important.

I'll give you a call in the next couple of days in order to make arrangements for a discussion.

Yours sincerely,

J. L. Fisher

ROLE AND COMPOSITION OF THE HOLDINGS BOARD

TESCO STORES (HOLDINGS) LIMITED

This memorandum describes our conclusions and recommendations on the role and composition of the Holdings Board (both now and after the appointment of a new Chief Executive). These conclusions are based on discussions we have had with members of the Holdings Board and on our own observations over the last few months.*

In summary, we have concluded that if the Board is to improve its effectiveness in carrying out its main role of determining the future of Tesco, it must make a number of changes in the way it operates and in its membership.*

1. It should exercise more self-discipline in interpreting its role and conducting its meetings.

2. It should assign to a Chief Executive's Committee (which would become the chief operating committee on appointment of a new Chief Executive) responsibility for day-to-day operating performance.

3. It should include additional outside directors, to provide fresh viewpoints and advice.

EXERCISE
MORE SELF-DISCIPLINE

At present, the Board does not fulfil its functions in the most disciplined manner. This weakness arises for two main reasons. First, the distinction between the responsibilities of the Board, the Chairman, and the Chief Executive is not at all clear, so that the Board tends to concern itself with issues that should be dealt with by the Chairman or the Chief Executive. Second, the Board does not conduct its meetings on a formal, systematic basis.

We believe the Board can overcome these shortcomings and thereby improve its effectiveness by:

- Concentrating at its meetings only on matters that are really its concern

- Formalizing the preparation for and conduct of its meetings.

Concentrate on Board Matters

Confusion about the exact role of the Board has resulted in its dealing with day-to-day issues that are more properly the responsibility of the Chairman or the Chief Executive. For example:

---

* The requirements we discuss in this memorandum are additional to the usual legal and statutory requirements of a Board of Directors.

- Purchase tax registration for food warehouses
- Company car policy
- Purchase of Heldrew Engineering offices
- Sale of Cadena property
- Sales of surplus properties
- Responsibilities of Holdings Board executive directors for transport, etc.
- Day-to-day Green Shield stamp responsibility.

The Board should not be spending its valuable time on issues of this kind, which could, and should, have been dealt with at lower levels of the organization. It should be concentrating on matters on which only the Board is qualified to take decisions, i.e.,

1. Setting long-term objectives for growth in turnover and profits, and translating them into agreed annual objectives for the Chief Executive, e.g., growth in turnover of 35 per cent for the next year and in profits of 25 per cent

2. Reviewing quarterly performance of individual divisions against agreed budgets, and providing guidelines and instructions for the Chief Executive where changes or improvements in performance are required

3. Deciding Tesco financial policy concerning, e.g., leasehold versus freehold, alternative methods of raising money, the annual dividend

4. Reviewing (a) performance of individual members of Tesco top management down to the level of executives reporting to the Chief Executive, (b) Tesco remuneration policy covering pay and performance, and (c) senior executives' salaries over, e.g., £8,000 a year

5. Agreeing changes in organizational structure, appointments at top-level management, i.e., positions reporting to the Chief Executive, and succession policy in relation to executives and directors

6. Reviewing and agreeing major proposed diversification efforts such as out-of-town shopping centres and chemists' shops, and major capital expenditure projects, e.g., those above £250,000

7. Ensuring that appropriate reports on Tesco performance are given to shareholders

8. Reviewing and negotiating proposed mergers and acquisitions on behalf of the shareholders, covering terms, offers, etc.

9. Agreeing additions to or resignations from the Holdings Board, and reviewing compensation to the Chairman and to Holdings Board members.

These activities, we believe, constitute the main role of the Holdings Board.

Formalize Preparation for
And Conduct of Board Meetings

The second area in which the Board (and the Chairman) should introduce more discipline is in the way it prepares for and conducts its meetings.

- It is not formally prepared for taking decisions

  - It rarely receives completed staff work, e.g., position papers, for review before Board meetings

  - The Chairman typically does not vet the agenda before it is distributed to ensure that the Board deals only with appropriate matters.

- Meetings are sometimes called at short notice, without proper preparation.

- The Board tends to be diverted easily into discussing issues that should not be discussed at Board level, thus wasting members' valuable time.

- The Board appears to waver in its decision making, thereby creating the impression that it favours compromise rather than firmness, and causing confusion among executives down the line who have not heard the discussions that may have led logically to a change of mind.

The Holdings Board, through the Chairman, should deal with issues firmly and decisively. Once they have been agreed in the Board meetings, responsibility for follow-up should be assigned to an individual Board member. When the Board is reviewing issues that concern other members of Tesco who are not members of the Holdings Board, they should be brought into the discussions. Finally, the Holdings Board, and the Chairman, should be seen to be passing over responsibility to executives down the line, such as agreeing significant authority levels in Store Development.

The Chairman will lead the Board in carrying out its responsibilities. He must therefore ensure that each member of the Board understands and accepts that his role as their leader is to:

1. Ensure that relationships between the Board and executive management, particularly the Chief Executive, are defined, under-

stood and followed (see next section on Chief Executive Committee)

2. Decide which questions of policy should be resolved by

   - The Chief Executive and line management

   - The Board

   - The Chairman unilaterally, e.g., when they are too urgent to wait for a full Board review

3. Ensure that proper staff work is carried out before issues are raised or discussed at Board level, so that the Board is given the information it needs to make decisions, and to arrange, where appropriate, for positions papers to be distributed in advance of Board meetings

4. Ensure that issues that arise in specific Board meetings but that are not the prerogative of the Board are either delegated to the Chief Executive or one of the other executive directors on the Board, or given to the appropriate staff department for review and resolution

5. Communicate effectively and properly, not only with the Board and executive managers, but with employees and the general public.

* * *

To start the process of improvement, he should institute the following steps now, and continue to take them as a matter of course for all future meetings.

1. Review the agenda prior to Board meetings so that the Board, as a matter of principle, deals only with areas within its own jurisdiction

2. Ensure that, where appropriate, proper staff work is reviewed with members of the Board in advance of meetings, so that they are properly informed and able to take decisive action (he may delegate this step to a subordinate)

3. Ensure that, in Board meetings, issues are dealt with quickly by assigning responsibility to executive directors or to other staff members for review and follow-up.

Finally, the Holdings Board should review the frequency of Board meetings, to determine whether it could be reduced from monthly to quarterly to coincide with the review of quarterly figures (particularly if the Board adopts our recommendation below to form a Chief Executive's Committee).

ASSIGN DAY-TO-DAY RESPONSIBILITY TO
A CHIEF EXECUTIVE'S COMMITTEE

We have pointed out above that the Holdings Board is not a proper forum for review of detailed operating performance and for decision making on day-to-day operating issues. Using it in this way, as at present, blurs the distinction between the responsibilities of the Chief Executive and those of the Holdings Board in respect of profit and turnover performance. Moreover, the Holdings Board does not contain the expertise needed to make day-to-day operating decisions, and we believe that bringing other executives onto the Board to provide this expertise would further blur this distinction.

We have already stated that the Chief Executive should be responsible for day-to-day operating issues and performance. At present, however, he lacks the formal mechanism he needs for obtaining sound and experienced advice on these matters. Tesco should therefore form a Chief Executive's Committee* designed to provide him with sound guidance and advice and to replace existing boards of subsidiaries. Establishing such a committee would have a number of benefits.

- It would provide a basis for involving important non-members of the Holdings Board in the policy-making process.

- It would ensure that executives and key operating officers are involved in decision making and that their advice and expertise was at least taken into account by the Chief Executive.

- It would, in the short term, be a basis for reviewing and agreeing on project team work, and, longer term, could provide a basis for the new Chief Executive's review process.

- It would meet the criticism that the Holdings Board does not take down-the-line people into its confidence when it would be desirable to do so.

- It would ensure that executives down the line feel fully committed to and convinced of the desirability of change.

- It would demonstrate conclusively to executives down the line that the Holdings Board is in fact turning over responsibility in line with its agreed responsibilities.

- It would reduce the importance of the subsidiaries, which should continue to exist only to provide the basis for titles for external use by present titleholders.**

---

* Throughout this section we have called this forum the Chief Executive's Committee. To give it both prestige and effectiveness, however, it may be desirable to entitle it the Holdings Board Executive Committee. Such a name would reinforce the importance of the Committee by attaching the Holdings Board name to it, and also give prestige and status to the members of the Committee.

** It has been agreed previously that no further appointments will be made to the boards of subsidiary companies.

APPENDIX FOUR
Severance Letter to Green Shield, 1977

Mr G. R. F. Tompkins,   8th May 1977
Chairman,
Green Shield Trading Stamp Co. Ltd.,
Green Shield House,
Station Rd.,
Edgware, Middx,
HA8 7AQ.

Dear Mr Tompkins

It is with regret that I write to inform you that my Board has instructed me to state that in the light of the failure to agree terms for the continuation of the trading relationship between our respective companies, we have no alternative but to confirm that the existing agreement with your company will be permitted to expire on the 7th June 1977.

In the intervening period we will, of course, continue to observe the terms in our Agreement and in order that we might do so without incurring the risk of an under-estimate of our trading stamp requirements we would be grateful if you would agree to the stamps acquired by us in that period, or already in our possession, being regarded as purchased on a sale or return basis.

You can, of course, rely on our co-operation in allowing your staff into our stores on Saturday 4th June or after the Jubilee holiday for the purpose of collecting unused saver books and catalogues.

L. Porter
Chairman

APPENDIX FIVE
Ten-Year Record, 1980–9

Year ended February
Results £m
Turnover excluding VAT

Operating profit
Operating margin[2]
Interest receivable less payable

Profit before property profits, employee profit sharing and taxation
Property profits

Profit before employee profit sharing and taxation
Net margin[2]
Employee profit sharing

Profit before taxation
Taxation

Profit after taxation

Earnings per share[3]
Fully diluted earnings per share (excluding property profits)[3]
Dividends per share[4]

Productivity £
Turnover per employee[5]
Profit per employee[5]
Wages per employee[5]
Weekly sales per sq ft[6]

Retail Statistics
Market share in food and drink shops[7]
Number of stores
Total sales area – '000 sq ft
Sales area opened in year – '000 sq ft
Average store size (sales area) – sq ft
Average sales area of stores opened in the year – sq ft
Full-time equivalent employees[3]

Notes
[1] 53 week period.
[2] Based upon turnover exclusive of value added tax.
[3] Adjusted in respect of 1985 rights issue and 1987 capitalisation issue.
[4] Adjusted in respect of 1987 capitalisation issue.

1980	1981[1]	1982	1983	1984	1985	1986	1987[1]	1988 Restated	1989
1,530.6	1,820.7	1,994.4	2,276.5	2,594.5	3,000.4	3,355.3	3,593.0	4,119.1	4,717.1
39.7	51.3	51.5	60.6	68.9	81.7	104.1	147.7	214.4	276.5
2.6%	2.8%	2.6%	2.7%	2.7%	2.7%	3.1%	4.1%	5.2%	5.9%
(3.2)	(15.7)	(8.8)	(7.1)	(1.5)	(0.4)	18.8	21.4	15.3	2.4
36.5	35.6	42.7	53.5	67.4	81.3	122.9	169.1	229.7	278.9
0.4	20.0	24.0	7.7	5.6	9.6	8.3	9.4	6.6	10.7
36.9	55.6	66.7	61.2	73.0	90.9	131.2	178.5	236.3	289.6
2.4%	3.1%	3.3%	2.7%	2.8%	3.0%	3.9%	5.0%	5.7%	6.1%
–	–	–	–	–	–	–	2.6	10.7	13.6
36.9	55.6	66.7	61.2	73.0	90.9	131.2	175.9	225.6	276.0
(1.4)	(5.5)	(12.0)	(11.5)	(25.1)	(13.2)	(47.4)	(56.9)	(75.1)	(89.7)
35.5	50.1	54.7	49.7	47.9	59.7	83.8	119.0	150.5	186.3
3.51p	4.93p	5.40p	4.88p	4.67p	5.79p	7.03p	9.51p	10.69p	12.35p
–	–	–	3.96p	3.83p	4.54p	5.84p	8.05p	9.66p	11.32p
0.82p	0.85p	1.00p	1.17p	1.37p	1.62p	1.93p	2.43p	2.85p	3.50p
38,398	46,913	49,341	56,384	64,279	71,404	77,227	79,386	82,067	89,449
996	1,322	1,274	1,501	1,707	1,944	2,396	3,263	4,272	5,243
3,478	4,401	4,731	5,227	5,800	6,304	6,907	7,355	7,809	8,695
5.10	5.57	5.75	6.32	7.10	8.26	9.14	10.23	11.00	11.51
N/A	N/A	N/A	5.9%	6.2%	6.6%	6.7%	7.1%	7.6%	8.2%
552	554	544	489	461	441	395	337	379	374
6,210	6,840	7,203	7,425	7,362	7,415	7,502	6,997	8,220	8,542
524	747	532	584	241	352	568	432	655	557
11,200	12,300	13,200	15,200	16,000	16,800	19,000	20,800	21,700	22,800
16,500	32,500	31,000	33,400	25,300	36,800	37,100	34,900	34,300	34,800
39,862	38,809	40,421	40,377	40,363	42,020	43,447	45,260	50,192	52,742

[5] Based on full-time equivalent number of employees, turnover exclusive of value added tax and operating profit.
[6] Based on weighted average sales area and turnover inclusive of value added tax.
[7] Based on Department of Trade and Industry data.
[8] Based on average number of full-time equivalent employees in the United Kingdom.

APPENDIX SIX
UK Grocers' Market Shares

	83/84 %	84/85 %	85/86 %	86/87 %	87/88 %
Tesco	11.3	12.0	12.5	13.1	14.0
J. Sainsbury	11.7	12.3	12.8	13.5	13.9
Dee	4.2	7.7	12.2	11.1	11.5
Argyll					
Presto etc	5.0	5.7	5.7	5.7	6.1
Safeway	3.0	3.2	3.6	3.9	4.6
Asda	7.2	7.4	7.5	7.4	7.6
Co-op	13.8	13.3	13.3	12.4	12.1

APPENDIX SEVEN
The Board, 1948–89

1948 J. E. Cohen (Chairman)
    T. E. Freake
    H. Kreitman
    A. A. Carpenter
    H. J. Hedges (Secretary)

1949 J. E. Cohen (Chairman)
    H. Kreitman
    A. A. Carpenter
    H. J. Hedges (Secretary)

1950 J. E. Cohen (Chairman)
    H. Kreitman
    A. A. Carpenter
    H. J. Hedges (Secretary)

1951 J. E. Cohen (Chairman)
    H. Kreitman
    A. A. Carpenter
    E. R. Collar
    H. J. Hedges (Secretary)

1952 J. E. Cohen (Chairman)
    H. Kreitman
    E. R. Collar
    A. A. Carpenter (Secretary)

1953 J. E. Cohen (Chairman)
    H. Kreitman
    E. R. Collar
    A. A. Carpenter (Secretary)

1954 J. E. Cohen (Chairman)
    H. Kreitman
    E. R. Collar
    A. A. Carpenter (Secretary)

1955 J. E. Cohen (Chairman)
    H. Kreitman
    A. A. Carpenter
    S. Berzin
    E. R. Collar
    C. W. Wales (Secretary)

1956 J. E. Cohen (Chairman)
    H. Kreitman
    A. A. Carpenter
    S. Berzin
    E. R. Collar
    D. Behar
    C. W. Wales (Secretary)

1957 J. E. Cohen (Chairman and
    Joint Managing Director)
    H. Kreitman (Joint Managing
    Director)
    A. A. Carpenter
    S. Berzin
    E. R. Collar
    C. W. Wales (Secretary)

1960 J. E. Cohen (Chairman and
    Joint Managing Director)
    H. Kreitman (Joint Managing
    Director)
    Leslie Porter
    David Behar rejoins the board
    E. R. Collar
    C. W. Wales (Secretary)

1961 J. E. Cohen (Chairman)

E. R. Collar (Vice Chairman)
Isaac Judah Klug
Hyman Kreitman
Leslie Porter
Frederick Albert Turner
Arthur Thrush
Laurence Don (Company
  Secretary)

1962 J. E. Cohen (Chairman)
E. R. Collar (Vice Chairman)
Hyman Kreitman
Leslie Porter
David Behar
Arthur Thrush
Laurence Don (Company
  Secretary)

1963 J. E. Cohen (Chairman)
Hyman Kreitman (Vice
  Chairman)
Leslie Porter
David Behar
Arthur Thrush
Laurence Don (Company
  Secretary)

1964 J. E. Cohen (Chairman)
Hyman Kreitman (Vice
  Chairman and Managing
  Director)
Leslie Porter (Assistant
  Managing Director)
David Behar
Arthur Thrush
Laurence Don (Company
  Secretary)

1965 J. E. Cohen (Chairman)
Hyman Kreitman (Vice
  Chairman and Managing
  Director)
Leslie Porter (Assistant
  Managing Director)
David Behar
Arthur Thrush
Samuel Charles Weiner

(Managing Director of
  Charles Phillips)
John Austin Wells (Director of
  Charles Phillips)
Laurence Don (Company
  Secretary)

1966 J. E. Cohen (Chairman)
Hyman Kreitman (Vice
  Chairman and Managing
  Director)
Leslie Porter (Assistant
  Managing Director)
David Behar
James Grundy
A. E. Thrush
S. C. Weiner
J. A. Wells
L. Don (Company Secretary)

1967 J. E. Cohen (Chairman)
Hyman Kreitman (Vice
  Chairman and Managing
  Director)
Leslie Porter (Assistant
  Managing Director)
David Behar
Laurence Don (also Company
  Secretary)
James Grundy
Arthur Thrush
John Wells

1968 J. E. Cohen (Chairman)
Hyman Kreitman (Chairman
  and Managing Director)
Leslie Porter (Assistant
  Managing Director)
Arthur Thrush (Assistant
  Managing Director)
David Behar
Laurence Don
John Wells

1970 Sir John Cohen (Life President)
Hyman Kreitman (Chairman
  and Managing Director)

Leslie Porter (Deputy
  Chairman)
Arthur Thrush (Assistant
  Managing Director)
David Behar
Laurence Don
James Grundy
John Wells
Ralph Temple (Company
  Secretary)

1971 Sir John Cohen (Life President)
  H. Kreitman (Chairman and
    Managing Director)
  L. Porter (Deputy Chairman)
  A. E. Thrush
  D. Behar
  Mrs D. Hart
  L. B. Leigh
  I. C. MacLaurin
  A. E. Singer
  J. A. Wells
  G. R. Wood
  R. Temple (Company Secretary)

1972 Sir John Cohen (Founder and
    Life President)
  H. Kreitman (Chairman)
  L. Porter (Deputy Chairman
    and Managing Director)
  A. E. Singer (Deputy Managing
    Director)
  D. Behar
  R. N. Behar
  Mrs D. Hart
  L. B. Leigh
  I. C. MacLaurin
  G. R. Wood
  R. Temple (Company Secretary)

1973 Sir John Cohen (Founder and
    Life President)
  H. Kreitman (Chairman)
  L. Porter (Deputy Chairman
    and Managing Director)
  A. E. Singer (Deputy Managing
    Director)

D. Behar
R. N. Behar
Mrs D. Hart
L. B. Leigh
I. C. MacLaurin
G. R. Wood
R. Temple (Company Secretary)

1974 Sir John Cohen (Founder and
    Life President)
  L. Porter (Chairman)
  L. B. Leigh (Managing
    Director)
  I. C. MacLaurin (Managing
    Director)
  D. Behar
  R. Behar
  S. Berwin
  Mrs D. Hart
  H. Kreitman
  G. R. Wood
  R. Temple (Company Secretary
    and on the board)

1975 Sir John Cohen (Life President)
  L. Porter (Chairman)
  I. C. MacLaurin (Managing
    Director)
  D. Behar
  S. Berwin
  M. Darnell
  D. G. Harris
  Miss D. Hyams
  H. Kreitman
  F. Krejsa
  R. Temple
  G. R. Wood
  M. Boxall (Company Secretary)

1976 Sir John Cohen (Life President)
  L. Porter (Chairman)
  I. C. MacLaurin (Managing
    Director)
  D. Behar
  M. Darnell
  D. Harris

Miss D. Hyams
H. Kreitman
F. Krejsa
R. Temple
G. R. Wood
M. Boxall (Company Secretary)

1977 Sir John Cohen (Life President)
L. Porter (Chairman)
I. C. MacLaurin (Managing
    Director)
D. Behar
M. Darnell
D. Harris
Miss D. Hyams
H. Kreitman
F. Krejsa
R. Temple
G. R. Wood
M. Boxall (Company Secretary)

1978 Sir John Cohen (Life President)
Leslie Porter (Chairman)
I. C. MacLaurin (Managing
    Director)
D. Behar
M. Darnell
D. Harris
Miss D. Hyams
H. Kreitman
F. Krejsa
R. Temple
G. R. Wood
M. Boxall (Company Secretary)

1979 Leslie Porter (Chairman)
I. C. MacLaurin (Managing
    Director)
D. Behar
M. Darnell
D. Harris
Miss D. Hyams
H. Kreitman
F. Krejsa
A. D. Malpas
H. F. Pennell

R. Temple
G. R. Wood
M. Boxall (Company Secretary)

1980 Leslie Porter (Chairman)
I. C. MacLaurin (Managing
    Director)
M. Darnell
D. Harris
D. D. Hyams
H. Kreitman
F. Krejsa
A. D. Malpas
H. F. Pennell
R. Temple
G. R. Wood
M. Boxall (Company Secretary)

1981 Leslie Porter (Chairman)
I. C. MacLaurin (Managing
    Director)
M. Darnell
D. Harris
D. Hyams
H. Kreitman
F. Krejsa
A. D. Malpas
H. F. Pennell
R. Temple
G. R. Wood
M. Boxall (Company Secretary)

1982 Leslie Porter (Chairman)
I. C. MacLaurin
M. Darnell
D. Harris
D. D. Hyams
H. Kreitman
F. Krejsa
A. D. Malpas
H. F. Pennell
R. Temple
G. R. Wood
M. Boxall (Company Secretary)

1983 Sir Leslie Porter (Chairman and
    Chief Executive)

I. C. MacLaurin (Managing
Director)
M. Darnell
D. Harris
F. Krejsa
A. D. Malpas
H. F. Pennell
R. Temple
V. Benjamin
H. Kreitman
J. Padovan
S. Young
M. Boxall (Company Secretary)

1984 Sir Leslie Porter (Chairman)
I. C. MacLaurin (Deputy
Chairman)
V. W. Benjamin (Deputy
Chairman)
A. D. Malpas (Managing
Director)
R. Temple (Managing Director)
M. Darnell
D. Harris
H. Kreitman
F. Krejsa
J. Padovan
H. F. Pennell
D. C. Tuffin
G. R. Wood
S. Young
M. Boxall (Company Secretary)

1985 Sir Leslie Porter (Chairman)
I. C. MacLaurin (Deputy
Chairman)
V. W. Benjamin (Deputy
Chairman)
A. D. Malpas (Managing
Director)
R. Temple (Managing Director)
M. Darnell
J. Gildersleeve
F. Krejsa
J. Padovan
H. F. Pennell

D. C. Tuffin
S. Young
M. Boxall (Company Secretary)

1986 I. C. MacLaurin (Chairman)
V. W. Benjamin (Deputy
Chairman)
A. D. Malpas (Managing
Director)
M. Darnell
J. Gildersleeve
F. Krejsa
H. F. Pennell
D. E. Reid
D. C. Tuffin
Sir Leslie Porter
Miss D. O'Cathain
J. Padovan
S. Young
M. Boxall (Company Secretary)

1987 I. C. MacLaurin (Chairman)
V. W. Benjamin (Deputy
Chairman)
A. D. Malpas (Managing
Director)
M. Darnell
J. Gildersleeve
F. Krejsa
H. F. Pennell
D. E. Reid
D. C. Tuffin
Sir Leslie Porter
Miss D. O'Cathain
J. Padovan
M. Boxall (Company Secretary)

1988 I. C. MacLaurin (Chairman)
Mr V. W. Benjamin (Deputy
Chairman)
A. D. Malpas (Managing
Director)
M. Darnell
J. Gildersleeve
F. Krejsa
H. F. Pennell

D. E. Reid
D. C. Tuffin
J. A. Gardiner
Miss D. O'Cathain
J. Padovan
M. Boxall (Company Secretary)

1989 Sir Ian MacLaurin (Chairman)
V. Benjamin (Deputy
Chairman)
A. D. Malpas (Managing
Director)

M. Darnell
J. Gildersleeve
F. Krejsa
D. Reid
D. Tuffin
Mike Wemms
Sir Leslie Porter
Miss D. O'Cathain
J. Padovan
J. A. Gardiner
M. Boxall (Company Secretary)

BIBLIOGRAPHY

Abel, W: *Agricultural Fluctuations in Europe*. (Methuen and Co, 1980)

Addison, P: *Now the War is Over*. (BBC Books, 1985)

Annual Abstract of Statistics, Vol 86, 1938–48

Barker, McKenzie, and Yudkin: *Our Changing Fare*. (MacGibbon and Kee, London, 1966)

Bell, D: *The Coming of the Post-Industrial Society*. (Peregrine, 1973)

Booth, C: *Life and Labour of the People of London*, Final Vol (Macmillan and Co Ltd, 1902)

Booth, General: *In Darkest England*. (1890)

Braudel, F: *The Wheels of Commerce*. (Collins, 1982)

Briggs, S: *Keep Smiling Through*. (Weidenfeld and Nicolson, 1975)

Britain: *Mass Observation*. (Penguin Special, 1939)

Burnett, J: *A Social History of Housing, 1815–1970*. (David and Charles, 1978)

Burnett, J: *Plenty and Want*. (Methuen and Co, 1983)

Calder, A: *The People's War*. (Jonathan Cape, 1969)

Calder and Sheridan: *Speak for Yourself*. (Oxford University Press, 1985)

Central Office of Information: *The Distributive Trades of Great Britain*, 1966.

Corina, M: *Pile it High, Sell it Cheap*. (Weidenfeld and Nicolson, 1971)

Course, E: *The Railways of Southern England*. (B. T. Batsford Ltd, London, 1974)

Crawford and Broadley: *The People's Food*. (Heinemann Ltd, 1938)

Darling, G: *The Politics of Food*. (The Labour Book Service, London, 1941)

Davis, D: *A History of Shopping*. (Routledge, 1966)

Department of Environment and the Welsh Office: *Development Control Policy Note 13, Out of Town Shops and Shopping Centres*.

Dimbleby and Reynolds: *An Ocean Apart*. (BBC Books, 1988)

Drummond and Wilbraham, A: *The Englishman's Food*. (Jonathan Cape, 1957)

Engels, F: *The Conditions of the Working Class in England*. (1844)

Fishman, W: *East End Jewish Radicals 1875–1914*. (Duckworth and Co, 1975)

Fishman, W: *East End 1888*. (Duckworth and Co Ltd, 1988)

Fishman and Breech: *The Streets of East*

London. (Duckworth and Co Ltd, 1979)

Flinn and Smout: *Essays in Social History*. (Oxford University Press, 1974)

Gainer, B: *The Alien Invasion*. (Heinemann Educational Books, 1972)

Garrard, J: *The English and Immigration 1880–1910*. (Oxford University Press, 1971)

Gartner, L: *The Jewish Immigrant in England 1870–1914*. (Wayne State University Press, 1960)

Gershuny, J: *After Industrial Society*. (Macmillan, 1978)

Graves, R: *The Long Weekend*. (Faber and Faber, 1939)

Green, O: *The London Underground*. (Ian Allen, 1987)

Hall, P: *Urban and Regional Planning*. (Penguin, 1975)

Halsey, A. H: *Changes in British Society*. (Oxford University Press, 1978)

Hammond, R: *History of the Second World War. Food Vol 1, The Growth of Policy*. (HMSO and Longmans, Green and Co, 1951)

Hammond, R: *Food and Agriculture in Britain 1939–1945*. (Stanford University Press, 1954)

Heren, L: *Growing up Poor in London*. (Hamilton, 1973)

Hirsh, F: *Social Limits to Growth*. (Routledge and Kegan Paul, 1977)

Hoggart, R: *The Uses of Literacy*. (Chatto and Windus, 1957)

Holdsworth, A: *Out of the Dolls' House*. (BBC Books, 1988)

Holmes, C: *Immigrants and Minorities in British Society*. (Allen and Unwin, 1978)

Hopkins, H: *The New Look*. (Secker and Warburg, 1964)

Huxley, E: *Back Street New Worlds. A look at Immigrants in Britain*. (Chatto and Windus, 1964)

Jackson, A: *Semi-Detached London*. (Allen and Unwin Ltd, 1973)

Jacobs, J: *Out of the Ghetto*. (Janet Simon, 1978)

Jeffreys, J: *Retail Trading in Britain 1850–1950*. (Cambridge University Press, 1954)

Johnston, J: *A Hundred Years of Eating*. (Gill and Macmillan Ltd, 1977)

Landes, D: *The Unbound Prometheus*. (Cambridge University Press, 1969)

Levy, H: *The Shops of Britain*. (Kegan Paul, Trenet, Trubner and Co Ltd, 1948)

Lewis, J: *Women in England 1870–1950*. (Wheatsheaf Books, 1984)

Liberal Industrial Enquiry: *Britain's Industrial Future*. 1928.

London, J: *People of the Abyss*. (1901)

Longmate, N: *How We Lived Then*. (Hutchinsons and Co Ltd, 1971)

McKendirck, Brewer, and Plumb: *The Birth of a Consumer Society*. (Hutchinson, 1983)

Marriot, O: *The Property Boom*. (Hamish Hamilton, 1967)

Marwick, A: *British Society since 1945*. (Allen Lane, 1982)

Mathias, P: *Retailing Revolution*. (Longmans, 1967)

Ministry of Agriculture, Fisheries and Food: *When Hard Times were on the Cards*, 1 and 2. (Bulletin Vol 26, no 5, 1982)

Ministry of Food: *How Britain was Fed in Wartime*. (London HMSO, 1946)

Minns, R: *Bombers and Mash*. (Virago, 1980)

Oddy and Miller: *The Making of the*

Modern British Diet. (Croom Helm Ltd, 1976)

Pagnamenta and Overy: *All Our Working Lives*. (BBC Books, 1984)

Pickering, J: *Retail Price Maintenance And Practice*. (George Allen and Unwin, 1966)

Quiney, A: *House and Home*. (BBC Books, 1986)

Roberts, E: *A Woman's Place*. (Basil Blackwell Ltd, 1984)

Royle, E: *Modern Britain*. (Edward Arnold, 1987)

Skeffington, A: *People and Plans*. (Ministry of Housing and Local Government, 1969)

Stevenson, J: *British Society 1914–1945*. (Penguin Books, 1984)

Storey, J: *Keep the Home Fires Burning*. (Nutrition and Food Science, no 85, 1983)

Thackeray, W: *Vanity Fair*. (Oxford University Press, 1983)

Thomas, M: *Built Environment Quality*. (Architects Journal, 1976)

Thompson, D: *England in the Nineteenth Century 1815–1914*. (Penguin Books, 1950)

Walton and Walvin: *Leisure in Britain*. (Manchester University Press, 1983)

Weiner, M. J: *English Culture and the Decline of the Industrial Spirit*. (Cambridge University Press, 1982)

White, H: *A Regional History of the Railways of Great Britain*, Vols 1 and 2. (David and Charles, 1961)

Woolton, Lord: *The Memoirs of the Rt Hon The Earl of Woolton*. (Cassell, London, 1959)

PHOTO CREDITS

East London street market *Tower Hamlets Local History Library & Archives*
East End Jewish school *Tower Hamlets Local History Library & Archives*
Well Street market *London Borough of Hackney Archives Dept*
Jim Harrow *Courtesy of Mrs P. Harrow*
Wartime rationing (2 pictures) *Imperial War Museum*
Queuing for food (2 pictures) *Imperial War Museum*
Mac cartoon © *Daily Mail*
Giles cartoon © *Express Newspapers plc*
Sir Ian MacLaurin © *Lord Snowdon/Tesco*

All other photographs supplied by Tesco

INDEX